Co-designing Infrastructures

ENGAGING COMMUNITIES IN CITY-MAKING

Series editors
Sarah Bell, Tadhg Caffrey, Barbara Lipietz and Pablo Sendra

This series contributes to the urgent need for creativity and rigour in producing and sharing knowledge at the interface of urban communities and universities to support more sustainable, just and resilient cities. It aims to amplify community voices in scholarly publishing about the built environment, and encourages different models of authorship to reflect research and pedagogy that is co-produced with urban communities. It includes work that engages with the theory and practice of community engagement in processes and structures of city-making. The series will reflect diverse urban communities in its authorship, topics and geographical range.

Engaging Communities in City-making aims to become a central hub for investigation into how disciplinarity, transdisciplinarity and interdisciplinarity can enable schools, teacher trainers and learners to address the challenges of the twenty-first century in knowledgeable and critically informed ways. A focus on social justice is a key driver. The series explores questions about the powers of knowledge, relationships between the distribution of knowledge and knowledge resources in society, and matters of social justice and democratisation. It is committed to the proposition that the answers to questions about knowledge require new thinking and innovation, that they are open questions with answers that are not already known and which are likely to entail significant social and institutional change to make the powers of knowledge and of knowing equally available to all.

Co-designing Infrastructures

Community Collaboration for Liveable Cities

Sarah Bell
Charlotte Johnson
Kat Austen
Gemma Moore
Tse-Hui Teh

First published in 2021 by
UCL Press
University College London
Gower Street
London WC1E 6BT

Available to download free: www.uclpress.co.uk

Text © Authors, 2023
Images © Contributors and copyright holders named in captions, 2023

The authors have asserted their rights under the Copyright, Designs and Patents Act 1988 to be identified as the authors of this work.

A CIP catalogue record for this book is available from The British Library.

Any third-party material in this book is not covered by the book's Creative Commons licence. Details of the copyright ownership and permitted use of third-party material is given in the image (or extract) credit lines. If you would like to reuse any third-party material not covered by the book's Creative Commons licence, you will need to obtain permission directly from the copyright owner.

This book is published under a Creative Commons Attribution-Non-Commercial 4.0 International licence (CC BY-NC 4.0), https://creativecommons.org/licenses/by-nc/4.0/. This licence allows you to share and adapt the work for non-commercial use providing attribution is made to the author and publisher (but not in any way that suggests that they endorse you or your use of the work) and any changes are indicated. Attribution should include the following information:

Bell, S., Johnson, C., Austen, K., Moore, G., and Teh, Tse-Hui. 2023. *Co-designing Infrastructures*. London: UCL Press. https://doi.org/10.14324/111.9781800082229

Further details about Creative Commons licences are available at
https://creativecommons.org/licenses/

ISBN: 978-1-80008-224-3 (Hbk.)
ISBN: 978-1-80008-223-6 (Pbk.)
ISBN: 978-1-80008-222-9 (PDF)
ISBN: 978-1-80008-225-0 (epub)
DOI: https://doi.org/10.14324/111.9781800082229

Contents

Figures	vi
Tables	viii
Voices	ix
Abbreviations	x
How to read this book	xi
Acknowledgements	xii
Glossary	xiv

1 Introduction	1
2 Urban communities	17
3 Infrastructures	33
4 Bottom-up research	51
5 Social housing decisions: demolition or refurbishment?	70
6 Reconfiguring the water-energy-food nexus: Engineering Comes Home	86
7 Collaborating for environmental justice: Somers Town air quality	109
8 Integrating water and urban greening: the Kipling Garden	135
9 Tools for co-design	165
10 Conclusions	186

References	197
Index	209

v

Figures

3.1	Infrastructure life cycle	37
4.1	Legend for 3Cs diagrams	58
4.2	Community as client	59
4.3	Community as contributor	59
4.4	Community as collaborator	60
4.5	Bottom-Up Infrastructure co-design method	62
5.1	Demolition or Refurbishment – community as client	71
6.1	Engineering Comes Home – community as contributor	88
6.2	Six step co-design method for Engineering Comes Home	89
6.3	View of Meakin Estate and the TRA meeting room from Decima Street	93
6.4	Raised beds at the Meakin Estate with the energy infrastructure renovations visible in the background	95
6.5	Participants discussing possible interventions on the estate using fact sheets and the LCA calculator	100
6.6	On a walk-about to decide locations for further rainwater harvesting tanks	102
7.1	Somers Town air quality – community as collaborator-client	110
7.2	Location of Air Quality monitors in Somers Town	116
7.3	Six step co-design method for Somers Town air quality	119
7.4	LEAI 1 km by 1 km background pollution grid covering Somers Town	124
8.1	Kipling Garden – community as collaborator	136
8.2	Joanna's view of the rooftop (image credit Joanna Vignola)	141
8.4	Results from the value elicitation	148
8.5	A modelled design for the garden	150
8.6	The water tank being installed by Robert	153
8.7	Measuring the roof in workshop 3	156

8.8	Using the rainwater and attenuation calculator in workshop 3	156
9.1	Nexy token	171
9.2	Engineering Comes Home tool table	172
9.3	Using the Nexy tokens to create resource stories	172
9.4	Participants using the LCA calculator in the Engineering Comes Home project	174
9.5	Food and Waste in the LCA calculator	176
9.6	The Kipling calculator	180

Tables

5.1	Demolition or Refurbishment project summary	72
6.1	Engineering Comes Home project summary	90
7.1	Somers Town Air Quality project summary	111
7.2	Recent major construction works in and around Somers Town	115
7.3	Ideas from the themed discussion groups at workshop 1	121
7.4	Source of emissions in 2013 from LAEI data for Somers Town	123
7.5	Criteria for STNF to assess evidence needs against STNF priorities	125
7.6	Results from the feedback form for workshop 3	131
8.1	Kipling Garden project summary	137
8.2	Aims, activities and participants in the three workshops	147
8.3	Participants' design ideas for the garden	150

Voices

1.1	Gemma	9
1.2	Kat	10
1.3	Charlotte	11
1.4	Hui	12
1.5	Sarah	13
5.1	Richard Lee's reflection on the impact of the project on Just Space's interactions with researchers	84
7.1	Donna Turnbull's reflection on initiating the collaboration with UCL Engineering Exchange	113
7.2	Reflection from Dr Claire Holman, Director, Brook Cottage Consultants	133
8.1	Clive's reflections on project initiation	138
8.2	Clive's reflections on the garden trip to Golden Lane Estate	151
8.3	Joanna's reflections	158
8.4	Clive's reflections on the research team's engagement	161

Abbreviations

AQO	Air Quality Objective
CAMELLIA	Community Water Management for a Liveable London
EIA	Environmental Impact Assessment
EPSRC	Engineering and Physical Sciences Research Council
ELF	Environmental Law Foundation
GLA	Greater London Authority
HGV	Heavy Goods Vehicle
JMB	Joint Management Board
LARRG	London Action Research on Regeneration Group
LCA	Life Cycle Assessment
LAEI	London Atmospheric Emissions Inventory
LTF	London Tenants Federation
NERC	Natural Environment Research Council
NRMM	Non-Road Mobile Machinery
RCUK	Research Councils UK
RAEng	Royal Academy of Engineering
RIBA	Royal Institute of British Architects
STNF	Somers Town Neighbourhood Forum
SUDS	Sustainable Drainage Systems
TRA	Tenants and Residents Association
UCL	University College London
UK	United Kingdom

How to read this book

This book is intended for anyone interested in using community-based co-design to improve urban infrastructure and neighbourhoods. If you are reading this book, you might be an engineer, a designer, a student, a researcher, a citizen, an urban planner, an infrastructure manager or simply curious about innovative approaches to solving environmental and social crises in cities. You can read the book from cover to cover, or dive straight into the case studies and tools. The early chapters provide the theoretical and historical background, while the second half of the book provides the practical detail and stories of each project.

This book is published under an open access licence so that it might be read as widely as possible. Open access publishing is specifically aimed to make research findings freely available to everyone with an electronic device, including people who are impacted by the work, might be able to implement its findings or who paid taxes to support the research. Given the content of this book and the diverse contributors to the work, it is important that it is openly accessible to all.

Acknowledgements

Sarah acknowledges the Wadandi people of the Noongar Nation, and the Wurundjeri people of the Kulin Nation, on whose lands she lived and worked while writing this book. She pays her respects to their elders, past and present.

This book is the outcome of a rich network of relationships, stretching across communities, universities, professional institutions, funding agencies and beyond. Hundreds of people participated in the Engineering Exchange and dozens contributed to the projects that are part of the book. This work has been nourished by countless interactions, and we acknowledge everyone who has been involved in or supported this research programme. We are especially grateful to the members of Just Space and the London Tenants Federation, the residents of the Meakin, Kipling and Carpenters Estates, the staff of the Leathermarket Joint Management Board and the members of the Somers Town Neighbourhood Forum, who were part of the projects in the book.

The Just Space network provided the inspiration and motivation for ever stronger collaboration between universities and community groups to achieve a fairer, healthier, greener London. Just Space coordinator Richard Lee has been a strong, critical friend and supporter of the Engineering Exchange and, with Sharon Hayward, was the client for the Demolition or Refurbishment project. Robin Brown was a member of the steering committee of the Engineering Exchange, and a generous collaborator and contributor to several projects.

The Engineering Exchange was initially funded through a UCL Public Engagement Fellowship, a scheme that was initiated by Head of Public Engagement Steve Cross. Steve and the public engagement team provided leadership and resources to support innovation in public engagement at UCL, which created an environment where the Engineering Exchange was possible. The Public Engagement Fellowship funding was matched by the Faculty of Engineering, led by Dean Anthony

Finkelstein, who was a strong supporter of engaging communities in engineering to *Change the World*.

Charlotte Barrow was the communications officer for the Engineering Exchange, supporting the work in countless ways with friendly professionalism and enthusiasm. The co-directors of the Engineering Exchange, Carla Washbourne, Aiduan Borrion and Ed Manley, helped engage a wide community of academics in the programme, and Vera Bukachi supported student and professional involvement as education co-ordinator. The steering committee members kept the programme on track. They were Robin Lee, Muki Haklay, Phil Stride, Kim Townsend, Donna Turnbull, Jack Stilgoe, Sharon Hayward, Agamemnon Otero, Nadia Berthouz, Diana Young, Hilary Jackson and Yasminah Beebeejaun.

It is not a coincidence that this work was done at UCL, a university with a strong culture of working with communities in research and teaching, and a few academic colleagues deserve special mention. Michael Edwards, from the Bartlett School of Planning at UCL, was a founding member of Just Space, and a role model for doing academic work in partnership with communities. Jane Holder, from UCL Laws, led the Environmental Justice Enquiry in Euston, which provided the background to the Somers Town Neighbourhood Forum project. Muki Haklay, from Geography, is a powerful leader of citizen science, and in driving institutional change to democratise knowledge production and access.

The research for this book was funded by UCL, the Royal Academy of Engineering and Research Councils UK through the following grants: *Bottom-Up Infrastructure* (EP/N029339/1), *Community Water Management for a Liveable London* (CAMELLIA) (NE/S003495/1), *Engineering Comes Home* (EP/N005902/1) and *UCL EPSRC Impact Acceleration Account 2017–2020* (EP/R511638/1).

Pat Gordon-Smith at UCL Press helped to strengthen the idea for this book, and saw it through commissioning, review and publication. The anonymous reviewers of the proposal and manuscript also pushed the ideas further and improved the outcome. Hilary Jackson read the final draft manuscript and provided important suggestions and questions. Enzo Lara-Hamilton joined the team in the final stretch as research assistant to make sure everything was in order.

Glossary

Action research: A process of collaboration between researcher(s) and others (such as, organisations, communities) to solve a problem, with a focus on generating solutions. It is research orientated towards bringing about change, often involving a range of people in the process of investigation.

Agile technology: Development methodologies and technologies based on iterative development.

Anthropocene: Time period, noting the commencement of significant human impact on Earth's geology and ecosystems.

Aquifer: A body of rock or sediment that holds water under the ground.

Beneficiaries: People or users who will benefit from a service or event or activities.

Biodiversity: The variability of living organisms on Earth, including the number and diversity of species.

Bottom-up: A term used to refer to activities being led by the community, as opposed to top-down initiatives led by other decision-makers.

Capacity building: The development of awareness, knowledge, skills and capability to achieve a purpose.

Co-design: The fundamental principle that an end-user of a particular design has the right to have a voice in the design process.

Combined sewers: Sewers that carry surface-water and wastewater in the same pipe. Surface-water comes from rain falling on streets, roofs and other spaces. Wastewater comes from toilets, bathrooms, kitchens, factories and other places. Wastewater is typically more polluted than surface-water. Most of the time, combined sewers take both sources of water to wastewater treatment works, before discharge into the environment. During heavy rainstorms, combined sewers overflow into rivers, streams and other water bodies, discharging polluted water directly into the environment, without treatment.

Community: Community is a term that is used in many different ways and can refer to many different communities (communities of place, communities of shared interest, communities of religion, communities of action, etc.). It usually refers to those living within a defined geographical area, also sometimes used to describe a physical area rather than a group of people.

Community Infrastructure Levy: In the UK, local governments can charge developers a fee on large developments. The money is used by local governments to invest in infrastructure to support development in their area.

Community organisation: Organisation operating at a voluntary and local level to represent a local community or interest group.

Community profiling: Covers a range of methods to understand the needs and resources of a community with the active involvement of community members and representatives.

Consultation: A process to seek and understanding people's views (but not necessarily involving them in decision-making).

Co-production: An approach that involves a group of people working together (on a project, service or activity), who constructively, through inevitable tensions and conflicts, negotiates outcomes with recognised power and responsibility sharing.

Council tenant: A household who rents their home from a local council in the UK.

Embodied carbon: Carbon dioxide emissions released during the production of a material or product, including extraction of raw materials, processing, manufacturing, transport and construction.

Environmental and climate justice: A set of related social movements that seek to address inequality in how environmental problems and climate change are caused and their effects distributed. Environmental and climate justice recognise that the people who are most impacted by pollution and climate change, and who have the least access to green spaces and natural areas, are often the most marginalised in society, including people of colour, Indigenous peoples and people living in poverty. At a global level, climate justice recognises that people and countries who have contributed the least to global carbon emissions are most vulnerable to the effects of climate change, such as rising sea levels and extreme weather.

Ethnography: A type of social research that aims to understand cultures and the points of view of people who are part of them. It involves a range of social research methods, including observations, analysis of media and texts, interviews and diaries. Ethnographic researchers immerse themselves in their study context to allow for a deep understanding of the community and culture they are working with.

Evaluation: The assessment of monitoring and other information in context (e.g., how successful it was, what difference it made, etc.). It is a process that involves reflecting on, assessing or making a judgement about something, regarding its quality or value. It is a useful learning tool to aid the improvement of processes or activities.

Green-blue infrastructure: Networks of green spaces, waterways and other natural and designed elements that are connected across a landscape, and provide benefits to the environment and people. Elements include rivers, wetlands, ponds, parks, gardens, green roofs and facades, street trees and natural ecosystems.

Housing association: In the UK, a not-for-profit housing provider for people on low incomes.

Impact: Broader or longer-term effects of a project's or organisation's outputs, outcomes and activities.

Infrastructure life cycle: Covers a range of stages – initiation, planning, design, construction, operation, maintenance and decommissioning.

Knowledge democracy: Making sure that different forms of knowledge are taken into account in decisions, including knowledge held by marginalised groups and people impacted by decisions. It is also about promoting open access for the sharing of knowledge, so that everyone who needs knowledge will have access to it.

Knowledge exchange: A range of mechanisms and approaches to share knowledge between different stakeholders (usually between researchers and external groups (e.g. practitioners, community organisations, community groups or policy-makers)). It is sometimes used interchangeably with a number of related terms including 'knowledge brokerage', 'co-production', 'engagement' and 'research impact'.

Life cycle assessment: A method for analysing the environmental effects of a product or service from raw materials, manufacturing, transport, use and disposal.

Local authority or local council: In the UK the form of government responsible for local public services, planning and regulation in an area (e.g., London Borough of Camden).

Metadesign: An approach to design that aims to create tools that increase participation in complex topics, to break design free of the economic context in which it has been operating, and to bridge the gap between community and state.

Neighbourhood forum: In the UK, a designated group or organisation that is authorised to lead the neighbourhood planning process in their area.

Neighbourhood planning: In the UK, a process that empowers local communities to influence development in their area by creating a set of guidance and strategies that form part of the local planning system. They aim to influence where new homes and commercial buildings are built, what infrastructure is needed to support development and what new buildings should look like.

Neoliberalism: A policy agenda promotes the market and competition as the means to distribute resources and deliver services. It aims to minimise the role of the state in the economy, reducing regulation and enhancing the role of the private sector.

Outcomes: The changes, benefits, learning or other effects that result from what the project or organisation makes, offers or provides.

Participation: Act of being involved in something, which can vary in terms of commitment (e.g. activity, event, project, programme).

Participatory democracy: Process that involves people directly in decision-making that affects them.

Policy-makers: People involved in making decisions in government. This includes politicians and people who work for government (e.g., civil servants and local government officers).

Qualitative data: Descriptive data not based on numbers – it is very varied as it includes any information that is not numerical. Qualitative data can include words and narratives, but may also include visual images, film or other media. Qualitative methods can include surveys, interviews, focus groups and observations.

Quantitative data: Numerical data, where numbers are gathered and used to describe something.

Rainwater harvesting: Collecting water that flows off roofs during a rainstorm and storing it in a tank to be used later.

Rebound effect: Describes how improvements in efficiency of resource use lead to higher overall consumption.

Resuspension: The distribution of road dust into the air by vehicular traffic.

Retrofit: Modification of an existing building, space or infrastructure to improve its performance so that it can better meet current needs. Retrofitting is particularly important to upgrade buildings, neighbourhoods and infrastructures to reduce environmental impacts and adapt to climate change.

Stakeholder: Person or organisation with an interest (in a project or programme or organisation) because they will be affected or may have some influence.

Sustainable development: A policy, social and business agenda that aims to continue to achieve the positive outcomes of development, such as reducing poverty and gender inequality, and improving education and health outcomes, while protecting the environment and avoiding climate change. Famously defined by the World Commission on Environment and Development in 1987 as 'development that meets the needs of the present without compromising the ability of future generations to meet their own needs'.

Sustainable drainage system: In the UK, this refers to surface-water drainage networks and elements that aim to mimic the flow of water through a natural landscape, within engineered systems. This includes increasing infiltration of rainfall into the ground, slowing down the flow of water during storms, using wetlands to store and clean water, and storing water in rainwater tanks and ponds. In Australia this is called 'water sensitive urban design', and in the United States it is referred to as 'best management practices' or 'low impact development'.

Social design: Design for improving human well being and livelihoods. It implies a social model of design that addresses the interface between people and the built and natural environment.

Sociotechnical systems: Consider social and technical elements as part of the same system, rather than separate. The interactions between people and technologies are of particular focus, as are the institutional and management structures that underpin the existence and operation of technologies and infrastructures.

Technical aid: Expert assistance provided to community groups for free or at a low cost. It refers to a diverse range of skills to support community groups, such as architecture, engineering, surveying, management, administration and evaluation.

Tenants and residents association: A group of people who live in the same neighbourhood or estate, who organise to achieve improvements in their homes and communities. In the UK, they are particularly associated with social housing estates, and provide representation and consultation between residents, landlords and local councils.

Urban infrastructure: Water, energy, transport, data and waste infrastructures supply the basic services needed for urban life. This includes the physical systems (e.g., pipes, wires, cables, wind turbines, reservoirs, treatment works, recycling centres, roads, airports and more) and management and governance systems that operate and finance the systems.

Value elicitation: In the early stages of co-design or consultation, a process for finding out what a community values, and what values are important to them in guiding design and decisions. A range of tools can be used to help people express and prioritise their shared values.

Value persistence: Throughout a co-design process, checking how well the design and decisions continue to be aligned with the values that the community expressed at the beginning, and checking how community values may be changing as the process evolves.

Voluntary sector: Non-statutory organisations funded by grants and sponsorship that provide goods and services to groups of people.

Water-energy-food nexus: The connections between the use of different resources and their environmental effects. The nexus highlights how resource use and infrastructures are interconnected, and how changes in one system impact on others. This can be mutually beneficial and can lead to unintended negative consequences. For instance, water systems require energy for pumping and treatment, energy systems require water for cooling and food systems require water for irrigation and energy for transportation.

Wicked problems: Problems that are so interconnected they are overwhelmingly complex and difficult to solve through one intervention type of knowledge alone.

1
Introduction

> My heart is moved by all I cannot save:
> so much has been destroyed
>
> I have to cast my lot with those
> who age after age, perversely,
>
> with no extraordinary power,
> reconstitute the world.
>
> *Adrienne Rich*
> 'Natural Resources', 1977 (Rich, 2018)

'You can go now. We need to figure this out.'

Gaye is huddled around a laptop with her neighbours, dragging and dropping bits of garden onto a map of a concrete rooftop, calculating how much water they will need to keep it alive and how much run-off they will keep out of London's sewers, preventing pollution of the River Thames. She waves her hand to dismiss the small phalanx of engineers and researchers hovering behind them.

The residents of the Kipling Estate have come together on an early summer evening for the third in a series of design workshops. It is a milestone on a long journey: one that started with a few folk looking down from their high-rise flats onto bare concrete and imagining a garden. The space they looked onto is a rooftop of a single-storey block of garages, linking two housing towers at first-floor level. In the 1960s, when the estate was built as social housing, this was a play area for children and the venue for fetes and parties. Over time it became blocked off, inaccessible, ugly. Gaye and her neighbours want to bring it back to life.

Residents building a garden on a concrete rooftop seems a pure vision of community life, urban greening and sustainability. An antidote to news of climate emergency, inequality, air pollution and social isolation. Turning visions into gardens in the middle of a hectic city requires determination, negotiation, soil, raised beds, plants and water. It also helps to have money.

Sarah, one of the engineers being brushed away, first saw the rooftop and fell for the vision when the Kipling residents were preparing a small funding application to Southwark Council, their local government authority. Joanna, one of Gaye's neighbours, was working with staff from the Leathermarket Joint Management Board (JMB), a tenant-led organisation that manages the Kipling and other estates, to raise funds to start the garden. They soon realised they would need a source of water for the plants, so they asked Sarah, who had been doing research with their neighbours on the nearby Kipling Estate, if she could help.

When she stepped on to the roof for the first time Sarah saw a water catchment. A few blocked drains left large puddles on the open surface and revealed the drainage pattern. The water draining from the roof could be stored and re-used for irrigation, to support the residents' vision, but that was just the start. Keeping that water out of the local sewers would help solve one of London's biggest environmental problems.

In Southwark, as in much of Central London, wastewater from toilets, bathrooms, kitchens and laundries is carried in the same pipe network as surface-water running off streets and rooftops. During heavy rainstorms, these 'combined sewers' fill up and overflow into the Thames, dumping raw sewage into one of the world's most iconic urban rivers. 'Combined sewer overflows' are a problem for cities around the world. In London, a £2 billion tunnel is under construction to capture and store the overflows under the river, preventing discharge into the river (Dolowitz *et al.*, 2018). Another part of the solution to this long-running environmental problem is to keep as much water out of the sewers as possible, to stop them filling up and overflowing in the first place. Slowing down water flowing into the sewers during storms helps reduce the chance of overflows, creating more time for water to flow safely through the sewers and on to the wastewater treatment works (Stovin *et al.*, 2013).

If the Kipling gardeners stored water for irrigation, that water would be kept out of the sewers. The garden would also soak up water that was rushing off the concrete roof. A garden on the Kipling rooftop could be beneficial to London's water infrastructure, as well as a nice place for children to play. Joanna and the Kipling gardeners agreed to join a research project with Sarah and a team of scientists, designers and engineers to find out how to create a garden that worked for the residents and functioned as a sustainable addition to London's water infrastructure network. A few years later, Gaye is in the Kipling Tenants and Residents Association (TRA) meeting room, part of a group optimising water impacts and garden design features on a Wednesday evening, eager to get on with it.

In the words of poet Adrienne Rich, the Kipling gardeners are among 'those who age after age, perversely, with no extraordinary power, reconstitute the world'. People working in their own neighbourhoods, navigating relationships with each other and powerful institutions around them, fixing things, making things better. The Kipling Garden project tested new ways of communities working together to create better places to live, using science, engineering and design to link those local aspirations to bigger urban and global challenges such as water security, air pollution and climate change.

The story of the Kipling Garden reveals the potential and the challenges of making change in local spaces, within complex urban systems. From the excitement of the research and design process, the gardeners then faced years of fundraising, organising, negotiating and hard work, much of it during a pandemic. The vision for the garden on the rooftop was ultimately not realised, but the Kipling residents persisted and redirected their efforts and resources to building a garden on a different site on their estate. The research project has come to a close, but the Kipling story remains open.

This book tells the stories of those who 'reconstitute the world'. It is about bottom-up approaches to some of the world's most vexing problems. It describes a philosophy and methods that bring extraordinarily powerful tools of science, engineering and design into the hands of people with deep knowledge of their local places and the vision and drive to make things better. It also tells of the limits of these powerful tools in delivering lasting change.

Urban struggles

These stories are set in London, but are relevant to communities, designers, engineers and scientists around the world. London is a vast, iconic metropolis, made up of people going about their lives in ways that are recognisable to urban citizens from many parts of the planet. London's long settlement has left layers of infrastructure and shaped its urban form, just as every city holds is own stories within its buildings, streets and spaces (Halliday, 1999; Hughes, 1993; Melosi, 2001). London's history as a colonial centre of power and its continued role as a global financial centre provide a peculiar and problematic political and economic context, extracting wealth from the global economy, attracting waves of migrants, and contributing to vast inequalities within its own population and between Indigenous and settler populations elsewhere (Zahedieh, 2010). Companies, families and individuals based in London profited from slavery and were generously compensated when it was abolished, and racism remains in the lived experience and unfair life outcomes of Londoners from minority ethnic groups (Draper, 2013; Gilroy, 1993). London's poor air quality is a significant public health problem, and its famous River Thames continues to be polluted (Analitis *et al.*, 2020; Bowes *et al.*, 2018; Walton *et al.*, 2015). Like many cities, London is struggling to reduce its contribution to global carbon emissions, while figuring out how to adapt to hotter summers, more intense storms, more frequent flooding and longer periods of drought (Charlton and Arnell, 2011; Symonds *et al.*, 2021). More than 24,000 people infected with COVID-19 died in London in 2020–2 and the economy and social life of the city was transformed through lockdowns and social distancing. London may be a global city, but everyday life for Londoners is experienced in local neighbourhoods full of the struggles and joys familiar to people living and working almost anywhere.

London faces some big problems: climate change, racism, inequality, air pollution, overflowing sewers, recovery from the COVID-19 pandemic. Big problems deserve big solutions through policy, regulation, technology, investment and economic change. These issues are complex, and top-down responses, led by governments, large institutions and corporations, are necessary. However, top-down solutions prove to be immensely difficult to negotiate and implement. Bottom-up approaches, emerging from community and citizen organisation and action, are not an alternative to top-down leadership, but provide complementary pathways to more sustainable, resilient urban futures. Big problems require solutions from every direction, drawing on all talents and sources of innovation. Perversely, as Adrienne Rich wrote, it may be those like the Kipling gardeners, with the least power and influence, who are able to contribute most to 'reconstitute the world' as cities find their way through immensely uncertain times.

A new role for science, engineering and design?

Science, engineering and design have traditionally served big institutions and corporations, working to solve big problems, driving innovation, progress and growth (Davis, 1998). These powerful ways of knowing and changing the world are central to solving global crises and making the most of emerging opportunities. Science, engineering and design have been less present in supporting bottom-up, community-based innovation and progress. This is partly to do with power and resources (Foucault and Gordon, 1980). Engineers, designers and scientists work for people who can afford to pay their wages and provide the investment needed for equipment and materials to realise their ideas (Davis, 1998). Professional and scientific expertise are entangled with structures and processes of power that shape cities and reinforce patterns of domination and discrimination according to gender, sex, race, class and disability (Perez, 2019; Wajcman, 1991; Wilson, 1992). Individual scientists, designers and engineers also work on big projects because they connect to their curiosity and ambition. For many of them, bigger scale, more complex problems may provide a greater challenge and professional reward.

Increasingly, scientists, engineers and designers, and those who employ them, are recognising the need for bottom-up solutions. It is also important to engage communities in big, top-down programmes and projects (Glass and Simmonds, 2007; Petrovic-Lazarevic, 2008). Big projects can be delayed or stopped by community resistance (Close and Loosemore, 2014; Teo and Loosemore, 2011). For some engineers, designers and scientists, this means finding better ways of convincing communities to accept the decisions and designs of powerful interests. For others, it means working meaningfully in collaboration with communities to find solutions that work for everyone (Hecker *et al.*, 2018; Irwin, 2002). Some go further still, finding ways to work directly in service of communities to put the powerful tools and methods of their professions into the hands of people who are rebuilding cities from the bottom up (Bell *et al.*, 2021; Stevens *et al.*, 2014).

This book

The stories in this book are about engineers, designers and scientists testing out ways of working with local communities to co-design infrastructure solutions to urban environmental problems. Three modes of working with communities emerge – community as client, contributor and collaborator. As clients, community groups define a specific technical task for engineers and researchers to deliver. As contributors, community groups participate in research projects testing new ideas and ways of working. As collaborators, communities bring their interests, knowledge and needs to the table and work together with designers, engineers and scientists throughout a project. Sometimes community groups operate in more than one role, spanning client, contributor and collaborator as projects and contexts evolve.

Engaging communities in infrastructure co-design requires understanding of urban communities, and some of the strengths and pitfalls of thinking about communities in cities. Community-based action has long been important to social and political movements working to address the environmental crisis. Environmentalists since the 1960s and 1970s have explored decentralised, off-grid technologies to support eco-communities. The climate and environmental crises have unequal impacts on different groups within cities and societies, prompting attention to environmental justice, where social and environmental inequalities intersect. Local communities are sources of mutual support in times of shared emergency, such as floods, bushfires and pandemics. We explore the idea of 'community' and the role of local communities in responding to global crises in Chapter 2, 'Urban Communities'.

Infrastructure systems for energy, water, waste, transport and communications provide the technical fabric that holds cities together, keeping the lights on, the water running and the traffic moving. They are also responsible for a substantial proportion of our resource consumption and pollution and are central to efforts to reduce human impacts on local and planetary life-support systems. Infrastructures are typically thought of as big engineering systems, designed and managed from the top down to provide services that are in the background of urban life, allowing people to go about their daily lives in safety and comfort. The infrastructure life cycle describes how infrastructures are created, operated and decline. Ownership and management of big infrastructure systems also reinforces powerful interests in modern societies. In Chapter 3, 'Infrastructures', we consider the role of infrastructures in responding to environmental and economic crises. The concept of 'communities of infrastructure' is introduced as the foundation for developing new ways to bring communities into the design and delivery of these complex urban sociotechnical systems.

A commitment to bottom-up approaches to reconstituting our cities is a technical challenge as much as a social and political movement. Urban scientists, engineers and designers who have developed tools and techniques to deliver top-down visions and systems are now reconsidering how they might contribute to more inclusive, generous, open cities and neighbourhoods. A small group at UCL set out to test new modes for communities, scientists, engineers and designers to work together. The Engineering Exchange was established to enhance collaboration and

CO-DESIGNING INFRASTRUCTURES

to provide a technical advice service to grassroots community groups in London. A series of research projects under a programme of Bottom-Up Infrastructure contributed a set of case studies, methods and tools, described in Chapter 4, 'Bottom-Up Research'.

The first case study chapter in the book exemplifies the role of community as client. The London Tenants Federation and the Just Space network worked with the Engineering Exchange in a project to review technical evidence for 'Demolition or Refurbishment of Social Housing in London'. Social housing estates in London are the focus of urban regeneration programmes, which often involve the demolition of homes. Tenants and residents across London identified the need for independent technical evidence to enable them to judge whether demolition was required and to compare it with refurbishment of existing buildings. Where analysis of options is done as part of regeneration planning, it is typically undertaken on behalf of the housing agency or their private developer partners, on terms that are limited by the scope that these organisations define. Tenants wanted a wider review of the environmental, health and economic implications of demolishing or refurbishing homes. The Engineering Exchange worked with the London Tenants Federation and Just Space to agree a project scope and terms, and set out to deliver a robust review of current evidence for their clients. The technical work was peer-reviewed by other engineers and researchers, and communicated in a report, fact sheets, videos and a policy briefing note. The story of the Demolition or Refurbishment project and its effects is told in Chapter 5.

Water, energy and food are fundamental to human survival, and their provision in modern cities has led to the creation of complex, intertwined social and technical systems. Engineering Comes Home was a research project that aimed to find out what would happen if communities were involved in designing new systems for provision that started with thinking about how people use and share resources every day, at home. Residents of the Meakin Estate were recruited to contribute to the research as participants. During the project, they shared their stories of resource use, contributing to co-design workshops to propose alternative systems to meet those needs while reducing environmental impacts. This story of community as contributor to an engineering research project is told in Chapter 6.

The impacts of pollution, climate change and other environmental crises are unevenly distributed. Poor and marginalised communities are more likely to live in polluted places, with limited access to green spaces and higher exposure to environmental risks such as flooding. Environmental justice aims to address the connection between social and environmental inequality. Somers Town is a neighbourhood in central

London with a rich history of social innovation and community action, but a high degree of deprivation. Situated between King's Cross and Euston railway stations, located close to a major arterial road, this part of London is perpetually under construction. Residents live with poor air quality and have limited access to green space. Working with UCL Laws and the Environmental Law Foundation, the Somers Town community identified air quality as a major issue of environmental justice, requiring further technical exploration and action. As both client and collaborator of the Engineering Exchange, the Somers Town Neighbourhood Forum worked with researchers to identify urban planning and monitoring measures to hold construction contractors and the local council to account in improving air quality. The story of the Somers Town Air Quality project is told in Chapter 7.

The Kipling Garden, the collaborative project introduced at the start of this chapter, is described in Chapter 8. Community ambitions for a garden coincided with researcher and industry interests in sustainable water management in London. Joanna, Gaye and the other Kipling gardeners participated in a co-design process to outline their garden and its wider benefits, helping them raise funds and put their ideas into action. The researchers from UCL, Imperial College, the University of Oxford and the British Geological Survey were part of the Community Water Management for a Liveable London (CAMELLIA) project. They developed and tested tools for working with communities to link urban greening projects to water infrastructure management, which they further developed for wider use. Community members and researchers worked together throughout, securing funding, recruiting people to join the project and supporting further work.

Each of the case studies in this book provides valuable, unique lessons, but this is not their sole purpose. The projects were testing grounds for developing tools and methods to enable stronger collaboration between communities and urban professionals. Chapter 9, 'Tools for Co-design', draws together the core methods and highlights some of the specific tools developed as part of this work. The case study projects worked with communities at various stages of the infrastructure life cycle. In the process of delivering these projects, various tools were developed and adapted to help communities address the complexities of infrastructure design. The definition of 'tools' is broad, including custommade software, hardware prototypes, games and fact sheets. Tools for engaging with a community will always need to be adapted to a specific context. However, the typology of tools in Chapter 9 provides the basis for starting to co-design infrastructure from the bottom up.

The case studies in this book were well-resourced research projects. The intention was to use those resources to create tools and methods that others can replicate and adapt in resource-constrained settings. Each of the case study chapters tells how the projects were funded to acknowledge the privileged context for the work with resources from the university and UK government research funding councils. They demonstrate resourcefulness and flexibility in using the big institutions of science and engineering to support community-based work. Directing research funding to community-based research reflects its small but growing importance in the professional landscape of science, engineering and design.

Collaboration

This book and the stories that it tells are collaborations. Each project involved a team of people, including a core group of committed community partners. The named authors of the book contributed to the projects and put the words on paper. Sarah and Charlotte were involved in all the case study projects, Kat worked on Engineering Comes Home with the Meakin Estate residents, Hui was part of the research team in the Kipling Garden, and Gemma joined the writing team to bring community voices into the stories and the text. They each have their own stories that brought them to this work, and of the impact that it has had.

Voice 1.1 Gemma

(*Continued*)

I am an environmental geographer; my background in geography means that I am used to and trained to work across different concepts, disciplines and methods. I like this variety – although sometimes it can feel like I am a 'jack of all trades'. I am currently working as a researcher; I take an engaged and applied approach to my work. I work on projects that I find interesting and enjoyable, and these it seems are projects that fall at the intersection between research and practice. I work with academics, policy-makers, specific professional communities and residential communities. All the projects that I am involved in have broad goals around creating healthy, sustainable urban environments – but most of my work focuses on the relationships between people, their local environment and decision-making processes. I value working with and learning from others, particularly those with different perspectives, experiences and knowledge to myself. Collaboration is important to me as, I believe, collaboration through diverse teams and experiences brings about innovation – and ultimately positive social change. I have mostly been on the periphery of the work and stories represented in this book – although at points I have been the funder and evaluator of some of these case studies. I joined the 'Co-designing Infrastructures' team to work with the team, the collaborators and the contributors, to tell the stories and support the involvement of multiple voices within those stories.

Voice 1.2 Kat

I want my work to help avert the climate crisis. As an artist working in multimedia installation, performance and participatory projects, I focus on human agency in addressing overwhelming environmental problems. I became involved with the bottom-up infrastructure projects via a circuitous route. I became interested in domestic water use while creating an installation for an immersive theatre show about the future of water in 2014. To that end, I started working with tech company iilab in the context of prototyping Open Droplet, an open-source device that would collect data on domestic water use while maintaining privacy in the home. Open Droplet stopped at the prototype phase, but Sarah saw that the principles of its development fit well with the Engineering Comes Home project. I led iilab's engagement in the project, where I developed the co-design workshops, worked with the team on tech prototypes and set the framework for the infrastructure co-design toolkit. Since then, I also project-managed the production of the bottomupinfrastructure.org website.

Voice 1.3 Charlotte

The projects in this book turned me into the researcher that I am today. I joined UCL in 2013 having just finished my PhD, an ethnographic study of urban infrastructure and social change. My PhD was in social anthropology and geography, and my interest in infrastructure was in its ability to make material the politics

(*Continued*)

and values of the society that built it. Moving to the Faculty of the Built Environment, my research moved away from social theory and into technical reality. I worked on fascinating interdisciplinary research, bringing together technical insights of how systems function with social insights on how systems relate to people's lives. However, the projects that I worked on through the Engineering Exchange allowed me to re-engage with the politics and power of knowledge production and not only to question how change could be achieved but to endeavour to support it. I worked on all the projects in the book. Typically, I was involved in establishing the processes and expectations for the research, seeking ethical approval from the university, carrying out contextual research, identifying stakeholders, creating qualitative research tools to learn about people's lives and aspirations for their neighbourhoods, facilitating workshops and writing up the results. Researching the climate crisis can be overwhelming, but these projects and the commitment of the people involved provide me with optimism.

Voice 1.4 Hui

Many years ago, I started to explore ways to create a better world for everyone to live in. At first, I became an architect. Who wouldn't want to help make enchanting places for people to live?

It was satisfying working with individual clients, creating new homes and new ways for them to live their lives, but I became discordant with the way that a fortunate few were able to make a small place lovely for themselves, but at the expense of what or whom? I needed to break out of the site boundary to find out! Now I research the connections between people and the ecological and infrastructural systems that support their lives. I aim to find ways that these connections can co-evolve to be sustainable in the future. For this project I developed and facilitated the first two co-design workshops for the Kipling Estate. I also drew the illustrations for this book.

Voice 1.5 Sarah

I am an engineer and an academic. Like most engineers and academics, I have spent my career in the employment of large public institutions and private corporations. Like most academics and engineers, I believe in the value of my profession to society. I think we (engineers and academics) have the power and potential to contribute to solving the world's most complex problems, but too often we fall far short. Engineers and universities have exacerbated underlying economic and social conditions, as well as inventing and perpetuating damaging technologies. I have a simple faith that widening access to science and engineering can bring more hands and minds to the

(Continued)

urgent task of transforming cities and societies to move beyond current crises towards restoration. Working with communities most affected by environmental and social problems provides vast potential to rapidly expand the positive impact of science and technology, to build more sustainable and resilient infrastructure and cities. In all the case studies in this book, I co-ordinated the team, raised the funds for the work and oversaw the research. I have benefited personally and professionally, winning research grants and being promoted in the UK, and being recruited to a well-paid job on the other side of the world, back in my home country, Australia.

Community voices

The writing of this book reflects the processes of co-design and community engagement that it documents. The different roles and resources of those involved affect their agency and the impact they have on the outcomes. The work of community partners and wider team members is represented in the case study chapters. Who tells these stories is important. Community voices are incorporated in the text as the means to attribute and acknowledge intellectual contributions from beyond the named authors of the book. The words of partners are presented as 'voices' in the case study chapters, short sections highlighted between the authors' text. Community partners in the text provided consent and approval for the representation of their contribution. Their work and their reflections are central to the intellectual development of this book and the source of its most significant content. Community contributors to the book are acknowledged at the start of each chapter, while the core authorship team was responsible for the overall development and writing of the book as a whole. This means that the authors' voices are the loudest in the text. In writing about the projects, the authors have endeavoured, along with contributions from community partners, to represent the rich, detailed stories of messy projects.

The intention was to integrate the personal and the political, the practice and the research, and voices of those who are key to these stories. However, like with any engagement activity, there was not one method or approach to how communities voices were included in the writing of this text. The contribution of different communities in the drafting (and redrafting) of the case study chapters varied.

The process started in January 2021 by looking at the case studies and existing materials to develop a list of who was involved and how. Gemma reached out to those involved in the case studies to share the authors' ideas about the book and gauge community interest in its creation. Community partners were presented with a range of options of how this involvement might work. They were offered a 'spectrum of co-authoring', acknowledging that different ways of working together to create the text might be appropriate for different partners and contributors, and involvement was entirely optional. A key word here is 'appropriate': making sure to account for different capacities and relationships with and within the case studies.

The strategies taken to include community voices were: community partners drafting or reviewing text; group and individual (online and in-person) meetings to discuss chapters; semi-structured interviews; site visits to see and discuss the case studies; the sharing of references and documents; and emails.

Providing different options to include a range of voices, aimed to counterbalance the inevitability of the hierarchal situation between the researchers' and community voices. Although the desire was to take a collaborative approach to co-authoring, it is worth mentioning the importance, and influence, of the researchers' positionality and role in the process. Positionality is 'one's position of power vis-à-vis other stakeholders inside and outside the setting' (Herr and Anderson, 2005, p. 41). Although the goal was reciprocal collaboration whenever possible, three key factors influenced the writing of this text.

First, although different communities were engaged in the stories documented in this book, the researchers made key decisions about the direction and narrative of the stories. For example, Charlotte proposed and drafted the initial framework for the structure of case study chapters, which all of them follow. However, unlike more conventional texts (where the writing process is closed), the drafts (and in some cases the skeleton outline) were discussed, shared and reframed as a result of the involvement of partners and contributors.

Second, the key drivers to write the book were motivated by academic interests, rather than being a priority for many of the partners and communities involved in the case studies. Even though the researchers are driven beyond the outputs of academia (e.g., papers, books, grants), they remain part of that system.

Third, the writing process was bounded by practical issues such as timing. The researchers managed the writing project, including the time available to engage, write, share and re-write, in line with committed

INTRODUCTION   **15**

deadlines (discussed and agreed between the authors and publishers, rather than with the community partners). These practicalities influenced what was possible and when.

Learning with communities

The methods used in the projects and the process of writing provide general principles and an overall structure for the stories; but working in communities is complex. Knowledge is contested. Local priorities may also be in conflict. Inevitably, outcomes fall short or miss the mark. Projects are moments in time in complex lifeworlds. These are small projects, but with a lot at stake for those involved. The detail reveals the specificity of each case, but also provides opportunities for wider resonance.

This is an account of a particular programme of work, in a particular place, undertaken by particular people. It is also a collection of stories by and about people who are working in their own neighbourhoods to address global problems, using methods that can be adapted to be used almost anywhere. It is part of a broader intellectual conversation and practical movement to reconstitute the structures of power and knowledge that shape our worlds, starting with communities of active citizens, such as Gaye, Joanna, their neighbours on the Kipling Estate and the creative, determined folk across London whose work is the foundation of this book.

2
Urban communities

Euston railway station is one of the busiest in London. As an unusually heavy snowstorm closes in, commuters scramble for early trains and the surrounding streets become quiet. Everyone wants to be at home and warm. A short walk from the station, down a side street and behind a blue door, a small crowd has gathered in the Basil Jellicoe Hall to hear the findings of an inquiry into environmental justice in the Euston area. A collaboration between the neighbourhood forum, the local voluntary service council, university staff and students, and environmental lawyers, the inquiry has heard from more than 90 residents about the cumulative impacts of development on their health and wellbeing (Holder, 2018). About half of them have defied the weather warnings to learn the outcomes and hold their local representatives to account.

The meeting hears from the report authors how decades of construction in and around the station have affected local people and the environment. Dust, noise, light and air pollution, as well as a loss of green space, trees and local heritage sites contribute to feelings of helplessness and despair, and mental and physical illness. A short film shows how a teenager struggles to manage her asthma, and an elderly woman with chronic obstructive pulmonary disease is fearful for her future, living in an area in breach of European health standards for air quality. The most vulnerable people living near Euston railway station bear the burden of years of disruption and pollution, while commuters rushing through to other parts of London, the UK and Europe benefit from faster, more reliable trains. This uneven distribution of benefits and impacts is worsened in Euston because development is relentless. The cumulative impact of many years of construction projects all over the neighbourhood exacerbates negative consequences on the health and wellbeing of residents and their environment.

The leader of Camden Council, the local government, listens to the presentations and faces questions about what the council will do. She knows many of the residents by name, and authentically sympathises with their plight. She recognises the seriousness of the inquiry and the weight of its findings. The council has control over some, but not all development in the area, which is a nationally significant transport node. The residents of Euston have lived with disruption and pollution for a long time and there is no quick fix.

The people in the hall in Euston are a community. They share an interest in acting to improve the quality of their local environment and their own health and wellbeing in the face of overwhelmingly powerful agents of urban change. At the same time, they come from many different communities. Regents Park and Somers Town, although geographically close and within the 'Euston area', form distinct neighbourhoods and local identities (Somers Town is the focus of Chapter 7). People at the meeting also reflect different ethnic communities, with a significant group of people of Bengali heritage living in the local area. Euston has been home to a strong working-class community for several generations, and is a place with a proud heritage of social innovation and organisation (Clarke *et al.*, 1977; Hanson, 2000).

Communities are groups of people, gathered together, beyond their families and workplaces, with a common purpose or identity. Community is a word that expresses the experience of belonging to something bigger than a household, more personal than a workplace, and smaller than the state or society. Community is a buffer between intimate lives and the rest of the world.

This chapter considers how urban communities, like those gathered in the Basil Jellicoe Hall, are understood in theory, policy and practice, and their potential as sites of action in response to global environmental crises. The chapter starts by providing a background on the conceptualisation of 'community' and how communities have been promoted in neoliberal policies as a tool for the delivery of services. This is followed by a focus on four key issues for urban communities: resilience; environmental and climate justice; sustainable development; and appropriate technological innovation. The purpose is to provide a foundation for community-based research and design for sustainability and resilience, while acknowledging its limits and potential for misappropriation. The chapter ends by noting that, in parallel with an increase in community mobilisation and action in response to climate change and environmental crises, there is an increase in community engagement by universities, scientists, engineers and designers. The chapter draws on two key mechanisms within this text: citizen science and participatory design. Together, these movements require better understanding of the nature of communities and their contribution to change, as demonstrated in the case study projects in Chapters 5–8.

Urban communities and politics

Community and the ideas associated with it (e.g., social networks, social relations, trust, social ties, cohesion and inclusion) are central to theories about modern society. Sociologist Ferdinand Tönnies famously distinguishes between the *Gemeinschaft* (the community), the social bonds based on similarity, and the *Gesellschaft* (society), the social bonds of interdependence and exchange (Tönnies and Loomis, 2002). Historically, romantic, nostalgic qualities of integrated, place-based, typically rural, social worlds contrast starkly with representations of urban areas as lacking in community. Cities have been imagined to be diverse, large-scale systems with ephemeral, anonymous, transient populations; the antithesis of community.

'Community' is both a hackneyed term and a key force in urban politics. Deployed by politicians, activists, advertising campaigns, scientists, health and social workers, and real estate developers, it carries heavy baggage. Even as community is promoted as the site of transformation to more sustainable and democratic ways of living, urban communities experience neglect, misrepresentation and marginalisation. The use of the idea of community for wildly different political and social purposes warns of the need to be critically alert to manipulation, but it also indicates the potential for agreement on fundamental values.

The community is often defined by a single dimension, based on geography (Pahl, 2005). 'Community' evokes visions of groups of people co-habiting the same space, with strong social networks, sharing common values and interests, manifesting themselves by formal and informal social activities and infrastructures (e.g., street parties and neighbourhood watch associations). Marilyn Taylor (2011) outlines three ways that community is used by policy-makers:

- Descriptive community – a group or network of people who share something in common or interact with each other. For example, people with a shared cultural heritage (e.g., the Turkish community in London); common economic interests (e.g., the business community); or a shared experience of power or oppression (e.g., the LGBTQIA+ community).

- Normative community – a place where solidarity, participation and coherence are found. For example, people living in neighbourhoods with dense, overlapping ties of kinship, friendship, class, work and religion (e.g., the Somers Town community).
- Instrumental community – community as an agent acting to maintain or change its circumstances, or the location or orientation of services/policies. For example, people impacted by a construction site; people using a local health service; people involved in delivering local services.

Community in an urban environment is diverse and complex. The city can be seen as 'the community of communities' (Amin, 2007 p. 109), being held together by a range of objects and connections. Urban sociologists have shown that what each person considers to be 'the community' varies, not only from person to person, but also depending on the setting and time (Hunter, 1974). Communities can be identified at various scales within cities, and individuals select a level of community that best satisfies their needs and interests at the time. It is therefore important to recognise that an individual may enjoy membership in multiple communities over both space and time, with varying degrees of attachment.

A community may arise when common concerns bring people together – for instance, communities may be constructed around a specific issue or project, or 'consensual concerns' (Olson, 2008), then dissolved once the issue is resolved or project finished. Within the field of local environmental planning, Patsy Healey (2006) describes these as 'place-based political communities'. These communities could be also categorised as 'instrumental' under Taylor's typology (2011). Communities engaged with infrastructure projects, through formal participation mechanisms, in opposition to development, or in co-design and collaboration processes, may be 'instrumental' or 'place-based political'. They may also fulfil longer-term, deeper functions as 'normative' or 'descriptive' communities.

Urban regeneration approaches that exclude local people through opaque decision-making processes may result in seemingly positive short-term outcomes for developers or government, but without support from local people, contribute to social marginalisation (Imrie, 1996; Imrie *et al.*, 1996; McInroy, 2000). Consequently, over the past 30 years there has been a significant movement for change in the organisational processes involved in urban initiatives to promote community organising and community engagement. This contributes to a recognition that community involvement could enrich the process of regeneration and ensure the sustainability of initiatives. Local 'ownership' through community organising has been shown to improve the sustainability of an initiative so that it continues when central support is no longer available, becoming self-sustaining.

Community participation in decision-making takes many forms. The US urban planner Sherry Arnstein (1969) famously suggested that participation was a 'progressive' concept, describing eight stages of participation in the form of a ladder. Non-participatory processes ('manipulation' and 'therapy') were located at the bottom of the ladder, leading to the semi-participatory processes of 'informing', 'consultation' and 'placation'. The higher stages of 'partnership', 'delegated power' and 'citizen control' were all levels where the public have more control in project processes, having some degree of power in influencing decisions. The top stages thus provided an opportunity for a two-way communication process between the public and the authoritative, decision-making bodies. Arnstein's ladder of participation suggested that some levels are superior to others (the aim is to be further up the ladder), and has been amended since its publication in the 1960s. Communities and individuals have different interests and will therefore wish to participate at differing levels. Decision-makers and designers may also be willing or able to account for various levels of citizen participation in different projects or issues. Clarity about the purpose of participation, what is at stake and what level of influence is achievable is as important in practice as encouraging stronger citizen control.

While Arnstein and others consider community and public participation to be a progressive movement, community-based action and social organisation are also consistent with conservative political values of self-reliance and small government. Preserving local traditions and community structures may be a site of resistance against modernising, progressive governments and social movements. 'Devolving' decision-making to the community level necessitates a shift in conventional power relations; citizens are no longer passive observers and consumers, but active participants in the delivery of key services (Raco and Flint, 2001).

Civil society, including 'communities', are important elements of neoliberal policy, which has encouraged deregulation, privatisation and markets-based mechanisms, and reduced the role of the state in welfare, services and development (Raco and Flint, 2001; Taylor, 2011). Communities have been promoted in neoliberal policy as a means of delivering services to local people, encouraging self-reliance and empowering local decision-making and choice. For communities that are relatively well-off, such models of devolved services and delivery may be welcomed. However, for poorer communities and individuals the roll-back of state funding and services has not been adequately compensated with an increase in community resources, capability and co-ordination, entrenching inequality. Community responsibility for services and decisions without sufficient resources or power to effect change can leave vulnerable people unserved, and community leaders burnt out and disillusioned.

Despite being referenced as a positive tool and outcome in policy and political circles, a community is as much about 'them' as it is about 'us' (Taylor, 2011). Conflicting, contrasting opinions and values occur between different communities, as well as between members of the same descriptive or instrumental 'community'. Communities may stifle individual freedom, enforce traditional identities and exclude or oppress people who 'don't fit in'. Communities can be sites of intense conflict. They may provide refuge for people with anti-social values and intent, fracturing society.

Urban communities are dynamic, constantly emerging and evolving. Talja Blokland (2017) conceives of community as an urban practice, something that is constantly shaped by interactions between citizens and the spaces and places where they live. Interactions may be weak or strong. They contribute to experiences of community and constructive community outcomes, such as a sense of belonging, mutual aid and resilience in times of disaster.

Community resilience

Community 'spirit' is often invoked in the aftermath of disasters. People speak of their community 'pulling together' to support each other to survive and recover. Resilience is most commonly understood as the ability to bounce back from an unexpected disruption (Holling, 1996). Resilience increasingly refers to the capacity of cities and communities to prepare for and learn from disasters, and to recover to a stronger, more sustainable position than before (Lowe *et al.*, 2021). Linking community and infrastructure resilience was the focus of the bottom-up infrastructure programme described in Chapter 4, and improving resilience is an implicit or explicit goal for all the case studies in this book.

Community resilience is a key element of disaster preparedness and recovery planning (Aldrich and Meyer, 2015; Cutter *et al.*, 2014, 2008). Community members may be able to support one another during disasters when emergency and government services cannot reach them. They also hold important local knowledge about the environment, local resources and vulnerable people that is unknown to formal agencies. Community networks are important for communication during and after disasters.

The increased emphasis on community resilience by governments, formal agencies and the media, aligned with neoliberal policy approaches, has been criticised as unfair by some people who have lived through disasters. Emphasis on 'resilience to' rather than 'protection from' disasters has the potential to leave some communities at higher risk. Over-reliance on 'community' resilience can leave vulnerable people without adequate support from emergency services and government recovery programmes. 'Don't call me resilient' has become a catchphrase from communities who are exposed to multiple hazards and vulnerabilities and experience the withdrawal of government services to reduce risks, survive disasters and recover in the months and years that follow (Kaika, 2017).

Environmental justice, climate justice

The Euston area environmental justice inquiry at the start of this chapter addressed a local manifestation of a global phenomenon. Environmental problems, such as poor air quality, noise, water pollution, exposure to toxic chemicals and higher vulnerability to natural and human-induced disasters, disproportionately impact on people who are already socially and economically marginalised. In the United States, Europe, Australia and other predominantly white societies, race is important in discussing environmental problems, especially in cities. Indigenous, Black, Latino, Asian and migrant communities are unfairly affected by environmental problems caused by urban development, industrialisation and climate change. Environmental justice was a driving motivation for the Somers Town Air Quality project described in Chapter 7.

The environmental justice movement emerged in the 1980s in the United States as the confluence of the environmental and civil rights movements (Bullard, 2008; Cole and Foster, 2000; Schlosberg and Collins, 2014). Community organising aimed to highlight the health impacts of waste and chemical facilities, to hold regulators and polluters to account and to oppose new or expanded polluting industries in Black, Latino and Indigenous communities (Cole and Foster, 2000). The concept of 'environmental justice' links wider movements for social justice related to housing, employment, health and poverty to environmental issues, and challenges the environmental movement's historic focus on wilderness preservation (Coolsaet, 2020). In Europe and the UK, environmental justice similarly links grassroots social movements to draw attention to structural injustice in the uneven distribution of environmental impacts and benefits (Walker, 2012).

Climate justice similarly draws attention to the relationship between race, class and other forms of social division, as well as the uneven impacts of climate change and the transition to a zero-carbon economy. Hurricane Katrina in 2005 starkly revealed racial inequality through its impacts in New Orleans. Black communities were more vulnerable to the storm and flooding, less able to safely evacuate and took longer to recover. This event contributed to more critical examination of the links between social and racial justice, natural disasters and climate change. Poorer communities, including Black and racial minorities, are more likely to live in locations that are vulnerable to flooding, houses that are susceptible to overheating and neighbourhoods with poor air quality. Globally and locally, poorer people also contribute much lower carbon emissions than wealthy elites, further demonstrating the uneven distribution of the benefits and impacts of development and its environmental effects.

The connection between social and political organisation and the environmental crisis has been a key concern for environmental philosophers and activists since the 1960s; however, without a critical focus on race. Social ecologists such as Murray Bookchin link human oppression and environmental destruction, and propose self-organised, autonomous communities as the solution (Bookchin, 2005). Drawing on political anarchism, social ecology resists centralised government authority and capitalist economy, and proposes localised political and social organisation that supports fairer distribution of resources within ecological capacity. Ecological feminism links the domination of women and nature within Western culture as a fundamental cause of the ecological crisis (Plumwood, 1993; Warren, 1990). The solution to women's oppression and ecological destruction is to replace hierarchical, patriarchal structures of power with relationships based on reciprocity, care and mutual respect. Local communities formed of rich, negotiated connections between people, non-human nature and wider ecosystems are the foundation of ecological feminist action and social organisation. Women's conservation movements and women-led environmental action against pollution or militarisation involve local organising and mutual support, typically in opposition to powerful, hierarchical structures of industry and government (Mies and Shiva, 1993).

Indigenous communities have an especially complex relationship with environmental movements (Pickerill, 2018). In seeking alternatives to the dominant Western worldview some environmentalists have turned to Indigenous philosophies as a source of wisdom and examples of 'living in harmony with nature'. Indigenous knowledge and worldviews are valuable in reorientating human relationships to the natural world and developing solutions to current crises. However, romanticism, appropriation and extraction of Indigenous knowledge without acknowledging and compensating for the brutality of settler colonialism, ongoing injustice and social disadvantage experienced by Indigenous peoples within modern settler societies reinforces structures of oppression (Dove, 2006; Liboiron, 2021a, 2021b; Whyte, 2016).

Indigenous knowledge systems present a fundamental challenge to research and expertise founded in European, colonial sciences, theories and philosophies. In the landmark book *Decolonizing Methodologies*, Linda Tuhiwai Smith (2021) demonstrates the connection between research and the experience of colonisation for Indigenous peoples and outlines an approach to research grounded in Indigenous worldviews and struggles. Tyson Yunkaporta's *Sand Talk* (2019) flips the usual extractive approach of environmentalists looking to Indigenous peoples for solutions to environmental crises, to analyse sustainability from an Australian Indigenous perspective. Philosopher and political theorist Mary Graham outlines the danger of colonial political and social systems grounded in a fear of scarcity leading to hierarchies of domination, in contrast to Australian Indigenous philosophies that emphasise relationalism and mutual obligation (Brigg and Graham, 2020).

Community-based environmental action and programmes offer a potential alternative to environmental policies that reinforce hierarchies of domination but are not immune to persistent patterns of social exclusion and injustice. Community development, organisation and activism to achieve environmental objectives are required to intentionally address issues of diversity, inclusion and justice to be effective and legitimate. Community leadership of environmental programmes and actions is important to ensure that those who are most impacted on by environmental degradation and climate change have the most influence on decisions.

Sustainable development

Community-based action is strongly linked to sustainable development in policy and popular imagination. At the 1992 Earth Summit in Rio de

Janeiro, world leaders signed up to 'Agenda 21', a commitment to the principles of achieving social and economic development while conserving and managing natural resources and ecosystems. While nation states are the focus of international conventions and high-level targets and goals, delegates at the Earth Summit also included local government leaders and non-governmental organisations. 'Local Agenda 21' provided a parallel set of commitments for local governments, in line with the slogan 'think global, act local'. International movements for sustainable development recognised that implementing change required more than national targets and legislation, and that local government services, planning and regulation have a direct impact on environment and development.

The 17 Sustainable Development Goals (SDGs), adopted by the United Nations (2015) to be achieved by 2030, are the most recent manifestation of international agreements to address intersecting environmental, social and economic problems (United Nations, 2022). 'Sustainable Cities and Communities' is the focus of Sustainable Development Goal 11, which is to 'Make cities and human settlements inclusive, safe, resilient and sustainable'. Specific targets within SDG11 address housing, participatory planning, disaster resilience, air quality, waste management and access to green spaces. These global issues of concern are reflected in community needs in the London case studies in Chapters 5–8, addressing housing (Chapter 5), waste (Chapter 6), air quality (Chapter 7) and green space (Chapter 8).

Appropriate technology

Technological innovation and dissemination are central to sustainable development. The environmental crisis and its relationship to development raises questions about the nature of technology and its role in social and economic development. In the 1960s and 1970s, British economist E. F. Schumacher drew on his experience as an advisor on international development to propose an alternative to the prevailing model of industrialisation. Schumacher travelled widely as an advisor to governments of developing nations while working as Chief Economic Advisor to the British National Coal Board. His book *Small is Beautiful* made the case for development based on 'intermediate' technologies that were appropriate to local environmental, cultural and social conditions (Schumacher, 1973). In contrast to economic development based on large-scale infrastructures, resource extraction and manufacturing, Schumacher presented development as emerging from local conditions, to meet the needs of local people, while protecting and preserving local environments. *Small is Beautiful* provided an economic and policy framework for the 'intermediate technology' or 'appropriate technology' movement, to use technology to improve human conditions within the boundaries of local and planetary ecosystems. This framing promoted decentralised infrastructures as the means of avoiding the ecological and social impacts of large, centralised systems.

The appropriate scale and mode of organisation of human technologies and societies has been debated within environmental activism and philosophy since the industrial revolution and became a central question for the emerging environmental movement in the 1960s (Kirk, 2001; Smith, 2005). It is also at the heart of the bottom-up approach described in Chapter 4 and explored in the case study chapters of this book. For some middle-class urban environmentalists, the ecological crisis alongside countercultural social movements of the 1960s and 1970s prompted efforts to live less resource intensive, polluting lifestyles, often associated with a 'back-to-basics' rural ideal. Goals of self-sufficiency in food, water, energy and materials promoted ecological innovations and decentralised, alternative technologies. Magazines, newsletters, demonstration sites and courses shared knowledge among networks of educated and resourceful environmentalists seeking to live out their political commitments and create a more ecologically grounded way of life (Anderson, 2012; Kirk, 2001; Penner, 2014; Smith, 2004).

Moving beyond individuals and families living 'off-grid', environmentalists have formed intentional communities, sharing resources and infrastructures to reduce collective as well as individual impacts (Pickerill, 2020). Eco-communities range from communes to suburban housing developments. Communities enable efficiencies of scale in infrastructure services, such as energy and water, sharing of resources and spaces, as well as mutual support and identity. Decision-making about shared resources and rules governing individual behaviours requires negotiation and administration, with varying levels of formality and different forms of structure. Establishing principles and processes for community organisations to support ecological and social goals has proven to be at least as important as the design of eco-efficient technologies, infrastructures and buildings.

Engagement by universities, scientists, engineers and designers

Movements to address environmental and climate injustice, achieve sustainable development, support ecological communities and promote appropriate technologies all reveal the complex intersection between society and technology. Improving public and community participation in decision-making to address environmental and climate crises is not limited to conventional social and political processes. It also includes participation in science, technology and design. Two key movements that underpin the work of *Co-Designing Infrastructures* are citizen science and participatory design.

Citizen science

'Citizen science' is a broad concept to describe public and community participation in science. Alan Irwin (2002) describes two aligned meanings of citizen science – science that serves the needs of citizens; and science directly involving citizens. Greater involvement of citizens in setting research agendas, and greater attention by scientists to the needs of less powerful groups in society, can be achieved through consultation and deliberation. Direct involvement of citizens in doing science includes a wide range of activities, from collecting and analysing data for large scientific projects, to directing and delivering scientific research to address questions of direct relevance to communities.

Citizen science has a long connection to environmental and ecological research. The engagement of bird watchers, or amateur ornithologists, in formal scientific research through the reporting of observations was a starting point for the recognition and promotion of citizen science by the US National Science Foundation (Bonney *et al.*, 2009; Strasser *et al.*, 2019). Citizen science has been important in environmental justice struggles. Citizen science methods and programmes have enabled communities affected by pollution, loss of green space or other issues to collect and analyse scientific data to document and understand their lived experiences, and to hold powerful interests to account. The Community Action Against Asthma project in Detroit assessed the effect of indoor and outdoor air quality on asthma in children (Parker *et al.*, 2003). The 'bucket brigades' in the United States developed a low-cost method of sampling air pollution from industrial facilities, which demonstrated the inadequacy of established pollution monitoring protocols and showed community exposure to chemicals with the potential to impact on their health (Ottinger, 2013, 2010). In the aftermath of the Gulf oil spill disaster in 2010, a group of citizen scientists known as 'Public Lab' used helium balloons and digital cameras to gather data to map the extent of the environmental effects. Public Lab expanded to become a platform for citizen science methods and tools, to support communities in gathering and analysing data on a range of environmental problems (Public Lab, 2022; Rey-Mazón *et al.*, 2018; Wylie *et al.*, 2014).

The involvement of citizens in designing and making technical instruments and software to collect and analyse data extends beyond citizen science to 'civic technoscience' (Wylie *et al.*, 2014). Aligned with movements towards widening access to fabrication equipment through community 'Maker Spaces' and 'Fab Labs', and open-source software communities, citizens can shape how scientific data is produced, analysed and used in decision-making.

Citizen science has become an element of a wider movement in universities for community-based research. Community-based research involves an equal partnership between the researchers and the community. Instead of research ideas being generated within a 'discipline' they are developed in collaboration with the community. The US National Institute for Environmental Health Sciences describes a community-based research approach as 'a methodology that promotes active community involvement in the processes that shape research and intervention strategies, as well as in the conduct of research studies' (O'Fallon and Dearry, 2002). Community-based research was a core aim of the Engineering Exchange, described in Chapter 4.

Just as urban communities are complex and dynamic, so are their relationships with researchers, scientists, engineers and designers. Muki Haklay defines four levels of participation and engagement in citizen science projects: crowdsourcing, distributed intelligence, participatory science and extreme citizen science (Haklay, 2013). Crowdsourcing involves citizens as data sources and providing voluntary computing to large scientific projects. Distributed intelligence involves citizens in the analysis of data. In participatory research, citizens are included in the definition of research problems and data collection. Extreme citizen science is collaborative, with citizens participating in problem definition, data collection and analysis.

In categorising different types of public participation in scientific research, Jennifer Shirk and colleagues present a spectrum of five models of projects: contractual, contributory, collaborative, co-created and collegial (Shirk *et al.*, 2012). The level of participation increases from contract through to colleagues, with most projects and innovation occurring in the middle – contribute, collaborate and co-create. This is similar to the three modes of engagement with communities described in the Introduction and explored in Chapter 4 – client, collaborator and contributor. Practices such as these, at the forefront of citizen science, also have the potential to feed back into environmental scientific research, including to help address entrenched colonial practices and foster diversity and inclusion (Austen and Hölker, 2022).

Participatory design

Nortje Marres (2016) extends traditional understandings of public participation in political processes to include the use of new technologies in everyday life, and engagement with demonstration projects such as display eco-homes. Her concept of 'material participation' recognises that values, needs and aspirations are expressed through everyday choices, experimentation and design, as well as through conventional political participation.

Extending participation into the 'material world' of cities has implications for the design of buildings, urban spaces, infrastructures and technologies. Design is inherently social and political, and begins with the definition of a design problem. Defining a design problem is highly subjective: it depends on a person's experience of a particular situation (Rith and Dubberly, 2007). A railway platform that is accessible only by stairs may be an adequate design for someone who can walk quickly and without pain, while for a wheelchair user it will be profoundly inadequate. In the design of infrastructure this subjectivity is important. As discussed in Chapter 3, infrastructure has traditionally treated users as homogeneous, concentrating on models and designs to fit assumed averages and peaks of demand, while disregarding diversity of behaviour, expectation and experience. As such, involving 'end users' in infrastructure design not only shapes solutions, but reframes the entire design problem space.

Since the 1960s, designers have been interested in increasing end-user participation. They have developed methods ranging from user-centric design, where character sketches of potential users have imagined interactions with designs, through to more radical social design and metadesign methods, which fall under the umbrella of co-design (Fuad-Luke, 2009).

Social design principles, which are well established in architecture, urban and industrial design, are of increasing relevance for infrastructure. Social design is commonly understood to be design for improving human wellbeing and livelihoods (Holm, 2006). It also implies a social model of design that addresses the interface between people – individuals or in groups – and environmental domains, including the environment and the built environment. Social design emphasises the need to identify stakeholders and to understand their motivations, as the basis for socially useful innovation. In social design, the designer focuses on providing enabling solutions, which extend the capability of the community or user. This includes building the capabilities of community members to reduce resource consumption and achieve sustainability goals, as described in the case study chapters.

All co-design is based on the fundamental principle that an end user of a particular design has the right to have a voice in the design process (Costanza-Chock, 2020). This premise acknowledges both the agency of the end designs – how a product, technology or infrastructure changes how people can interact with both it and the world – and the consequent power of designers. The co-design process at its most fundamental is a challenge to the established dynamic of infrastructure provision, with all the intricacies of power, capital, exclusion and inclusion that are built into it.

There are a number of co-design methods that allow for more or less participation from community members (ADB and RISE, 2021). Co-design is idealised as involving community members from the initial ideation stage and promotes learning between all members of the process – no matter what their position. It is particularly suited to situation-driven design contexts where there are common human experiences that provide a starting point for the process.

Metadesign is an emerging framework for design posited as crucial for addressing sustainability challenges (Wood, 2013). It aims to create tools that increase participation in complex topics, break design free of the economic context in which it has been operating, and bridge the gap between community and state (Vassão, 2017). Considering design from this contextualised standpoint helps to facilitate participants' engagement with unfamiliar problems, such as intervening in infrastructure design by developing tools and methods that make complex systems comprehensible to urban residents. Metadesign methods were used in developing the tools used in the Engineering Comes Home project in Chapter 6, described in detail in Chapter 9.

Community collaboration and urban change

The environmental justice inquiry in Euston that was the purpose of the meeting in a community hall on a snowy night in London was an example of collaboration between community groups, university researchers and engaged professionals (lawyers). The outcomes of the inquiry demonstrated the strength of what can be achieved through strong community participation in research. It was part of an ongoing, evolving partnership between the university and the community, and led to the Somers Town Air Quality project described in Chapter 7. The enthusiasm for the environmental justice inquiry indicates the commitment of community members, and their hope that working with urban researchers and professionals will provide useful knowledge to help solve some of the complex, long-running problems that they face.

Urban communities persist and change. They are shaped by the long arc of history, economics and politics, and their built and natural environments. Communities entail their own internal complexities, as well as myriad relationships with outsiders. Communities formed intentionally in response to ecological and climate crises grapple with questions of technology, infrastructure and design, as well as social and political organisation. Engagements with scientists, researchers and designers are typically focused on projects, which may have varying levels of participation, but are experienced as moments in longer stories of urban change and resistance.

Community is a valid and important scale of organisation and point of engagement with vast global and environmental crises. Urban communities are sites of innovation and holders of knowledge that might otherwise be beyond the grasp of researchers, scientists, engineers and designers. Working productively in collaboration requires an understanding of community dynamics and how they relate to wider structures of power that continue to shape cities and the infrastructures that connect them to the resources on which they depend.

3
Infrastructures

The bath in Hellene's flat is a source of concern to her. Hellene is a social tenant on the Meakin Estate and her flat, like most of her neighbours' flats, comes with a bath not a shower. As a contributor to the Engineering Comes Home Project (Chapter 6), Hellene tells Charlotte that when her children were young, they would happily share a bath, but now her teenager refuses and demands her own bath water. Hellene feels a shower would be less wasteful but lacks the space and means to add one. She also faces the disincentive that, as a tenant, she may have to reverse any changes that she makes inside her flat if she moves out. Consequently, after her son has bathed, Hellene watches hot water disappear down the plug hole into London's overburdened sewer system, before refilling the bath with more hot water for her teenage daughter. She is not on a metered supply, so she does not pay for the extra bath water, but she says she finds it 'depressing to see it go up and then down'. Hellene's concern about the bath and her children's bathing habits is not about the impact on the household budget, but rather the impact of her household on the city's water resources (Hellene is a pseudonym, and this story is adapted from Johnson *et al.*, 2020).

The water for the bath in Hellene's flat is heated in a boiler room which serves Hellene and her neighbours. The same system provides heating to radiators in each flat. The heating system is currently undergoing a much-needed upgrade, and the hot-water pipes are visible in open trenches for the first time in decades. The boiler runs on gas, connected to London's gas supply network, which in turn is connected to pipelines that span Europe.

Hellene's worries about wasting water hint at an everyday awareness of the connection between household behaviours and environmental impacts, mediated by vast systems of pipes. While young people have heroically been at the forefront of recent movements to avert the climate emergency, the teenage years can also be a time of high sensitivity to social norms about personal hygiene and privacy. Hellene's daughter's very reasonable expectation of her own bathwater is easily accommodated by the water and energy networks that connect her flat to the estate, the estate to London and London to rivers, groundwater and far-away gas fields. And yet, when Hellene sees the water go up and down, she knows the changes in her household are having an effect somewhere else, and she feels bad about it. Hellene sees the bathwater. The invisible systems that bring water and heat from somewhere else to make bathing possible are water and energy infrastructure.

Infrastructures are the sociotechnical systems that make cities work. Water, energy, transport, data and waste infrastructures supply the basic services necessary for urban life. Infrastructures shape communities and the environment, and embody social and political values, although they remain largely unnoticed (Shove *et al.*, 2018; Graham and McFarlane, 2014).

Infrastructures underpin economic and social activity, converting resources from the environment into a form that is useful, and taking away waste materials and contaminants to keep people healthy and safe. Water infrastructure collects and treats water from rivers and aquifers and distributes it to buildings and spaces across a city, then drains away dirty water, treating it and returning it to the environment. Transport infrastructure moves people and goods around, using energy from fossil fuels, electricity and bodies. Energy infrastructure converts energy in the wind, sun, other environmental elements or fuel reserves into electricity, heat or fuels that can be used by people, and distributes it to where it is needed. Waste infrastructure collects unused, potentially dangerous materials, removes them from the urban environment, treats them and either returns material to the economy or to the environment. Communication infrastructure converts information into data that can be transmitted, received, stored and retrieved. Infrastructures transform, distribute and store materials, people, energy and information as a foundation for modern society.

Infrastructures take care of people – at least those who live in wealthy, politically stable cities, with able-bodies and enough money to pay the bills. Every morning, millions of people safely make a cup of tea or coffee, take a shower, dress in clean clothes, check the weather forecast and get to school or work because of different forms of infrastructure. Mostly, people in the Global North do not worry if the water is safe to drink and bathe in. They do not think about where it goes beyond the plug hole. At the flick of a switch, the kettle boils. The internet sends the news. The bus arrives at its destination. Infrastructures are the background to modern lives (Edwards, 2003).

Typically, people only notice infrastructure on those rare mornings when the power is off, the taps are dry or, more frequently, the internet is slow and the trains are delayed. Infrastructure is most noticeable in cities where it has not been built, or has failed, which is often the case in the Global South (Graham, 2009). Infrastructure is acutely important to a household that does not have enough money to pay the bills. People who use wheelchairs become experts in the details of transport infrastructure, of which the able-bodied can remain ignorant. Cyclists become viscerally aware of infrastructure when a car comes too close to their bike in traffic. A growing number of citizens are paying attention to infrastructure as essential to solving the climate emergency, improving air quality, cleaning up local rivers and making cities healthy and safe (Rey-Mazón *et al.*, 2018).

To co-design sustainable and resilient infrastructure that meets the aspirations of urban communities, it is important to understand how urban infrastructures work. The projects described in this book intersect with vast networks of infrastructure in different ways, addressing specific problems for London communities in their interactions with the big sociotechnical systems of their city. This chapter provides a general backdrop for those specific struggles and opportunities, reviewing broad, global trends in infrastructure provision. It focuses mostly on urban infrastructures of the Global North, although the core themes may be relevant globally. The chapter defines infrastructure as sociotechnical systems and describes the infrastructure life cycle. It then explores who owns infrastructure, and opportunities for change. The idea of 'communities of infrastructure' is introduced as a new way of thinking about urban communities, opening up previously opaque black boxes to co-design sustainable, resilient, healthy urban futures.

What is infrastructure?

The physical systems of infrastructure – the pipes, wires, cables, wind turbines, reservoirs, treatment works, recycling centres, roads, airports and more – come to mind most readily. Infrastructures are also made up of the management and governance systems that keep things running, set standards for safety and performance, and pay for it all. Without the required legal and financial structures in place, the technical system starts to physically fall apart. Infrastructures are sociotechnical systems (Edwards, 2003) that need both social and technical elements for them to work (Star, 1999).

Infrastructure is made by people and, like technology, reflects the values that underpin its design and operation (Feenberg, 2012). It allows some things, and not others. It includes some people, but not others. It keeps people safe and comfortable, but too often comes at the cost of the natural environment. Infrastructure embodies social and political values (Star, 1999). Universal provision of clean drinking water and sewage services demonstrates the high social value of public health. Railway stations with stairs and escalators, but no lifts, reflect a society that values the mobility of people who can walk easily more than people who cannot. A society that throws millions of tonnes of material into gigantic holes in the ground values fast, simple disposal of waste more than conserving resources.

Conventional infrastructure systems are big (Hughes, 1993; Sofoulis, 2005). Electricity is transmitted across continents. Gas pipelines cover thousands of kilometres. Transport networks literally span the globe. Such large systems cost a lot to build and operate, are usually owned by governments and big corporations, and have extensive environmental effects (Loftus *et al.*, 2019).

The United Nations Sustainable Development Goals (SDGs) recognise the importance of infrastructure in Goal 9 – 'Build resilient infrastructure, promote inclusive and sustainable industrialization and foster innovation'. Infrastructures are important in delivering many other goals, especially those related to water (SDG6), energy (SDG7), economic growth (SDG8), cities and communities (SDG11), consumption and production (SDG12) and climate action (SDG13). The infrastructure goals provide the link between reducing poverty and improving health and education, and protecting and conserving the land, ocean and atmosphere (Waage *et al.*, 2015).

Infrastructures make connections. They can be thought of as networks of relationships – between the environment, the technical and physical components, management and expertise, buildings and urban spaces, the everyday habits and cultures of people who use services, and the industries, businesses and governments who own, operate and regulate the systems (Edwards, 2003; Star, 1999; Star and Ruhleder, 1996).

The infrastructure life cycle

Infrastructure networks emerge, stabilise, grow, decline and reconfigure over time. Infrastructures are initiated as ideas or solutions to problems, then become projects that are planned, designed and constructed, to be operated and maintained for decades or centuries, to eventually reach an end of life where they are decommissioned, to be re-purposed or replaced (see Figure 3.1). Opportunities for community engagement and co-design vary throughout the stages of the infrastructure life cycle.

Initiation

Infrastructures begin as ideas. Often, they start with addressing a problem (e.g., traffic congestion, water pollution or slow railway speeds). The definition of the problem determines the nature of the solution; hence the importance of communities and other stakeholders being involved at these earliest stages. For instance, if traffic congestion is defined as a problem causing long commuting times for drivers, wider roads may be the solution. If traffic congestion is defined as a problem causing pollution for local communities, more public transport or road-user charges to reduce road use may be the solution.

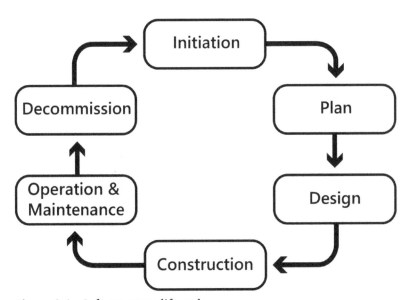

Figure 3.1 Infrastructure life cycle

Planning

The formal planning process is typically where most formal public and community consultation occurs, because of legislative or other government requirements (Bal *et al.*, 2013; Reed, 2008). Planning for infrastructure projects takes account of economic costs and benefits, and environmental and social impacts. Deciding which projects to build may be the outcome of decades of analysis and lobbying. Project appraisal and evaluation methods provide data to compare projects and their costs and benefits, but decision-making in infrastructure is also influenced by powerful actors and political interests.

Design

Designing infrastructure is usually the work of engineers. Architects, urban designers and product designers may also be involved in designing some elements of infrastructure systems, such as railway stations, buildings to house waste incinerators or the display interfaces for operators to control the systems. Infrastructure systems engineering and design includes many sub-stages, from overall concept design (e.g., a pipe to transfer water), to the core structure of the system (e.g., the location of the pipeline and pumping stations), detailed design of components (e.g., the size of pipes and valves to ensure safe and reliable operations), and design of the sequencing for construction and operation (e.g., which bits get built when, control systems for the pipe network) (Sage and Rouse, 2014). Much of this work is highly technical, requiring specialist knowledge and large teams of experts. Communities may be involved in decisions about some elements of the design, such as the open space outside a pumping station or the appearance of buildings but are typically excluded from this phase of the life cycle, despite the social and community impacts of design decisions.

Construction

Construction can be one of the most contentious phases of the infrastructure life cycle in urban communities (Close and Loosemore, 2014; Glass and Simmonds, 2007). Despite the best intentions of infrastructure planners, for many people, the first they learn of a new infrastructure project is when a construction site appears in their neighbourhood. Construction can be highly disruptive for local communities, as a source of noise and pollution. It may also provide opportunities for local employment and other benefits provided by construction and infrastructure firms as part of community engagement strategies. Local communities are often powerless to change construction plans and activities at this stage and may live with extensive disruption for many years (Teo and Loosemore, 2010).

Infrastructure construction projects are complex to deliver and require large, specialist organisations. A small number of large firms compete for infrastructure contracts within countries and internationally. Infrastructure projects typically involve many complex layers and types of contract, down to subcontracts with labour-hire firms and individual workers. Each contract transfers risks and responsibilities, along with money and profit margins. Workers on infrastructure projects may be employed by many different firms or by themselves.

Operation and maintenance

Maintaining infrastructure requires judicious planning. Maintenance operations often require systems to shut down, potentially disrupting service to customers, but are needed to avoid breakdowns that result in uncontrolled disruptions to service and dangerous risks to public, worker and environmental safety. Reducing maintenance budgets can decrease the overall costs of infrastructure operation, reducing government spending, keeping down user fees or increasing short-term profits for private owners and contractors. However, failure to allocate sufficient resources and expertise to maintenance increases the risk of catastrophic accidents, with disastrous consequences for workers, the public and the environment.

Infrastructure providers, both public and private, are typically large organisations requiring complex administration. Accounting, finance, human resources, public and media relations, planning, regulatory compliance, billing, customer relations, environmental management, information technology, health and safety, and quality control are among the many departments and professions employed by infrastructure companies. These people and the work they do is typically unseen, and may be transferrable to many other workplaces, yet they are as much a part of the sociotechnical system of infrastructure as the pipes, wires, tracks and roads.

As in many industries, automation has reduced requirements for workers to operate and administer infrastructure. Ticket machines and then contactless payment replaced ticket-booth operators and conductors on public transport. Automated number-plate recognition replaced toll-booth workers and car-park attendants. Water and wastewater treatment plants can now be monitored and controlled remotely, reducing the requirement for onsite workforce to intervene in treatment processes.

Decommissioning

The end of the life of an infrastructure system or facility may result in mixed impacts on local communities. It may be the end of pollution, noise and other disruption, but it may also lead to job losses and declining local economic activity. The transition from fossil fuels to renewable energy requires the decommissioning of existing infrastructures such as coal-fired power stations and oil refineries. The Just Transition movement, at the intersection of climate and environmental justice, aims to ensure that local communities and workers benefit from new investment and opportunities in renewable energy and other economic opportunities (McCauley and Heffron, 2018).

Decommissioning infrastructures may require specialist decontamination and management of pollutants accumulated over several decades. Iconic infrastructures may also be re-purposed into new buildings, such as the Tate Modern art museum in London, which was once a power station.

Who owns infrastructure?

The origins of current infrastructure systems can be found in the nineteenth century. In the early decades of modern infrastructure, many developments were led by the private sector. Providing new services, such as water and electricity to growing cities and the emerging middle classes, was a potentially lucrative business opportunity. The first water and energy companies in many cities were privately owned (Halliday, 1999; Hughes, 1993). Railways that criss-crossed countries and continents were highly competitive private enterprises. A proliferation of private companies led to different technical standards, even within the same city (Hughes, 1999). Private companies connected to households or businesses that were profitable for them, leaving poorer and more remote or hard-to-access homes and businesses outside the network.

By the middle of the twentieth century most infrastructures in most countries were under government ownership and control. Infrastructure was seen as a public service, to provide the background on which other economic and social activity could grow (Marvin and Graham, 2001). Public works departments or similar built and operated water supply, sewers, postal services, telephone networks, electricity and gas supplies. Transport agencies built road and rail networks, and government authorities owned and operated airports and airlines. Infrastructure investment generated direct economic activity by creating jobs and demand for materials and services during construction, operation and maintenance. It also provided the services necessary for industrialising economies and growing cities.

As the SDGs attest, providing equitable access to infrastructure is fundamental to economic and social development (Thacker *et al.*, 2019). Paying for infrastructure has reflected its public and private benefits, and ideologies about the role of the state (Della Croce and Gatti, 2014; Furlong, 2020). State investment in building infrastructure supports private sector investment and economic growth (Aschauer, 1989; Bom and Ligthart, 2014; Romp and de Haan, 2005). Government spending on infrastructure is a well-established economic stimulus strategy (Egert *et al.*, 2009; OECD, 2021). Big project announcements often include projections for the jobs created in construction. Infrastructure spending provides immediate economic activity through construction, and a long-term legacy to support further economic growth and development (Romp and de Haan, 2005). The private sector also plays a significant role as owners, builders or operators of infrastructure in many countries, a trend that has increased since the 1980s (Marvin and Graham, 2001).

There are a variety of ways that infrastructure is paid for by users and taxpayers (Klein, 2012; Rioja, 2013). Some infrastructures, including most roads, are now free to use. Others, such as railways, require users to pay for the service. Users may pay the full cost, a price that includes some profit margin, or a price that is subsidised, either by the government or other users. In some cities, services such as water and waste collection are paid through general government revenue, with no connection between payment and service. This means that revenue for infrastructure is subject to government budgetary processes and may reflect political priorities rather than the costs of running, maintaining and improving the service (Rioja, 2013). Local government property taxes or rates may include a charge for waste collection or water and sanitation services. This provides an assured revenue for the infrastructure services and links user charges to property wealth rather than service use. Fuel taxes may be directed towards transport budgets, so that users contribute to the cost of operating the roads and transport networks, without a direct link between how much they use the network and how much they pay (Rioja, 2013). Road tolls, public transport fares and metered supplies of gas, electricity and water are direct 'user pays' revenue collection systems.

Well-managed infrastructure systems with user charges provide constant, reliable revenue (OECD, 2021). This is partly an outcome of the 'background' nature of infrastructure. Whatever else happens in the economy, households still require water, energy, waste and data services. Revenue from infrastructure services is therefore more reliable than from other goods or services, or tax. Households under economic stress, such as loss of employment or reduced business income, may reduce their use of heating or water to save money, but utility bills are usually not 'discretionary' and cannot be delayed in the way household spending on other services and goods may be. Tax revenues also fall during an economic downturn, while infrastructure revenue remains relatively stable. Infrastructure requires large capital investment to build but it can deliver steady, long-term incomes from user charges if it is well managed (OECD, 2021).

The stability of revenue from infrastructure makes it attractive to private investment (Della Croce, 2011). Since the 1980s, many infrastructure services and systems have been privatised (Marvin and Graham, 2001). Full or part-privatisation of infrastructure, including national airlines and airports, telephone networks, waste management, electricity and gas, railways and buses, were key elements of neoliberal policy agendas in the 1980s and 1990s (Sager, 2011).

Neoliberalism promotes the market and competition as the means to distribute resources and deliver services (Bockman, 2013; Sager, 2011). It aims to reduce the role of the state in the economy, minimising regulation and enhancing the role of the private sector. In this model, the private sector is thought to be more efficient and responsive than the public sector, and competition and choice are thought of as the best means to achieve lower costs and better outcomes for consumers. Neoliberalism is also associated with the objective of reducing government debt and budget deficits, providing fiscal constraints on public sector capacity to invest in large capital projects such as infrastructure (Streeck, 2014). Private sector access to capital markets has therefore been a further driver of infrastructure privatisation. Large institutional investors seeking stable long-term returns, such as pension funds, have become significant owners of infrastructure in recent decades (Croce, 2011).

Privatisation of infrastructure takes different forms and has been pursued to different extents in different countries (Helm and Tindall, 2009; Sager, 2011). Private companies may provide contracted services to government-owned utilities such as maintenance, operations or revenue collection, while the infrastructure itself remains in public ownership. Infrastructure companies may be created that are fully owned by the government but are operated as cost-recovery or profit-making enterprises. Public-private partnership contracts allow private companies to build and operate infrastructure, with government guarantees of income and management of risks, often with ownership of the infrastructure transferring to the government at the end of the initial contract. Governments or private companies may own different parts of an infrastructure system. Power stations or renewable energy supplies may be owned by different companies or agencies, while energy distribution networks may be owned by others, and customers may receive services from retail suppliers.

Neoliberal policy creates market competition as a means to improve efficiency, reduce costs and meet demand (Sager, 2011). Due to the natural monopolies of many large networked systems, privatisation of infrastructure typically involves separating out production, distribution and retail activities in order to create markets at these different points. Privatisation in natural monopolies requires strong regulation of pricing, investment and services, to ensure that owners are not exploiting customers. Within neoliberal infrastructure policy, the private sector is meant to provide services and investment in the most economically efficient manner, while the government sets the conditions to protect consumers and the environment. At the same time, neoliberal policy advocates argue for reducing regulation, to enhance innovation, competition and efficiency. Large owners and investors in infrastructure are powerful political actors and stakeholders. They can also push against regulatory reform to maintain their incumbency and protect their dominance over existing markets or resist, for example, the requirement to increase environmental protection.

The problems with infrastructure

When infrastructure systems are working as they are designed, they provide limitless access at the flick of a switch for the ideal consumer (an able-bodied, working-age adult, with sufficient income to pay the bills). The water never stops running, even during a drought. Homes stay warm in the coldest winter and cool in the hottest summer. Streets do not flood, except in the most extreme rain events. It is possible to get in a car and drive and never reach the end of the road. A lifetime spent watching television would not be long enough to view all the content on streaming services delivered by data infrastructure. These vast systems shape modern life, bringing safety, convenience and creativity, but they also raise significant problems and challenges. Some key concerns for modern infrastructure are resource consumption, environmental impacts, interdependence, lock-in, basic provision, maintenance, gender and participation.

Resource consumption

Infrastructures tell consumers that there are no limits. Everyday habits are shaped by infrastructure and this message of limitless supply. Sociologist Elizabeth Shove (2004) has pointed out that our water-using practices have co-evolved with infrastructure and technologies. Constant water supply and drainage connections to homes have enabled modern technologies such as automatic washing machines, which in turn have created higher social expectations of always wearing clean, freshly laundered clothes. People now use more water washing laundry more often than previous generations, despite improved water efficiency of washing machines, an example of the 'rebound effect'. People change their clothes-washing and wearing routines in response to water conservation campaigns (e.g., to only run the machine on a full load), but higher water use has become the norm thanks to changes in water infrastructure and laundry technology.

Infrastructures are also subject to the 'rebound effect' first described by economist William Jevons (1906). The rebound effect describes how improvements in efficiency of resource use leads to higher overall consumption. Jevons observed the increase in coal consumption in England following improvements in the efficiency of steam engines based on the Watt steam engine. The Watt engine was vastly more efficient in its use of coal than the previous Newcomen design and it became economically viable to operate in a wider range of industries, leading to an overall increase in coal consumption despite the improved efficiency of individual engines. Similar patterns have been observed in improvements in the efficiency of domestic appliances, with consumers using improvements in efficiency of devices to increase their use, rather than reduce resource consumption or cost (Borenstein, 2014). Improved efficiency of heating has been associated with stable or increased use of heating, as it becomes affordable for householders to raise the temperature on the thermostat or heat a whole house where once people chose to heat only specific rooms (Volland, 2016). Drivers of fuel-efficient cars tend to drive further than those with less efficient models. Infrastructures are known to 'induce demand', creating demand for a resource or service that did not previously exist. New roads are built to ease congestion on the existing network, only to fill with cars driven by people taking advantage of the new connections (Hymel *et al.*, 2010).

Environmental impacts

Infrastructures are the systems that transform environmental resources into useful services for people (Waage *et al.*, 2015). Consequently, they separate the users of the resources from their environmental impacts. This is a significant benefit as it provides safety, security, efficiency and convenience, but it also means that environmental impacts increase without widespread awareness until resource limits are reached or ecosystems are in crisis (Bell, 2015). It has become easier to believe that access to endless energy and clean drinking water is normal and right, than to understand that these are limited resources to be shared with other people and the environment.

Resource use and environmental impacts come together across infrastructure systems (Kurian, 2017; Leck *et al.*, 2015). The water-energy-food nexus, which is the focus of the Engineering Comes Home project in Chapter 6, describes how infrastructures and resources are connected. Increase in demand for one infrastructure service drives up demand for others and, conversely, resource constraints in one infrastructure impacts on others. Water is needed to cool power stations, so a drought can lead to power cuts. Energy is needed to pump water to irrigate crops to grow food. Energy is also needed to transport food from farms to market, including global supply chains for some commodities. Increasing fuel costs therefore increase food prices. Water shortages may be addressed by installing desalination plants, which use a lot of energy to remove salt from seawater to make clean drinking water.

Interdependence

Infrastructure interdependence is an area of concern for disaster management and resilience (Little, 2002). Large sociotechnical systems are complex and interconnected. As the water-energy-food nexus described in Chapter 6 shows, failure in one infrastructure system has consequences for other systems. Flooding of an electricity substation that supplies a water treatment works may lead to a disruption of water supply, leaving people surrounded by water but without clean water to drink from their tap. Electricity and data failures can also disrupt transport systems, such as when traffic lights fail and rail networks cannot operate. Wastewater treatment plants require energy to operate, and power failures can result in sewage being dumped in the environment without treatment.

Lock-in

Adaptation to environmental, social and economic change beyond their original design assumptions is challenging for large, centralised infrastructure systems. Infrastructures get 'baked in' to a city (Hommels, 2008; Sofoulis, 2005). If a city has been built with roads and private cars as the main form of transport infrastructure, it is difficult to shift everyone on to public transport. Prior investment to build infrastructure creates 'fixed assets' that serve a single purpose and cannot be sold and moved if they are no longer needed. A state that has built a big dam to supply water to factories cannot sell the dam to another country when the industry moves offshore (Brady, 1985). Power stations that use water from local rivers for cooling are vulnerable to declining rainfall due to climate change (Linnerud *et al.*, 2011). A power network built for a one-way flow of electricity from constant generation by coal-fired power stations to homes and businesses must be reconfigured to be able to distribute energy from renewable sources located across a landscape. For instance, the electricity grid in the United States was built to distribute power from large power stations to consumers, in some cases across states. This ageing infrastructure requires major new investment to be able to connect to renewable supplies distributed across the network (Jansson and Michelfelder, 2008).

Not only are physical systems difficult to move or change, but ownership, management, regulation and knowledge are also hard to shift. Large corporations and government departments have evolved to manage big, centralised infrastructure, and can resist changes to infrastructure systems that might reduce their income and influence. Management and regulation of a water system to supply clean, safe water through one centralised utility seems easier and more efficient than monitoring thousands of water systems located in individual buildings, owned and operated by thousands of homeowners, landlords or service companies (Dolowitz *et al.*, 2018). Changing systems of ownership, regulation and management of infrastructure can be at least as complex and difficult as changing the physical technologies and systems.

Social values baked-in to infrastructure systems are also exceedingly difficult to shift. A famous, though contested, example from New York is the low bridges built over parkways (high-speed roads) in the middle of the twentieth century. These prevented buses from travelling to state parks on Long Island, allegedly excluding poor Black residents from travelling to beaches and recreation sites (Winner, 1988). Roads and railway lines become social barriers, dividing urban communities, with poorer people living closest to noisy and polluting infrastructure while wealthier commuters travel through. In the United States, waste and industrial facilities are located in neighbourhoods with higher proportions of Black people (Cole and Foster, 2000). Environmental justice movements, discussed in Chapter 2, highlight the impact of pollution, noise and climate change on poorer, marginalised communities, such as the residents of Somers Town in Chapter 7.

Basic provision

The absence of infrastructure in cities of the Global South is a major challenge to be addressed by the SDGs. Large, centralised infrastructure systems require large capital investment and stable economic and political conditions to ensure ongoing operation and economic returns. Rapid urbanisation, neoliberal policy agendas, local political instability and corruption have left billions of people without access to basic infrastructure services (Anand *et al.*, 2018). Initiatives to promote decentralised, lower-cost systems to deliver infrastructure services aim to address this gap, but raise concerns about equality of access, reliability and high user charges (Ranganathan and Balazs, 2015).

Maintenance

Infrastructure systems of any scale require maintenance to ensure a safe, reliable, efficient service. As discussed earlier, maintenance receives relatively little attention compared to design and construction in infrastructure discussions and debates, yet poor maintenance can lead to catastrophic failure, environmental harm, reduced lifespans for assets and a general decline in service and experience. Maintenance budgets are vulnerable to being cut to save costs for operators or to run down assets towards the end of their life. The geographer Jamie Peck (2012) argues that after the global financial crisis of 2008 some cities in the United States experienced what he terms 'austerity urbanism'. Underfunded municipal authorities with declining revenues looked to defer or cut maintenance programmes. Detroit, for example, removed most of its streetlights, suggesting residents could keep their porch lights on instead

(Peck, 2012). In the UK, housing activists have argued that years of poor maintenance and neglect turn liveable estates into targets for demolition, an issue explored in Chapter 5.

Gender

The professions and trades that plan, design, build and operate infrastructure remain dominated by men in most parts of the world (Adeyemi *et al.*, 2006; Ness, 2012; Patel and Pitroda, 2016). Women are under-represented as employees in almost every part of the sector. Infrastructure is associated with masculine characteristics of control, mastery and domination of natural elements, despite the important roles that infrastructure services play in domestic life and care for citizens and communities, which are traditionally feminine (Bell, 2015; Wajcman, 1991). The gendered associations of infrastructure jobs being done by men, and infrastructure functions as large, technical systems of control and domination, are separate but linked. They structure women's experience of the city and capacity to participate in decision-making and public life (Wilson, 1992).

Participation

When it is so clear that the physical fabric of infrastructure has implications for society and the environment, questions arise about whose voices, knowledge and opinions should be considered when designing infrastructure. There have been increasing efforts to engage with infrastructure 'consumers' – the citizens who use infrastructure daily. In some accounts, this opens the door to rethink the roles of consumers, turning them into 'co-managers' of infrastructure, exploring the complexities of better resource management (van Vliet, 2016). In other accounts this engagement can be seen as prescriptive and limiting the opportunity for real citizen engagement in decision-making. Analysis of public engagement policy for new UK energy infrastructure found that the formal decision-making processes had become less open to citizens, limiting the types of decision that could be debated to streamline development (Cowell and Devine-Wright, 2018). The authors also noted the increasing use of community benefits funds by infrastructure developers, suggesting these 'frame publics as local communities rather than as active citizens', by offering them money to host infrastructure rather than allowing them to have a voice (Cowell *et al.*, 2011; Cowell and Devine-Wright, 2018, p. 509).

New sociotechnical systems

The drive to decentralise infrastructures is a response to environmental limits, and a means to improve the reliability of access to services compared to increasingly vulnerable and unstable centralised networks. Rescaling infrastructure to a community level creates a sense that these two are aligned – the infrastructure will serve the community and the community will manage the infrastructure. This alignment will not happen unless systems are designed in that way – physically designed to allow for active participation, and supported by regulations, business models and governance structures that allow for a group to take responsibility for a decentralised part of the system. Decentralisation has the potential to increase, rather than decrease social inequality. Without appropriate management and policy, people with plentiful resources will exit large networks and receive cheaper, greener services. Meanwhile, poorer and more vulnerable people will be left paying higher prices for national-scale infrastructure networks, or they may be disconnected or find themselves in an infrastructure black spot (Marvin and Graham, 2001).

Innovation in technology, governance and business models have changed the boundaries of what is considered infrastructure and the actors involved in infrastructure provision. For example, where previously the electricity network stopped at the meter boundary, smart metering and demand management now mean that appliances and behaviour inside homes are considered part of the energy infrastructure. Decentralised systems, such as rooftop solar cells and batteries, and rainwater harvesting and water recycling, may now connect to larger systems of distribution. Households and communities may now be 'prosumers' of infrastructure services – becoming both producers and consumers – with significant impact on resource sustainability (van Vliet *et al.*, 2005). The community energy movement, including community-owned batteries and renewable energy technologies, demonstrates how infrastructure innovation has the potential to change models of ownership, governance and decision-making, as well as technologies of supply (Hewitt *et al.*, 2019).

Communities of infrastructure

Infrastructures are not finished or bounded in space or time; far from being static, they are constantly changing socially and physically (Larkin, 2013). Thinking of urban infrastructure in this way highlights the co-evolution and interdependency between social and physical infrastructures, with important implications for resilience and sustainability. The link between physical and social conditions is, nevertheless, complex. This re-think of sustainable infrastructure as both social and physical has the potential to generate both questions and conflicts: What qualities are valued? Whose decisions, interests or values should be counted? What processes influence the urban realm and drive the processes to deliver change?

Infrastructures therefore provide another form of community. Communities of infrastructure share connections to urban technical systems – for example, water, sewers, electricity, data and transport (Johnson *et al.*, 2020). These impersonal systems form the background to the city; designed and managed by invisible experts, they enable urban life, but form part of the unknowable modern world, bigger than everyday experience. Communities of infrastructure open these black boxes, revealing connections between people, environments, governments and institutions. In so doing, communities of infrastructure may find new modes of meeting everyday needs that support stronger, more nourishing relationships with each other and the local and planetary systems on which they depend.

4
Bottom-up research

In the spring of 2012, the Provost of UCL announced plans to build a new campus. UCL had outgrown its home in central London and, with the right land deal, it made sense to expand operations elsewhere. The Olympic Games were drawing world attention to the east of the city, along with government investment in transport and data infrastructure, and urban regeneration plans were emerging to make the most of this legacy. The east of London seemed like a smart place for university expansion. The problem was that the site that had been chosen was a housing estate. UCL's plan, under negotiation with the London Borough of Newham, was to demolish the Carpenters Estate, home to hundreds of people for more than four decades, and to build a new campus. Carpenters' residents organised to resist the plan, and students and staff from UCL joined in.

Within the university, the main proponents of the new campus were from Engineering, the faculty most constrained by the lack of space to build big equipment and run big experiments. The main opposition was from the faculties of Built Environment and Social Sciences, disciplines familiar with the negative consequences of grand schemes for urban revitalisation for the people they are supposed to help. Engineers came back from the site and spoke about the rail connections and data speeds. An urban geographer reported back from a visit to the Carpenters Estate, mentioning the local school and carefully tended flower boxes in home gardens. Social scientists saw a community. The engineers saw infrastructure.

In its marketing to recruit students, the UCL Faculty of Engineering promised to teach students how to 'Change the World'. The enthusiasm of engineering teaching and research staff for a project that disrupted the homes and lives of hundreds of fellow Londoners raised questions about who they would be changing the world for. This gap between engineers' claims to be serving social needs and their apparent inability to engage with the society affected by their work is not unique to UCL or to universities. It presents a fundamental challenge to engineering education and professionalism around the world, and it reflects a deeper structural problem in modern technological societies.

Technical knowledge, central to decision-making in complex modern societies, is largely owned and used by people with power and money: universities, governments, corporations. Too often it is out of reach from those most impacted by the outcomes of such decisions: local communities. Engineers change the world, but not always for the better.

The negotiations between UCL and the London Borough of Newham eventually broke down over who would pay 'site clearance costs', the euphemism for relocating residents and demolishing their homes. The Olympic Games were a glorious success, and before long a new proposition emerged for a UCL campus on the Olympic Park itself, which was previously industrial land, and the Carpenters' residents continued to organise their own plans to regenerate their estate.

The gap between the intent and the outcome of the Faculty of Engineering's mission to 'Change the World' that had become apparent in the dispute over the Carpenters Estate inspired the Engineering Exchange. The Engineering Exchange provided a structure to enable UCL engineers to work directly with local London communities, to put the slogan into action on their doorstep. In time, the Bottom-Up Infrastructure research programme evolved from this platform to explore the potential for co-designing infrastructures with communities.

This chapter explains how a bottom-up approach to engineering and infrastructure evolved through the experience of engaging with communities in engineering research and teaching at UCL. It uses the Carpenters Estate as an example of the democratic deficit created by unequal access to technical knowledge. It tells the story of the Engineering Exchange as a small attempt to address the gap and explores the origins and potential for community co-design of infrastructure. The chapter outlines the co-design method of the Bottom-Up Infrastructure programme, which was applied in different ways in case studies described in Chapters 6–8, and describes how research ethics issues were addressed.

Knowledge democracy

At the centre of the Carpenters Estate are two high-rise residential buildings. Long before UCL's brief involvement with the site, an analysis for the estate owner, the London Borough of Newham, recommended that they be demolished. The technical report concluded that it would be too expensive to refurbish the towers to meet energy efficiency and living standards. This would also have the benefit of providing a cleared site for future real estate deals and developments, such as a university campus. The residents were not convinced, but they were not qualified to question the technical analysis and cost estimates in the engineering report that justified demolition. Unlike the London Borough of Newham, they did not have the money to pay for an engineer or access to the necessary data to check the analysis and consider alternatives to demolition.

The Carpenters' problem is emblematic of a deficit in democratic decision-making in a complex technological society (Hall and Tandon, 2017). Technical information is at the heart of many important political decisions, but only the most powerful political interests can afford to commission technical work and steer its direction (Davis, 1998; Foucault and Gordon, 1980). Engineers and other technical professions are ethically bound to provide advice based on sound analysis using the best available data and methods. They are obliged to keep the public safe and contribute to sustainable development (Institution of Civil Engineers, 2017). They must also act in the best interests of their client, and the client pays their wages (Davis, 1998).

What if the engineers and designers were acting directly in the interests of the community, rather than on behalf of the usual powerful actors? Would the technical answer be different? It is impossible to know without intense, specialist interrogation of the specific piece of work. Basic material properties, like the load-bearing capacity of a beam or the insulation coefficient of a wall, do not change. Design options, building methods and costs for labour, materials and engineers' time, do. The calculation about whether it is cheaper or more environmentally efficient to refurbish or demolish a block of flats includes constants, such as insulation coefficients, but it also includes variables, such as the price of insulation materials. If insulation materials are assumed to be expensive in the calculations, then refurbishing the existing building may turn out to be uneconomical compared to demolishing it and rehousing the residents. If the price of insulation materials goes down, or if a different design strategy using less insulation is chosen, then the results of the calculation might be different. If the energy efficiency of heating an old building is compared to a new one, it looks good for the environment to demolish it and start again. If the whole life cycle environmental impacts of disposing of the waste from the old building, and manufacturing the steel, concrete, wiring and other materials for the new, then the environmental benefits may stack up differently.

Engineers make choices about designs and assumptions about prices and other variables. They draw boundaries around what they include in their calculations. Such decisions are typically based on sound data and collective experience, but they are made in the interests of the client, in line with the scope of work as they define it. If the interests of the client are to maximise the economic return on a site in need of regeneration, then the scope of work and the subsequent decisions made by the engineer or designer may be different than if the interests of the client are to minimise environmental impacts and provide safe, sustainable homes for the people already living there.

The people most impacted by engineering recommendations are often those least able to influence the terms on which engineering and design work is done. The residents of the Carpenters Estate were not able to define the scope of work or scrutinise assumptions made and boundaries drawn by the engineers acting on behalf of the London Borough of Newham. They did not have the funding to engage experts to act on their own behalf and their own expertise as residents of the buildings was not powerful enough to counter the technical report used to justify demolition.

Reflecting on four decades of leadership of participatory research in Africa, India and Canada, Hall and Tandon (2017) explain that 'knowledge democracy acknowledges the importance of the existence of multiple epistemologies and the knowledge of the marginalized or excluded everywhere'. Knowledge democracy is about understanding that knowledge is a powerful tool for taking action in social movements to deepen democracy. It is also about open access for the sharing of knowledge, so that everyone who needs knowledge will have access to it, and everyone's knowledge is taken into account in decisions that affect them.

There are several pathways to bring knowledge democracy to life in urban decision-making. The first is to strengthen policy processes so that a wider range of interests are represented in the commissioning of engineering work and deliberations over its outcomes. In contentious situations, such as housing-estate regeneration, this can become highly controversial and politically impossible. Another pathway is for engineers to raise their ethical obligations to the safety of the public and sustainable development to equal standing to their commitment to their clients, ensuring that their technical work takes account of wider interests by default. In the everyday world of commercial consulting, this is a laudable, but naïve, ambition. A third option is to expand access to specialist expertise beyond those who can afford to pay for it.

Throughout their efforts to resist the destruction of their estate and to create alternative plans, the Carpenters' residents were supported by the LTF, which represents social housing tenants across the city. The LTF is part of Just Space. This network of grassroots community groups works to increase community influence on strategic planning in London, and to share knowledge between local groups. Just Space works closely with academics and students in UCL's Bartlett School of Planning and was part of a series of workshops in 2013 organised by the UCL Urban Lab about how universities, residents and others might work together on research about estate regeneration in London. A breakout group on 'Technical Aid' discussed the need for communities to access advice and data about decisions and issues affecting their homes and neighbourhoods. This became a founding aim of the Engineering Exchange.

The Carpenters Estate provided more than inspiration for the Engineering Exchange. The Engineering Exchange went on to work with Carpenters' residents on their own plans for regeneration. A student group project outlined an infrastructure plan for the neighbourhood, an engineering consultancy firm did a *pro bono* sustainability assessment of their neighbourhood plan, and the Carpenters' problem, shared by thousands of social housing tenants across London, was motivation for the demolition or refurbishment project, as told in Chapter 5.

The Engineering Exchange

In 2013, UCL opened a funding scheme for 'Public Engagement Fellowships'. Over the past 15 years, there has been a gradual shift within universities to widening their main functions of teaching and research to include a third mission that includes their engagement with, and impact on, wider society (Hewitt *et al.*, 2020). This movement has been aligned with the expansion of citizen science initiatives, as described in Chapter 2. Using UK EPSRC money, the scheme would support staff to undertake special projects to improve the relationship between research and the public.

Having participated in the 'Technical Aid' workshop with Just Space and the LTF, Sarah proposed to take a year out from her teaching to build a small unit that would allow engineering researchers to work directly with grassroots London communities. The idea was that London community groups who otherwise could not afford to pay for expert engineering advice would be given access to UCL's world-leading researchers for free. The researchers might be inspired by new research problems and would benefit by seeing their work change the world in some small way. This would become the Engineering Exchange. Sarah won the fellowship and met with the Dean of Engineering to explain the project. He offered to extend the funding for a second year, include some cash for projects and events, and pay for a part-time administrator. Riding the tide of increased student tuition fees and numbers, it was a time of plenty in the Faculty. A time to build new campuses and support worthy ideas from earnest academic staff.

The purpose of the Engineering Exchange was not to engage directly in the struggles of communities but to raise the quality of public debate by widening access to technical knowledge. The intention was to support grassroots groups through the provision of high-quality technical advice and analysis, enhancing their capacity to scrutinise decisions that affected them and to propose technically viable alternatives. It was based on the concept of knowledge democracy: if technical knowledge is important in democratic decision-making, then technical knowledge should be widely accessible.

The Engineering Exchange aligned with a model of universities as more than simply sites for knowledge production and teaching. Delanty (2003) suggests that universities should become sites of public discourse rather than sites of exclusive expertise, so that they can become 'important agents of the public sphere, initiating social change rather than just responding to it'. The Engineering Exchange also drew on long-standing models of community engagement with research, especially the Science Shops of the Netherlands, the UK and elsewhere in Europe that had been established since the 1970s (Schlierf and Meyer, 2013; Wachelder, 2003).

Engineers working with communities through the Engineering Exchange were held to the same professional standards as if they were working for a government or private-sector client. Engineers and clients agreed to abide by protocols guiding their role and expectations. Community groups and engineers agreed a project scope, including aims, methods and deliverables at the outset. Milestones and interim progress reviews were included as needed, and significant project outcomes were subject to peer review by established, independent engineers and technical experts. The projects delivered by the Engineering Exchange were in the interests of their client, but the engineers who worked on them were no more community activists than engineers working for an industrial corporation are lobbyists. They were simply discharging their services to a client who would typically be excluded from technical expertise because they lacked the ability to pay.

The Engineering Exchange provided networks and systems for initiating and managing projects, and support for reviewing and disseminating outcomes. It consisted of a director, a communications and marketing officer, and a teaching fellow, in part-time paid roles, with three co-directors from different departments helping to deliver the programme as part of their academic roles. It trained graduate engineers and research students in how to work with communities. In addition to core funding from the UCL Faculty of Engineering, the Engineering Exchange won grants from the RAEng, the NERC and the EPSRC. In the five years that the Engineering Exchange operated it completed 22 projects, involving staff and students from 14 departments or institutes at UCL. The work was overseen by a steering committee, including equal numbers of community representatives and UCL staff, and an external engineer.

Engineering Exchange projects were led by academic or research staff at UCL and provided opportunities for students to apply their engineering learning. Topics including housing (Chapter 5), air quality (Chapter 7), transport, energy efficiency, neighbourhood security, building ventilation, canal barge design, emergency shelter for homeless people and pedestrian signalling. The model of working with communities evolved from the client relationship to research contribution and collaboration, as shown in Chapters 5–8. The Engineering Exchange provided proof of concept and a track record of community-based engineering consultancy and research, which then became the basis for larger funded research projects, including Engineering Comes Home (Chapter 6) and CAMELLIA (Chapter 8).

The nature of the relationship between community groups and researchers evolved throughout the life of the Engineering Exchange. It developed a track record of delivering outcomes that addressed community needs and respected community knowledge and skills, built trust and methods of working that enabled deeper collaboration. As an active research unit, the Engineering Exchange was able to access university and research council funding to enhance the impact of research in the community.

In 2019 the Community-University Knowledge Strategy for London (COLLABORATE!) project was initiated by Just Space, funded by the UCL EPSRC Impact Acceleration Account, and delivered in partnership with the Engineering Exchange. It provided equal funding to engage grassroots community groups and university staff to identify principles and actions to improve how universities in London work with local communities. COLLABORATE! produced a booklet of case studies of best practice in community-university partnerships in research and teaching, a video summarising the project, a charter and a strategic action document (Bell et al., 2021). The success of the project in meeting both university and community aims revealed the strength of the partnership that had developed over more than five years between the Engineering Exchange and its founding partner, Just Space.

The 3Cs

Working with communities to provide technical advice on specific problems through the Engineering Exchange revealed different forms of partnership between communities, researchers and the built environment professions. The Engineering Exchange experience revealed three roles for communities in research projects – as client, contributor and collaborator. These roles reflect different relationships between the community, the researchers and their contexts (see Figure 4.1). These are similar to three of the five models for public participation in scientific research outlined by Jennifer Shirk and colleagues: contractual, contributory, collaborative, co-created and collegial (Shirk et al., 2012)

Community as client (see Figure 4.2) was the foundation for the Engineering Exchange and exemplified by the Demolition or Refurbishment project (Chapter 5). To fulfil the role of client, community groups must have the capacity to define a problem, commit to the project and provide feedback and direction to the research team. The client has the most influence over the scope of the project, and the outcomes are intended primarily to meet their objectives. The researcher negotiates the scope of the project, to ensure that it can be achieved with the time and resources available, and ensures the work is delivered to a high standard. The researcher may achieve outcomes from the project, but these are subordinate to the outputs that serve the client.

The Engineering Comes Home project (Chapter 6) with residents of the Meakin Estate provided an opportunity to test infrastructure

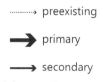

Figure 4.1   Legend for 3Cs diagrams

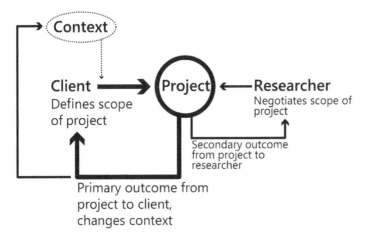

Figure 4.2 Community as client

co-design methods through a community as contributor model (see Figure 4.3). In this mode of working, the researcher defines the project scope and the outcomes are primarily intended to meet their needs and influence the context in which they are working. The community as contributor to the project negotiates the scope of their involvement to ensure fairness and feasibility. They should receive some benefits from the work, but these are secondary to the researcher's outputs.

Opportunities for working with community as collaborator (see Figure 4.4) on the Kipling Estate emerged through the CAMELLIA project

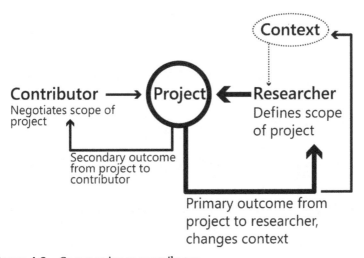

Figure 4.3 Community as contributor

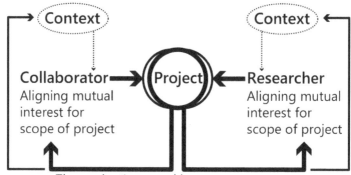

Figure 4.4 Community as collaborator

(Chapter 8). As collaborators, the community and the researcher mutually agree a project to meet each other's interests. Both collaborators bring their own objectives to the project, in response to their context, and the outcomes of the project serve the researcher and the community, in turn enabling them to influence that context.

Bottom-Up Infrastructure

The evolving programme of research and action found a source of support in 2015 when the UK EPSRC put out a call for early career research fellowships to address the question:

> How can our cities, their hinterlands, linking infrastructure, rural surround and the regions they are in, be transformed to be resilient, sustainable, more economically viable and generally better places to live?

Sarah submitted an application based on her experiences with the Engineering Exchange. She proposed a research programme of 'Bottom-Up Infrastructure' guided by a vision of:

> Infrastructure provision based on direct engagement of communities in engineering design and decision-making to deliver resilient, sustainable systems that meet the needs of people and the environment under conditions of uncertainty.

She won the grant. A research fellowship is a career changer for academic and research staff in universities. Research fellowships are competitive and only 20 per cent of people who apply are successful. Other people in universities take you seriously if you have a research fellowship: it signifies that your work is important, creative and novel. Most importantly, it means you have the time, money and credibility to do good work.

The premise of Bottom-Up Infrastructure is that engaging communities in infrastructure design and delivery will improve both infrastructure resilience and community resilience, areas that are conventionally thought to be distinct. The research considered different scales of infrastructure, from community-initiated and owned infrastructure, such as community energy co-operatives, to large, nationally significant infrastructure projects, such as major transport and water schemes. Researchers on the programme were embedded in different projects, documenting and evaluating engagement practices. A website was built to publish the tools and methods, described below and used in case study projects, including those showcased in Chapters 6–8 (Bottom-Up Infrastructure, 2022).

A co-design method

Bottom-Up Infrastructure frames community engagement as engineering work. Case study projects are positioned within the infrastructure life cycle: initiation, planning, design, construction, operation, maintenance and decommissioning (as described in Chapter 3). Co-design methods are defined according to project stages, based on engineering systems development: setting aims, characterising communities, capturing requirements, analysing options, crafting solutions and evaluation (described in detail later in this chapter). Tools are presented in a form familiar to engineers and other technical professionals, and are organised by the stage of the method they apply to (as summarised in Chapter 9).

Putting powerful engineering tools into the hands of communities is a core aim of Bottom-Up Infrastructure. The overall co-design method provides a framework that guides the kind of tools to be used in each specific process. The case study chapters describe how different tools were developed and used, and they are described in detail in Chapter 9. The remainder of Chapter 4 describes the co-design method developed and tested through the Engineering Exchange and Bottom-Up Infrastructure research programme at UCL, in partnership with community members, research collaborators and a wide network of stakeholders and supporters.

The Bottom-Up Infrastructure co-design method follows six steps (see Figure 4.5). In practice, the method is usually structured around three community workshops, which deliver the core functions of steps 3–5 (capturing requirements, analysing options, crafting solutions). Significant work is done before and after the workshops to gather data, prepare design tools, support community learning about technologies,

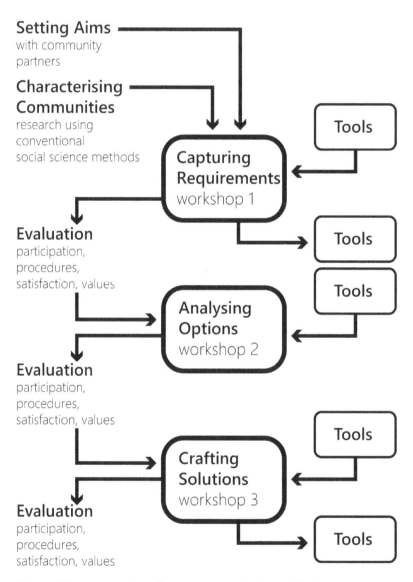

Figure 4.5 Bottom-Up Infrastructure co-design method

governance and management, and evaluating the process and outcomes (setting aims, characterising communities, evaluation).

1. Setting aims

A co-design process aims to create a shared understanding of the expected level of change, nature of the outcomes, level of community engagement, time frames, values and evaluation activities that review process and outcomes. The aims are defined at the beginning of the process to create a framework to measure success. They are context-specific and should be developed in collaboration with community partners. Once recorded, they should be used for continuous assessment against progress. Community members may have different degrees of influence on a project. In cases where the process is less open or part of the outcome has already been established, this needs to be clearly agreed. Expectations and anticipated outcomes can evolve throughout the project, and these changes can be updated at each stage.

2. Characterising communities

Before working with communities, it is important to understand their strengths, needs and aspirations. Community dynamics may be complex, requiring a good understanding of community members, relationships and issues. Recruiting participants will be influenced by what works and may be a mix of: engaging local gatekeepers and resident leaders; outreach (face to face, posters, email, flyers through letter boxes); asking people to identify others who should participate; or incentives such as financial reward, access to desired local resources or influence on decisions. This must be done with an understanding of barriers to participation, such as competing work and other priorities in the community, accessibility, varying levels of engagement and local community dynamics.

Characterising communities draws on conventional social science methods. For instance, the research team may undertake a series of recorded research activities (e.g., semi-structured interview, home visits, site visits, diary analysis) designed to understand the social and technical context to inform the co-design process. This phase also provides the data on shared values, which, when evaluated with all other project data and documentation, can help track how well the processes and outcomes align with the core values of the community.

3. Capturing requirements

This is a crucial step in bringing together different community members and stakeholders to collaboratively decide on the design directions and specific requirements to be explored in further steps. A clear list of requirements is the basis for choosing between design options and evaluating the success of the final system design and performance.

This stage often works best as a workshop facilitated by someone external to the project, and it can be useful to design props and materials that will allow for an initial open-ended exploration of the design space before discussion to reach a consensus. Workshops offer more than an opportunity to collect data from community participants in the project. They can build relationships and share information to enhance transparency throughout the project.

4. Analysing options

Community requirements can be typically met by many different design options. Options are identified by the design team, accounting for the local context and values, or generated by the community. Community participants are then involved in choosing the best options to meet their requirements. Participatory voting techniques or consensus decision-making are used to select a preferred option for further development.

In some projects, the professional designers and engineers may provide the community with a shortlist of viable options generated from previous stages and horizon scanning of potential technical solutions. Long lists of potential technologies are refined by the professional designers according to desirability and feasibility in the local context, before being presented to the community. Participants are provided with information about each option, in the form of fact sheets, models and by questioning the designers.

Alternately, the community can develop, analyse and select design options. Co-design games can be played to encourage creative thinking and scenario telling, with gentle competition to develop the most desirable and feasible options. Game props such as cards, models, toys and video cameras support community members, designers and stakeholders to work together to explore possibilities and pathways to achieving them.

Analysing options can be supported by software tools that help to make judgements on complex technical requirements, such as embodied carbon or air quality. The development of technical tools to support community decisions brings powerful engineering design tools, such as life cycle assessment or air quality modelling, into local contexts. This provides community participants with the capacity to account for the material impacts of their decisions at the same time as working through a process to express their social values and preferences.

5. Crafting solutions

Crafting solutions takes a preferred option and develops it into a proposal for change. This stage revisits the previous steps to review how the design was developed and to confirm core values and requirements driving the process and decisions. It involves looking again at the local environment and community to decide how best to implement the solution. Structured walking tours and audits allow participants to explore their neighbourhood for opportunities and constraints to inform the solution. Further technical information provided in fact sheets or other formats helps to extend participants' capacity to make decisions about design details. Prototype systems are also useful to learn how technologies perform in context. Software tools can also be useful to support calculations for sizing systems and optimising environmental, energy and other material impacts, alongside social or aesthetic requirements. Participatory voting or consensus decision-making are again useful to make choices about the final form of the system to be implemented.

6. Evaluation

Evaluation occurs throughout the life of a project. This enables adjustment of the design and activities to better meet values, needs and objectives. It also ensures that data is collected at the right time, to be able to judge the success of the process as well as outcomes. Five main principles are established to guide the evaluation of the co-design process:

- equality of participation;
- quality of participation;
- effectiveness of procedures;
- stakeholder satisfaction; and
- value persistence.

Equality of participation
Equality of participation means there is an opportunity for any community member to have a voice, to take action or to influence the outcome of

the co-design process. This is evaluated at two levels: representation and engagement. Community representation refers to the extent to which people who engage with the co-design process reflect the community of concern. Engagement can be recorded for attendance at workshops and activity during the workshops. Systematic exclusion may occur due to recruitment bias, practical arrangements (e.g., workshop timing, other commitments) or interest and motivation. Evaluation should assess who is attending and who is absent. While it is not expected that everyone will want to participate equally, the evaluation of equality of participation balances opportunity with activity.

Quality of participation

Measures of quality of participation can relate to the levels of engagement in terms of production of new information, disclosure of personal experience and creation or representation of novel or diverse ideas or experiences. This should not preclude diverging perspectives, contradicting experiences or disagreement. However, discussion should be free-flowing and require minimal prompting while following the structure of activities. These can be evaluated through measures of frequency of facilitator intervention, divergence from topic and turn-taking. Evaluation should consider the extent to which these features help progress towards desired outcomes.

Effectiveness of procedures

Across the stages of co-design, the overall aims and objectives are achieved through activities. Each activity includes sub-goals, data collection requirements and outputs. For each co-design workshop a procedure is designed, which includes activities, expected outcomes and timings. This can include assessment of keeping to time, use of physical space and suitability of materials, and should consider the equality and quality of participation as they relate to the methods used.

Participant satisfaction

Evaluation should take account of the extent to which community partners and stakeholders feel that their needs are being met, that activities and procedures support them in moving towards fulfilment of their needs, and whether they are achieving satisfactory equality and quality in participation. Satisfaction can be assessed for the overall process through explicit feedback (e.g., anonymous questionnaires) and through implicit feedback such as participant retention rates, wider community engagement and participant diversification, as well as observations regarding the quality of participation. Informal feedback from participants can also be included in the assessment.

Value persistence

Identifying core, community values is a prominent feature of the co-design process. All activities of co-design should be grounded in these values. Evaluation includes how well these values persist through the design, whether needs are met and whether the co-design process has raised or altered these values. While crafting solutions, values are explicitly referenced and evaluated against the design proposal. Open discussion can support extensive discussion of the values, and a satisfaction questionnaire can be used to explore changes in the values.

Research ethics

Bottom-Up Infrastructure was a research programme within a university. This brought specific institutional, administrative requirements, including the need to address ethical issues associated with participation in the research. The most significant projects within the programme, including the case studies in Chapters 5–8, were officially considered to be research projects and fell under the university's research ethics principles and processes. The requirement to carry out research ethically is a fundamental academic responsibility (Israel and Hay, 2006; Pimple, 2002). Research ethics marks out academic research and helps to delineate it from other types of research such as commercial research or journalism, and other ways of co-producing knowledge such as knowledge exchange activities or public engagement projects.

Research ethics asks researchers to reflect on the harm that may be caused through their research and to acknowledge the very real consequences of knowledge being power (Boser, 2006). In the context of projects examining local infrastructure and its social and environmental effects, this means thinking about who gets to participate, on what terms and with what consequences. Is there reputational risk for a participant in discussing the approach that their organisation takes in public consultations for infrastructure? Is there emotional harm done if, for example, the research reveals high levels of pollution and associated high incidence of lung diseases? How should the intellectual contribution of participants to a co-designed intervention be acknowledged? Can the right to anonymity be offered if a project focuses on the material opportunities of a specific housing estate to install a specific communal infrastructural intervention? These kinds of question help the researchers to consider the practicalities of the research through an ethical lens, thinking broadly about the research design, methods, process and dissemination to identify the most ethical ways of operating.

Research ethics is, however, also a formal process that relates to the legal responsibilities of an academic institution (Iphofen and Tolich, 2018). The process involves submitting numerous written accounts to various internal bodies related to data privacy and protection, health and safety of researchers and participants, mechanisms that can be used to explain and record consent. Each project that involved working with people – 'human participants' in ethics language – went through a formal ethics approval process. This was a chance to think broadly about how we could design participation in a way that suited the project and the community members' interests and availability. For example, for the STNF project where the members may not have had much time or even a shared vision of what the group should be focusing on, we devised an 'active consent' process. Workshop participants did not have to give their names or contact details, and they did not have to sign a formal consent sheet. Instead, if they opted to join in with any activity, a vote or a discussion for example, this was taken as their consent to participate in that activity. This was the most light-touch process and a way to offer anonymity. For the participants at the Meakin Estate in the Engineering Comes Home project (Chapter 6), we were asking for a lot more participation and the sharing of potentially sensitive personal data. We were asking residents to independently complete several research activities such as diaries, interviews and home tours. Here we required a written consent to participate and provided a fee to reimburse people for their time. By contrast, the refurbishment or demolition project (Chapter 5) did not require ethical approval because it was a literature review and did not involve any element of qualitative research with participants.

Research in action

The residents of the Carpenters Estate, their supporters in the LTF and Just Space, Hellene and her neighbours on the Meakin Estate, the STNF, and Joanna and the nascent gardeners of the Kipling Estate are communities working to improve their homes, neighbourhoods and city. They were patient and generous in sharing their time, knowledge and aspirations with a group of researchers in a university, through the Engineering Exchange and Bottom-Up Infrastructure research programmes. In return they received access to technical and design knowledge and outputs, to use in long-running efforts to effect change in complex urban systems. The researchers saw their technical expertise being used to solve important local problems, tested new methods of design and engagement, and collected data to publish in academic journals and books (like this one!). Together the researchers and community groups contributed in small ways to enhancing knowledge democracy in London (Hall and Tandon, 2017).

The general structure and working methods in the Engineering Exchange and Bottom-Up Infrastructure programmes emerged and evolved through experience and reflection. The methods and tools were grounded in engineering and design research and practice, and they were pragmatic and flexible to enable positive outcomes rather than strict adherence to codes. The four case studies in Chapters 5–8 show how the working relationships and methods evolved, and how they were adapted to specific contexts, challenges and communities. The earliest project, Demolition or Refurbishment in Chapter 5, does not follow the co-design method, but laid the foundations for working with communities on technical issues. The core method first appears in Engineering Comes Home in Chapter 6, and then changes to suit the different objectives and contexts of Somers Town air quality in Chapter 7 and the Kipling Garden in Chapter 8. Chapter 9 describes how tools were developed to support the different stages of the co-design method and provides detail of specific tools used in the projects.

5

Social housing decisions: demolition or refurbishment?

Community voices

This chapter includes contributions from Pat Turnbull, representing LTF (and a housing association tenant), and Richard Lee, representing Just Space (and a council tenant). They were clients for the project. As part of the process of writing the chapter, Gemma spoke with them about their reflections on the project seven years after it was completed. They also provided feedback on the draft text, specifically making invaluable suggestions on the section on 'Social housing history and politics' and the framing (and reframing) of the outcomes from this case study. Richard's reflections are included in Voice 5.1. The chapter was also informed by discussions with users of the research, including a staff member from a housing association and a PhD student at UCL.

Over the past 40 years, many London neighbourhoods have been the focus of urban regeneration programmes, which often involve the demolition of homes. As the experience of the Carpenters Estate in Chapter 4 shows, urban regeneration is a contentious issue and a contested process. The history of urban regeneration in the UK shows a shift from the initial economic drive of physical regeneration in the 1980s, to interest in the social and community impacts of regeneration in the 1990s (Atkinson and Cope, 1997; Colomb, 2007; Holden and Iveson, 2003; Mutale and Edwards, 2002). Numerous studies highlight the shortcomings of early efforts of regeneration, which were mainly property-led, with some initiatives contributing to negative social impacts, such as excluding local interests and increasing social marginalisation and social-economic inequalities. Coinciding with a shift to considering the wider social and environmental impacts of regeneration, the organisational processes involved in regeneration initiatives have also changed, with an increase in the promotion of public participation and stakeholder engagement in aspects of decision-making. Having a range of different stakeholders, notably residents and tenants, involved in decision-making about regeneration brings in different viewpoints and perspectives. However, the kinds of decision that are open to participation and the mechanisms for consultation often fall far short of this ideal.

Residents and communities are often excluded from decisions about demolition or refurbishment of housing. These decisions are typically justified in complex economic and technical terms, using language, data and arguments that are hard to access without professional training and expertise (Crawford et al., 2016). The Demolition or Refurbishment project aimed to provide social housing communities with technical information about the impacts and benefits of different options for estate regeneration, in formats that could be clearly understood and communicated. This was the first project undertaken by the Engineering Exchange and exemplifies the community as client model (see Figure 5.1). The clients and partners for the project were the LTF, representing social housing tenants, and Just Space, a London-wide

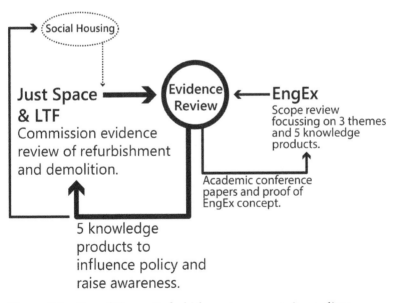

Figure 5.1 Demolition or Refurbishment – community as client

Table 5.1 Demolition or Refurbishment project summary

Project title	Demolition or Refurbishment of Social Housing
Project budget	£5,000
Funder	UCL EPSRC Impact Acceleration Account
Duration	Nine months in 2014
Research team (UCL)	Sarah Bell (lead), Kate Crawford, Charlotte Johnson, Felicity Davies, Sunyoung Joo
Collaborating groups	Just Space, LTF
Relationship type	Community as client
Outputs	• Report on evidence review • Three factsheets • Policy briefing • Community toolkit • Academic book chapter • Two academic conference presentations
Outcomes	• Proof of concept for Engineering Exchange • Contributed to changes in GLA guidance for estate regeneration and whole-life environmental assessment for new developments
Future developments and collaborations	EngEx established and delivered 22 projects Just Space and LTF collaboration on EstateWatch
Tools used in this project (refer to Chapter 9)	Factsheets, feedback forms

network of grassroots community groups with a special interest in urban planning. The Engineering Exchange acted as a consultant to deliver a review of evidence of the environmental, economic and health outcomes of demolishing or refurbishing social housing in London. This chapter documents the project and its policy impacts, while considering how the experience informed future research-community collaborations. Table 5.1 summarises the inputs, outputs and contributors to the project.

Project initiation

As a grassroots network, Just Space argues that residents should be at the forefront of decision-making around housing and planning, to ensure that the policies and decisions are fairer towards communities (Just Space, 2022). As discussed in Chapter 4, where analysis of options is done as part of regeneration planning, it is typically undertaken on behalf of the housing agency or their private developer partners, on terms that are limited by the scope they define. Existing housing was being demolished by local authorities and housing associations in London to open the way for investment, and was often justified on energy performance grounds or the comparatively high cost of refurbishment. In response to London Assembly's Housing Committee investigation in 2014 into the demolition of social housing, Just Space recognised a need for a review of technical evidence that could be used to decide whether to demolish or refurbish existing social housing.

Just Space works closely with academics and students in UCL's Bartlett School of Planning, and was part of a series of workshops in 2013 and 2014 to establish LARRG, organised by the UCL Urban Lab. The LARRG workshops discussed how universities, residents and others might work together on research about estate regeneration in London. A breakout group on technical aid discussed the need for communities to access advice and data about decisions and issues affecting their homes and neighbourhoods. The Engineering Exchange was in its early formation, and Sarah had joined the LARRG conversations to explore potential projects. In the technical aid breakout, she saw an opportunity to start building relationships between engineering researchers and local communities in London.

Establishing productive research relationships takes time and commitment. LARRG provided the first connection with Just Space and the LTF, and the first step of the Demolition or Refurbishment project. This project was an opportunity to put into place the aims of the Engineering Exchange to connect researchers and communities.

The Demolition or Refurbishment project was supported by the UCL internal grant that established the Engineering Exchange. The conversation on technical aid at LARRG, initiated by Just Space and LTF, echoed the aims of the Engineering Exchange, and the Demolition or Refurbishment project provided a chance to test the model. Following the encounter at LARRG, the Engineering Exchange worked with LTF and Just Space to agree project scope and terms, and set out to deliver a robust review of current evidence for its clients. LTF brought expertise, experience and research questions from across London, through its structure as an umbrella organisation that co-ordinates and represents social housing tenant groups from different local government areas.

Just Space shared the experience within its London-wide network of voluntary and community groups working together to influence planning policy at the regional, borough and neighbourhood levels. The academic team brought together two doctoral students, Sunyoung Joo and Felicity Davies; two post-doctoral researchers, Kate Crawford and Charlotte; and Sarah, who liaised with Just Space and LTF and managed the project.

Social housing history and politics

In 2014, the London Assembly Housing Committee started an investigation into the demolition of social housing. There were two key questions that Just Space and LTF raised in relation to this: 'How are decisions made to either refurbish existing buildings or to demolish and rebuild housing estates?' and 'What impacts do these programmes have on communities, households and individuals?'. These questions were not just in response to the investigation but were founded in wider concerns about decision-making in relation to housing provision, particularly social housing in London. This section provides some contextual background to this issue that helps to explain the wider origins of the Demolition or Refurbishment project.

Council housing, in particular, is threatened by regeneration, as political and financial support has changed over the past 100 years. London's Boundary Estate was the UK's first social housing, completed by London County Council in 1900. There was an increase in social housing construction in the 1950s, 1960s and 1970s, during shifts in policies from both Conservative and Labour governments. For example, 804,921 council homes were built under Labour between 1945 and 1951, with 190,368 in 1948 alone. However, by the 1980s there was less investment by local authorities and less support from central government. Under successive Conservative governments between 1979 and 1997, by far the largest single privatisation of public goods was the sale of council homes – worth an estimated £22 billion in 1997 (Boughton, 2018).

Council tenants were given the 'right to buy': the purchase of council homes by sitting tenants. This was not a new policy, but the 1980 Act enabled all council tenants who had rented for three years or more the right to buy their homes. It gave the Environment Secretary powers to intervene against any council held to be resisting the letter or the spirit of the new programme. Crucially, there were generous discounts applied to the purchase price, starting at 33 per cent of market value for those with three years' tenancy and rising to a maximum of 50 per cent (to the value of £50,000) for longer-term residents. Furthermore, there was no expectation that new council housing was to be built to replace homes lost to the market. In 1978–9, 79,160 new council homes started construction in England and Wales; by 1996–7, this figure had fallen to 400. Further legislation in 1984, which extended the right to buy to tenants of two years' standing, and increased maximum discounts to 60 per cent, only underlined the radicalism of this policy of privatising local government-owned housing. More than 1.8 million council homes were sold by 1997 – around one in four of the total. Council housing, which had formed 31 per cent of total stock in England, now formed around one-fifth (Boughton, 2018).

Adding to this shift was the level of maintenance budgets, which were high. The central government subsidy to council housing construction and maintenance fell from £2.13 billion in 1980-1 to £1.21 billion by 1990 – a cut of 43 per cent. At the same time, local authorities were forced to increase council housing rents – they tripled from an average £7.70 a week in 1980 to over £23 by 1990.

New models of housing investment encouraged private finance in order to reduce public spending on housing. Housing associations, or registered social landlords, are private companies that provide social, affordable housing to tenants. In 1979, housing associations provided around 1.9 per cent of Britain's total housing stock. The rate of transfer from council to housing association ownership averaged 50,000 properties annually under the Conservative government, but reached 100,000 a year between 2000 and 2002. Of 1.4 million homes transferred between 1988 and 2008, around 80 per cent occurred under the Labour government voted into power in 1997. By 2010, when Labour departed office, housing associations had overtaken councils as the country's main social housing providers, managing 2.2 million homes in England compared to the 1.8 million remaining in council hands.

Waiting lists for social housing in England peaked at 2.5 million English households in 2012. A reduction of 700,000 had been reached by 2016, reducing the waiting list to 1.8 million households. This reduction was not accounted for as a result of an upsurge in those being housed, but instead by stringent local council efforts to purge their lists by altering eligibility criteria or compelling those already on the list to reapply (Boughton, 2018).

A more recent threat to social housing is demolition. Estate Watch (Estate Watch, 2022) states that since 1997, 55,000 homes on 166 council estates in London have been demolished and about 131,000 tenants and leaseholders have been displaced. Demolition of social housing to make way for higher density urban development has been presented as a simple, if difficult, solution to London's housing crisis. However, there was a perceived gap in understanding of drivers behind such a 'simple' decision and the information informing it. A member of staff involved in strategic policy and research within a housing association, who was involved in some of the early conversations for the Demolition or Refurbishment project, reflects:

> I was sitting in the mix room of people, some residents, some activists, some technical, all asking 'yes, but why?' [i.e., why decisions were being made about demolition in the way they were]. And there were enough people asking why. So, it became obvious there was a hole. It felt there and then was a beginning of a rethink.

As noted in Chapter 4, decisions about whether to demolish or refurbish a building have historically been based on technical assessments that inform a series of cost and performance indicators. The technical assessments are based on surveys of building conditions and models of building performance. Factors that are considered within these assessments include energy performance of the building (compared to standards for new buildings), and assessment of environmental and energy impacts of the building from construction to demolition. Woven into technical models are assumptions about the building, and the economic and policy context in which regeneration will take place, which must be examined and justified in each case.

Evaluation of the economic case for refurbishment is sensitive to external drivers and factors, such as the retrofit supply chain and market, tenure types and management capacity, as well as access to finance. Typical economic indicators that are used include capital expenditure, operational expenditure and capital investment appraisal. Estimating the costs and impacts of refurbishment or demolition is complex, uncertain and subjective. Despite the complexity, Just Space and LTF wanted to question traditional approaches and open-up the considerations behind these decisions, to involve a wider range of perspectives in such decisions. Thus, Just Space and LTF commissioned the Engineering Exchange to review the technical evidence for demolition or refurbishment of social housing.

Review of technical evidence

The project involved four key stages, which were interlinked:

1. Review of technical evidence.
2. Series of events with community groups.
3. Creation of outputs (e.g., report, policy briefing, factsheets, community toolkit).
4. Engagement with policy.

The community as client process involved the Engineering Exchange team working with Sharon from LTF and Richard from Just Space. Together, they defined the scope, reviewed early outputs and decided on knowledge products. Richard and Sharon drove the project forward, setting clear aims for the Engineering Exchange team to work towards and reviewing early outputs. They argued for the focus on embodied carbon (outlined in the section about the three main themes of the review, below), which was an important outcome from the review.

The research team shared its review with Just Space and LTF in 2014. The review explored technical models, evidence and case studies about decision-making related to retention and demolition of social housing. It drew on evidence from industry as well as peer-reviewed academic articles, synthesising a range of evidence from different disciplinary fields. The literature the Engineering Exchange team reviewed emerged from different fields – engineering, energy modelling, planning and public health. It showed useful results, but it illustrated that it is often hard to disaggregate the evidence in a way that shows how the effects of refurbishment and demolition play out for different groups of people. The review showed that many aspects of decision-making about refurbishment and demolition are complex and interact with each other: what was needed was a more balanced interdisciplinary view of what housing interventions mean for people, who the winners and losers are, and over what timespans (as these may be different over the short and longer term).

The review of the technical evidence focused on three themes. First was the health and wellbeing of people living with regeneration projects, to understand the experiences of and impacts on social-housing tenants of such projects. Improving the quality of social housing stock is essential to reduce health inequalities in the UK. Housing has significant impacts on mental and physical health and wellbeing and should be a key factor in regeneration decision-making. Refurbishment can deliver improvements in housing quality at a faster rate than demolition and rebuilding of social housing, but health issues such as ventilation and indoor air quality can be complex to address in refurbishment.

The second theme was building performance, understood in terms of energy, water and waste. The operation of renewable energy systems also provides opportunities for community development through refurbishment of buildings and estates. The review found that most studies on retrofit compare 'before and after' energy performance, but some assess the potential savings that could be achieved if occupants were rehoused in new low-energy houses. At that time, only a few included the embodied carbon, that is, the total carbon dioxide emitted in the whole process of demolishing and replacing buildings.

When a building is demolished, energy is used to deconstruct it, and remove, process and dispose of the waste. Carbon dioxide and other greenhouse gases may also be released through associated chemical processes. Building a new building requires more materials and energy, creating more embodied carbon. Furthermore, when renewable energy is supplied to homes, it becomes less important to improve buildings' energy performance and more important to avoid the embodied emissions of demolition and rebuilding. Reusing or recycling building materials can reduce the embodied carbon of demolition. This was a significant outcome of the report and was an emerging issue at the time of publication.

The final theme dealt with conflicting assumptions underpinning the economic and environmental calculations applied to refurbishment and demolition. The review concluded that the ability of communities to engage in decisions would be enhanced by a consistent and transparent approach to the reporting of life cycle costs, energy and carbon, water and waste, and monitoring the wellbeing of those affected by refurbishment and demolition.

Events

The review ran alongside events in the university, community and local settings. These events were a key step of the process, as they provided an opportunity to present the review and gather feedback from the clients LTF and Just Space, housing and engineering experts, and community groups.

This iterative development process created opportunities for project partners and other interested parties to check and challenge the early findings of the work: it was a form of peer review. Funtowicz and

Ravetz (1991) have advocated for the incorporation of a broader set of views in the quality assurance of scientific and research processes from an 'extended peer community'. Extended peer review is the process of including a range of non-academic stakeholders with relevant expertise and experience in the processes of assessing and validating the quality of research (Liberatore and Funtowicz, 2003). The 'peers' could be comprised 'not merely of persons with some form or other of institutional accreditation, but rather of all those with a desire to participate in the resolution of the issue' (Ravetz and Funtowicz, 2015, p. 683). Liberatore and Funtowicz (2003, p.149) state that: 'A plurality of perspectives is considered as enhancing both procedural legitimacy (through inclusiveness) and quality of knowledge (through extended peer review)'. The processes organised within the Demolition or Refurbishment project were aligned to the process of 'extended peer community' and provided a space for questioning and direction of the review.

During the review process and the discussions, the team found that rather than contradictory or conflicting evidence, most studies were highly context-specific and patchy in their coverage of different places, groups of people and the impacts that had been assessed. There was a stage of referencing and mapping out the positive, negative, vague and absent evidence on key topics: embodied carbon, lifespans and decisions, health and wellbeing. It also became clear that although academic literature is potentially available to communities, developers and local authorities, it is not always free to download from academic journals or fast to review. There was a key issue around accessibility: relevant documents were not always in the public domain, and emerging evidence appears to be or is categorised as anecdotal. There also seemed to be a tendency to publish and republish simple, convenient numbers as universal rules of thumb when the original source research was out of date or based on a very few or specific cases that were hard to disentangle or generalise about (Crawford *et al.*, 2016). Scrutiny of the evidence, and discussion of the limitations of the studies, was a key step to ensure transparency.

Knowledge products

Alongside the technical 80-page report a range of other documents were produced, which included a policy briefing, factsheets and a community toolkit (Crawford *et al.*, 2014). The team also produced a series of short videos to accompany the factsheets.

The factsheets explore embodied carbon, lifespans and decisions, and health and wellbeing. LTF and Just Space had requested these factsheets to ensure that there is concise, readable, accessible information to share with community groups. These factsheets also allow the team to visualise the key messages of the technical report. Factsheets are a tool described in Chapter 9.

This community toolkit is a 'live' document and is designed to help social housing tenants and residents when decisions are being made about demolition or refurbishment of their homes. It aims to build an inventory of the environmental impacts of different options, and signpost when to get professional advice on the costs and benefits of different options. A strong thread around residents' and tenants' rights runs through the toolkit, as well as how these different rights might affect the options for tenants. There are three basic steps outlined in the toolkit:

- questioning decisions – finding out what information has been used to make decisions;
- taking stock – collecting information to start making your own case for refurbishment; and
- getting advice – getting help when there is missing information or when further support is needed.

In addition, a policy briefing note that summed up the state of the evidence was produced with support from UCL's public policy unit.

Policy engagement

Since 2014, there have been some important positive changes to policy, which support residents and tenants to be involved in urban regeneration decision-making. As well as local authorities, local residents have an essential role to play in regeneration processes. During this period, there has been political change in leadership in London from Conservative Mayor Boris Johnson to Labour's Sadiq Khan.

The commissioned review was used to support community input into the London Assembly's Housing Committee investigation into the demolition of social housing. This was the subject of the committee's meetings in June and July 2014. The following year, the committee published 'Knock It Down or Do It Up? The challenge of estate regeneration' (London Assembly, 2015). The report outlined principles for boroughs and housing providers, councillors and residents' groups to inform decision-making processes around regeneration. This reported figures of 8,000 net social housing units lost in 50 regeneration schemes, over a decade, as of its publication in February 2015. Alongside this report, the committee's activities raised the profile of the extent of demolition taking place and, crucially, the need for residents to be at the heart of such decisions. They reiterated the need for better collaboration between landlords and residents in exploring and evaluating the options concerns estate regeneration.

Impacts from the Demolition or Refurbishment project reached beyond the London Assembly's Housing Committee. A case study taken out of the research was used in mayoral guidance on estate regeneration as an example of bottom-up community engagement. The 2018 'Better Homes for Local People' report used the Carpenters Estate as an example of how the residents successfully opposed plans for demolition, and then produced a community-led vision for the estate (GLA, 2018). It stated: 'funding from the London Tenants Federation for a community-based organisation and technical support from University College London enabled residents to explore alternative options and undertake their own resident engagement'. The report notes a lesson for successful community engagement in estate regeneration is 'ensuring access to independent technical advice to assist tenants and residents in making informed decisions about the costs and benefits of the options for estate regeneration'. Furthermore, key points in the Mayor's guidance included: alternatives to demolition of social housing should always be considered first in estate regeneration schemes; and options appraisals should be open and transparent. The guidance stresses that this should include technical and financial appraisals that have influenced any decisions. The guidance also noted how information must be set out in an accessible format with non-technical summaries.

Evaluation

A diversity of outcomes, or changes, have arisen from the Demolition or Refurbishment project since it was completed in 2015. This project was a first step of the Engineering Exchange journey, and was fundamental to shaping its systems, relationships and ways of working. The key outcomes for this project fall across three main domains: conceptual (shifts or change in knowledge and attitudes); instrumental (shifts or changes in policies and plans); and capacity-building (changes to or shifts in capacities for designing, doing, learning).

Conceptual: changes to knowledge and attitudes

The report was an early contribution to what became an important discussion in estate regeneration in London. As a strategic policy staff member from a housing association said: 'There wasn't anything with authenticity questioning demolition, and now there is ... It was the kind of document that helped turn a corner.'

By exposing the structures and steps behind the decisions relating to the physical redevelopment of housing, the Demolition or Refurbishment project shared the challenges and opportunities these options posed for London's social housing stock. The review responded directly to a need and contributed to addressing a knowledge gap.

This project shifted the perceptions of the clients, of research and of the role of research. However, when opening-up science it can be challenging to avoid the pitfalls of tokenistic engagement. Just Space developed a protocol for research collaboration between community groups and researchers on planning issues (Just Space, 2018). The protocol was drafted in 2012, but is a work in progress, capturing experiences from such collaborations. The underlying message in the protocol is for equal 'benefits' between collaborating researchers and community partners. The protocol states:

> It could be that research aims formulated in theorctical terms might need to be adjusted to the practical aims and concerns of collaborating groups. It is very good to be open to this: it will mean that your results are likely to challenge and extend knowledge, rather than just reproduce well known academic debates. And it is certainly more likely that they will be more immediately useful to the groups you are working with ... Working collaboratively, then, can be a space for innovative thinking and creative tension as well as practical support and impact.

The Demolition or Refurbishment project challenged the traditional research model, to include a much broader set of voices in setting the agenda for research. The project helped to build the structure and the processes for the Engineering Exchange – putting into practice the community as client approach. The project illustrated the value of stronger engagement between university researchers and community groups: Just Space and LTF were able to draw on the expertise and lived experience of their members to articulate research needs. As the client, Just Space and LTF were key in proposing the scope of the project, steering and reviewing the work and ensuring delivery of accessible outputs that could be applied in a range of contexts. This aligns with a wider shift over the past decade with an emphasis on participatory, collaborative and transdisciplinary processes within research. As Michael Gibbons states, 'reliable knowledge can only be socially robust if society sees the process of knowledge production as transparent and participative' (Gibbons, 1999, p. C83). Catherine Durose and colleagues argue that 'opening up science beyond scientists is essential, particularly where problems are complex, solutions are uncertain and values are salient' (Durose *et al.*, 2018, p. 32). The complexity of infrastructure challenges, such as urban regeneration, requires the integration of diverse and varied perspectives to devise effective and innovative solutions.

Instrumental: changes to policies and practice

The review is still being used and applied in practice. A member of staff involved in strategic policy and research within a housing association said:

> I think it has lasted well ... I get the feeling, with some reports the tech moved on or the arguments changed ... Some reports that just pull everything together, and it doesn't matter if some things are out of date, it provided a good overview.

The Demolition or Refurbishment project sits within a wider context of changes and viewpoints on demolition. There have been recent shifts away from demolition in industry, motivated by the climate emergency. For instance, 'RetroFirst' is an *Architects' Journal* campaign to prioritise retrofit over demolition and rebuild. More than 200 architecture practices, organisations and individuals have supported the campaign (*Architects' Journal*, 2022). Furthermore, RIBA has advocated halting demolition in order to lower carbon emissions and help the UK reach its net-zero targets by 2050 (RIBA, 2020). It stresses that there should be a 'presumption against demolition', and that instead of being demolished and taken to landfill, buildings should be re-purposed and materials should be salvaged and re-used whenever possible.

In 2022 the Mayor of London adopted the London Assembly's 'Whole Life-Cycle Carbon Assessments Guidance' (London Assembly, 2022). The guidance requires large developments in London to show how they have calculated and minimised carbon emissions of the materials, construction, use and future demolition. Embodied carbon is included in analysis of new developments. Development of planning guidance involves multiple stakeholders and sources of evidence. The Demolition or Refurbishment project provided Just Space with evidence to be an early advocate for including embodied carbon and life cycle impacts in planning and assessment of development and regeneration.

> ### Voice 5.1 Richard Lee's reflection on the impact of the project on Just Space's interactions with researchers
>
> Being involved in this project gave us the encouragement to explore the issues surrounding refurbishment. Many tenants and residents didn't feel that they were being listened to, so working with the Engineering Exchange team helped us build knowledge, bridges and ultimately impact upon policy … Since it was completed, I feel we can trace a line from this original idea, to our work with other research projects, to our work on Estate Watch.
>
> Richard Lee, Just Space

Capacity-building: changes to skills and expertise

From 2018, Just Space and the LTF worked with the University of Leicester and King's College London on a research project that since 1997 has provided detailed evidence of the displacement of London council tenants and residents through regeneration schemes. As the research was in its final stages, a website (Estate Watch, 2021) was developed as a resource to help communities on estates facing regeneration understand their rights. The aim is to create a tool to hold the Mayor and councils across London to account, making sure that future regeneration schemes benefit existing local communities.

Finally, the review has been cited widely (including in Kate Raworth's bestselling *Doughnut Economics*, 2017) and has also provided the foundations for further research and studies (especially as it identified gaps in evidence). Ke Zhou, a UCL PhD student, notes:

> I was referring back to the report as source of information on how I do my research. I was impressed by the range the factors considered in decision making in regeneration. I try to use in it my work,

linking with my modelling (of the decision-making process). It is inspiring, it pushes me to think about how my work can add to UCL colleagues.

Conclusion

For Sarah, and the rest of the team, this project was the start of a community-university collaborative trajectory. On this trajectory was a growing ambition and openness to challenge the research process and the role of engineering. The Demolition or Refurbishment project provided proof of concept for the Engineering Exchange, and a track record of community-engaged engineering research that was essential in raising funds for the co-design research presented in Chapters 6–9.

For LTF and Just Space, this was a first step leading to a line of other opportunities and initiatives concerning demolitions. Richard and Pat, and their respective organisations, have continued working in this field, and this continuity has been crucial to build on the foundations laid by this project.

6
Reconfiguring the water-energy-food nexus: Engineering Comes Home

Community voices

This chapter includes contributions from Andy Bates, representing Leathermarket JMB, who was interviewed five years after the project ended to provide contextual information for the project inception and the Meakin Estate. Andy also reflects on the role of this project in developing a long-term relationship between residents and the research team.

The provision of water, energy and food is essential to meet basic needs. Climate change, environmental degradation and economic and political instability present risks to current and future supply. The immensity of these challenges becomes even more complex with the realisation that they are interconnected.

The water-energy-food (WEF) nexus refers to the interdependence between essential resources and the infrastructure systems that deliver them (Hoff, 2011; Kurian, 2017). For instance, water supply systems require energy for pumping and treatment, thermal electricity generation requires water for cooling, much of the world's agriculture requires water for irrigation, and energy is needed to transport food to market and on to consumers. An environmental disruption like drought can impact on all three elements of the nexus. Low rainfall can lead to shortages of water into municipal supply, crop failure due to limits on irrigation and electricity disruption due to insufficient water for cooling power stations. On the flipside, responses to resource limits in one part of the nexus can have an impact on others. For example, providing water for agricultural irrigation to secure food production by building desalination plants or pumping water in pipelines over long distances increases demand for energy. Ensuring resilience of one resource must not be at the expense of another. These complex relationships present challenges to typical resource and infrastructure management approaches based on separate sectors. The WEF nexus gives rise to a multitude of 'wicked problems' that are so interconnected that they are overwhelmingly complex and difficult to solve through one intervention alone (Churchman, 1967).

Most policy and design initiatives to address the WEF nexus focus on interactions at the supply side of big infrastructure systems that deliver water, energy and food, for example, water treatment works, power stations, large-scale farms and vast networks of distribution. This is extremely important, but it overlooks demand-side opportunities to find solutions and implement change.

Water, energy and food also come together in everyday life, at home. Cooking a meal integrates water, energy and food in the simplest of kitchens and the most mundane of daily rituals. Engineering Comes Homes was a research project that proposed to address the nexus from this perspective, the opposite end of the infrastructure system to where most engineers and researchers work. It proposed to start from inside the home and to look outwards, to find solutions to nexus problems that cannot be seen from the usual point of view of big infrastructure engineering.

If engineers are to step inside people's homes and ask them how they used nexus resources, then it makes sense to involve those people in designing infrastructure systems to deliver those resources more sustainably. Engineering Comes Home aimed to explore the possibility of involving communities in co-designing nexus infrastructures from the bottom up. The project expanded the scope of the nexus to include household waste, which is both an environmental problem linked to water, energy and food, and an opportunity to recover resources within a circular economy.

Engineering Comes Home worked with residents of the Meakin Estate in south-east London. Hellene, introduced in Chapter 3, and her neighbours contributed to the project by allowing researchers into their homes, explaining how they used resources and interacted with infrastructures, and participating in a series of workshops to design new systems of provision. The project tested whether community co-design methods could be applied to infrastructure design, and developed new tools to support decision-making at the nexus of water, energy, food and waste.

Engineering Comes Home was conceived by the research team, and the Meakin residents fulfilled the role of community as contributor (see Figure 6.1). The community gave time and knowledge to the research team, and the outputs of the project primarily met the needs of engineers and designers. The six-step Bottom-Up Infrastructure co-design method presented in Chapter 4 was first developed and tested in Engineering Comes Home (see Figure 6.2).

This chapter tells the story of Engineering Comes Home. It describes the origins of the project and how Hellene and the residents of the Meakin Estate came to be involved. The chapter shows how the research team delivered the co-design process, designed tools to support technical decision-making by the residents and produced a toolkit for use by other designers and engineers (the tools and the toolkit are described in detail in Chapter 9). Finally, it reflects on the outcomes and experience of the project, as an early step in testing and refining new ways of engaging communities in complex urban systems design. Table 6.1 summarises the inputs, outputs, contributors and tools involved in the project.

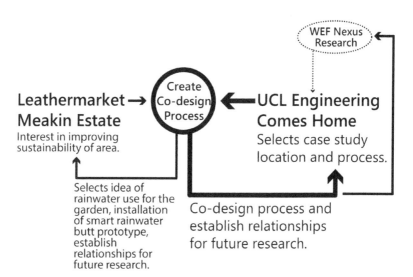

Figure 6.1 Engineering Comes Home – community as contributor

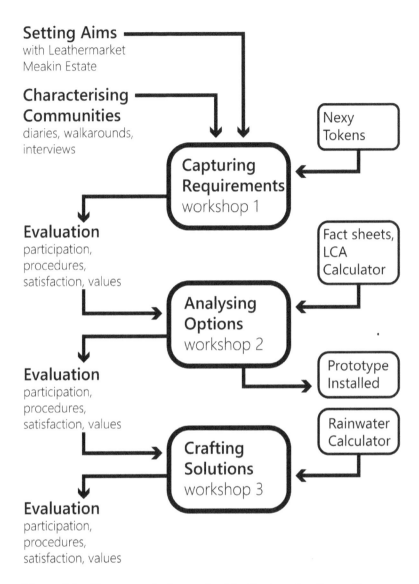

Figure 6.2 Six step co-design method for Engineering Comes Home

Project initiation

Engineering Comes Home started as a speculative research idea. In 2014 the EPSRC called for expressions of interest for researchers to 'Design the Future' (EPSRC, 2014). Participatory infrastructure design was not the focus of this or any other research funding call, but the scope

Table 6.1 Engineering Comes Home project summary

Project title		**Engineering Comes Home**
Project budget		£300,000
Funder		EPSRC
Duration		Nov 2015–May 2018
Research team	UCL	Sarah Bell (lead), Aiduan Borrion, Charlotte Johnson
	Newcastle	Robert Comber
	iilab	Kat Austen, Jun Matsushita, Alex Shure
Collaborating groups		Leathermarket JMB, Meakin Estate TRA and residents
Relationship type		Community as contributor
Outputs		Infrastructure co-design toolkit: • Nexy tokens • LCA calculator • Rainwater harvesting calculator • Method statements Three journal papers Three conference presentations
Outcomes		Demonstrated feasibility of community co-design of infrastructure
Future developments and collaborations		New research collaboration with Leathermarket JMB through CAMELLIA (see Chapter 8)
Tools used in this project (refer to Chapter 9)		Diaries, home tour, stakeholder interviews, Nexy tokens, story creation, value elicitation, LCA calculator, rainwater harvesting calculator, feedback forms, Engineering Comes Home toolkit

was wide enough for the Engineering Exchange, with academic and designer collaborators, to apply. Demonstrating sufficient fit with the remit of the call, the research team drew on expertise from engineering design, participatory research, ethnography, environmental impact assessment and agile technology. The bottom-up approach, along with the co-design, community engineering and social research expertise of the team, held the potential to increase the impact of the project on society and the economy, another key aim of UK research councils. The research team included Sarah, Charlotte and Aiduan Borrion from UCL; Kat, Jun Matsushita, Pierre Allix and Alex Shure from social technology enterprise iilab; and Rob Comber from Newcastle University.

Engineering Comes Home aimed to get behind the front door of the home, so that the practices, perspectives and experiences of residents could be included in infrastructure design (Bell *et al.*, 2017). The water-energy-food-waste nexus was chosen as the focus for the project to align with emerging priorities for UK research and policy.

The primary focus of the research proposal was to engage a community in infrastructure design. To do this the team proposed to develop tools that facilitated this process, and a toolkit intended for other infrastructure designers who wanted to include communities in projects. The project intended to adapt powerful engineering analysis methods that are used to address the WEF nexus into tools that could be used with communities with no prior technical expertise. The project was entirely conceived by the research team, who were awarded a grant of £300,000 without having a community partner. The track record of the Engineering Exchange (described in Chapter 4) in working with communities provided the research funder with sufficient confidence that the team would be able to recruit a community to contribute.

Life cycle assessment (LCA) is one of the engineering methods that was proposed to be adapted for use in community co-design. LCA is frequently used by engineers and designers to calculate the environmental impact of different materials, products and design choices, by providing quantitative assessment of the energy and material requirements, over the course of the entire life cycle. For instance, when looking at a choice between using a pen or a pencil, LCA will take into account the materials used – where the pencil's wood is sourced, the oil to make the pen's plastic body – along with the energy required to manufacture and transport each, the number of times the pen can be refilled and how each will be disposed of at the end of its useful life. The LCA data allows the decision-maker to weigh these impacts against each other before choosing their preferred writing tool. LCA is a powerful tool in helping designers to take nexus interactions into account in their decisions because it has the potential to show the full scope of environmental, energy and resource impacts associated with design choices. The focus of an LCA can be tuned depending on the types of decision that need to be made. In the case of Engineering Comes Home, the focus was on systemic environmental impacts of different small-scale infrastructure interventions.

Co-designing nexus infrastructures

The bottom-up, demand-side focus of Engineering Comes Home required working with people to share knowledge about what goes on inside their homes, and in turn provided the motivation for engaging communities in designing alternatives to reduce WEF nexus resource impacts. If part of the solution to the challenges of the WEF nexus is to reduce resource consumption through changing infrastructure, then communities and consumers who are impacted by those infrastructures should contribute to their design. Engineering Comes Home adapted conventional design methods for community co-design to address this need, which evolved into the six-step process (see Figure 6.2).

Setting aims

The London borough of Bermondsey bustles with activity, with a shining skyscraper, the Shard, dominating the skyline. Moving south, away from its base at London Bridge railway station, the streets become rapidly more residential. Buses trundle through traffic, past the terraced shops lining the busy pavements of Tower Bridge Road. At the corner with Decima Street, next to a row of telephone boxes and bicycle racks, flat-topped terraces give way to the three and four-storey blocks of the Meakin Estate. The buildings' red and yellow brickwork facades are fronted with blue-railed balcony access on the upper floors (see Figure 6.3). This complex of blocks, dating from 1935, comprises 121 flats with between one and four bedrooms (Leathermarket JMB, 2015).

In looking for a community to contribute to Engineering Comes Home, Charlotte began cold-calling community-based organisations to gauge their interest in addressing resource management. Through these initial conversations, which set the aims for community engagement in the project, the Leathermarket Joint Management Board (JMB) agreed to contribute and facilitate relationships with its residents.

The JMB is a resident-managed housing organisation, responsible for 1,500 homes in Borough and Bermondsey in London. JMB estates are represented by five different TRAs, which interface between residents and JMB staff, and organise community events and activities. The relationship between UCL and the JMB developed further and led to the Kipling Garden project (discussed in Chapter 8). Engineering Comes Home began working with the Decima Street TRA, focusing co-design activities on the Meakin Estate.

As Andy Bates from the JMB remembers, the relationship developed through shared goals and interests: 'The way that I got involved with Sarah was accidental … Sarah was looking for somewhere sympathetic to come and try kind of a low-key, and not very much money project. I do have interest in greening and sustainability of housing estates.'

Figure 6.3 View of Meakin Estate and the TRA meeting room from Decima Street

The committed approach from Sarah, and the inclusion of discussions about sustainability, were welcome: 'I ... remember Sarah sitting through long meeting [with residents], where we argued about repairs and … anti-social behaviour, so to talk for 5 to 10 minutes about the sustainability projects that was kind of lovely.' From these seeds grew a collaboration that led to the Engineering Comes Home project, and from there a larger partnership in the CAMELLIA project (Chapter 8): 'And because of that connection we got involved in a much bigger project.'

Through the JMB, people living on the estate were recruited to participate in a co-design process that began with a study to explore nexus resource use in their homes, followed by a series of co-design workshops. The residents' engagement with the project was extensive. The project funding from EPSRC paid residents for their time contributing to the project (a total of £100 per person), but it was also clear from the start that a strong motivation for residents was in addressing infrastructure problems that were a barrier to environmentally positive living.

Characterising the community

On the ground floor, the Meakin Estate flats have small private gardens that front onto communal outdoor areas. The walkways, a few grassy knolls and the estate's playground are open to public access. When the research team first visited, the estate was in the middle of renovations to the communal heating system. Fenced-off areas of pavement revealed piles of paving slabs ringing pipe-filled holes dotted around the footpaths and gardens.

While energy infrastructure was laid bare in the walkways of the Meakin Estate, the way that people were interacting with resources provided by this and other infrastructures in their own homes was far harder to see. The Engineering Comes Home team wanted to 'get behind the front door' to focus on the needs and knowledge of the residents, taking a social design approach to the estate's infrastructure possibilities. As discussed in Chapter 2, social design aims to create a solution that satisfies human needs, rather than creating a commercially successful product (Fuad-Luke, 2009). Involving community members who will be affected by the outcome allows for a more successful design to be achieved.

Over a series of visits to people's homes, Charlotte began characterising the community in the context of the project by discussing the WEF nexus as experienced through everyday life. Residents completed diaries of their daily routines involving WEF resources, they gave Charlotte tours of their homes and they participated in interviews. Diaries and home tours are tools described in more detail in Chapter 9.

Many of the residents were highly conscious of existing issues with water wastage. Residents shared, for instance, that the infrastructure in the estate meant that they would have to run the tap for a long time before the water reached the required temperature. Residents also highlighted that they were using mains drinking-quality water to water plants because there was no alternative water source, and they had concerns over the amount of water used in toilet flushing. Resource use sometimes meets indirect needs. For instance, some residents talked about leaving the radio or television on, even when they weren't actively interacting with it, so that they would feel less lonely at home.

Co-creation workshops

The results from characterising communities provided the foundation for detailed planning of co-design workshops. The challenge with the Engineering Comes Home co-design was to work with community members to identify the connections between Meakin-specific WEF nexus problems, and to create a prototype solution that would address some of them within the time frame, practicalities and budget of the project (see Figure 6.4).

Figure 6.4 Raised beds at the Meakin Estate with the energy infrastructure renovations visible in the background

Three co-creation workshops iteratively addressed site-specific infrastructure issues in the Meakin Estate. Not all the community members who took part in the household-based research came to the workshops, and there was some discontinuity in workshop participants over time (this is discussed later in the chapter). Committee members of the Decima TRA, some of whom were living on the Meakin Estate, were present at all the workshops.

Workshop methods built on co-design and co-creation practices. These practices focus on facilitated discussions, allowing the participants to work with the research team to explore which problems should be addressed and how this might be done. For each workshop, bespoke workshop plans and materials were prepared to foster discussion and facilitate working with the complex relationships between resources at the WEF nexus. Engineering Comes Home began with aspects that had emerged from characterising communities and were explored further with the help of co-design tools developed specifically for the project (see Chapter 9).

Workshop 1: capturing requirements

The purpose of the first workshop was to define what residents required to improve the WEF nexus on their Estate. Using the characterising communities results as a guide, Kat and the iilab team developed a set of methods and tools to invite the participants to express their values and to share their experiences of water, energy, food and waste resource-use and management on the estate.

The first workshop was run by an independent facilitator, who did not have any other role in the project or stake in the outcome. The facilitator was recruited because the team was entirely engaged with other tasks during the workshop. The design team needed to observe the use of the tools and the outcomes of discussions about them, as this would inform the next design iteration. Charlotte followed the dynamics of the workshop in her role as community mediator, Sarah had an interest in the overarching methodology and Rob was evaluating. Finally, Aiduan was involved in bringing the context of LCA to the discussion.

The first task was to investigate the underlying values held by the workshop participants. This was done using a value elicitation tool that encouraged exploring the roots of values that participants expressed, to find the underlying motivator for decision-making (refer to Chapter 9). Discussions during the exercise made it clear that many of the workshop participants had significant altruistic environmental and social motivations.

The next step was to examine the physical, infrastructural challenges experienced by the community, using the 'Nexy tokens' developed as part of the project (described in Chapter 9). These palm-sized, weighty, upcycled acrylic hexagonal tokens were stamped with icons representing different aspects of the nexus as it related to the Meakin Estate and possibilities for change. The tokens represented composting, rainwater capture, gardening, solar panels and more, leaving some blank so that the participants could add anything that was missing.

The hexagonal design was intended to allow for participants to build up a story of how different elements of the nexus are connected by placing the tokens next to each other. For instance, a garden token might connect to a food token, and then to a compost token, showing a closed cycle of nutrients. The garden token could also connect to a water token, which could connect to a tap representing the mains water supply, or a rainwater tank, representing rainwater harvesting on the estate. There is a full description of the Nexy tokens and related tools in Chapter 9, along with links detailing how they can be made.

The workshop was far busier than anticipated and, consequently, the team were running low on resources. As such, the workshop was reconfigured on the fly, accommodating the extra participants by sharing resources. The team provided the Nexy tokens, magnetic boards, pens and paper, and photographs of different sites around the estate that had been highlighted through the characterising communities study. The participants worked in pairs to frame a story about resource challenges in specific parts of the estate using the tokens, the photographs and their own drawings and words. Story creation is a tool described in more detail in Chapter 9.

The stories that the groups told initially focused on waste (both composting and waste management) and food (including food-growing and sharing). However, rainwater capture and wastewater reuse also emerged during the workshop discussion. At this point, there was a great deal of discussion about how practical any potential solutions might be, even though potential solutions had still not been designed and their impact had not been calculated. The outcomes of the workshop provided data for the research and design team to identify potential technologies to address residents' needs and aspirations, aligned with their shared values. It also provided information to inform the development of a bespoke LCA software tool to help residents to explore options and make choices in workshop 2.

The intention of this workshop had been to focus on the values, needs and requirements of the community members in relation to the WEF nexus, as a starting point for exploring options for infrastructure interventions. However, open-ended discussions to achieve this were sometimes cut short by participants, based on concerns over the practical implementation of a proposed solution. Existing power dynamics in the group made these points of tension difficult to overcome despite expert facilitation.

Workshop 2: analysing options

The gap between first two workshops was a few months, partly due to the necessity to design and build the LCA software tool for use in the second workshop, as described in the section 'Metadesign of tools for co-designing infrastructure' later in this chapter, and in Chapter 9. Consequently, only some of the workshop 1 participants returned for workshop 2, although numbers were maintained by the presence of new participants. Efforts made during the recruitment process meant that most of the participants were familiar with the general idea of the project already.

In between the workshops, the design team undertook a horizon scan of all possible known technologies that could provide solutions to the nexus problems on the estate identified during workshop 1. This long list of technologies was assessed in terms of desirability and feasibility, based on the values expressed in workshop 1 and early discussion of the practicalities of change on the estate. Five possible technologies were selected by the design team as the basis for discussion in workshop 2 – composting using a wormery, a waste compactor, rainwater harvesting, urban food-growing and food-sharing apps.

The intention behind workshop 2 was to narrow down the exact problem that residents wanted to address, and to select a preferred solution to develop in more detail in workshop 3. While workshop 1 aimed to keep options open, to gather lots of ideas, workshop 2 intended to explicitly address feasibility: if somebody pointed out potential problems with the design, the group would address whether there was a solution, or the design option would be eliminated from discussion. Thus, in workshop 2 a space was created in which it was possible to address hidden assumptions. It was also vital to see how options proposed by the team fitted into the reality of participants' lives and the practicalities of managing the estate. A staff member from the JMB was present to help inform these discussions.

As with workshop 1, the team planned a three-hour workshop. After the initial introduction and recap of workshop 1, and an explanation of what was happening workshop 2, some time was spent discussing the overall nexus problems on the estate. The design team shared the shortlist of five potential solutions that might meet some of the needs identified by the community in the previous workshop and then introduced the LCA calculator software.

The LCA calculator is a tablet-based prototype software application to show co-designers the nexus impacts of different design options (refer to Chapter 9). Workshop participants could change parameters in the calculator (e.g., the number of garden beds growing food), and see the resource impacts (e.g., the change in water demand). The LCA calculator included five pre-determined scenarios that were defined by the team based on the outcomes of first workshop, built around the shortlisted technologies. The team also provided photographs of solutions and spaces around the estate, and factsheets for background information about the five technologies that became components of the different scenarios presented in the software (refer to Chapter 9). The LCA calculator and the factsheets are described in Chapter 9.

The first scenario in the LCA calculator referred to the problem of food waste on the estate and the possible impacts of a waste compactor. The whole group worked through this scenario together to explore functionality of the calculator, such as collecting waste from one household or many, and calculating the carbon emissions associated with food purchase, consumption and waste. Kat guided the participants through this scenario with the example of wasting carrots, a problem that had been raised in workshop 1.

The workshop then moved on to more complex scenarios. Participants worked in groups to calculate the impact of introducing a garden into the food waste scenario. As demonstrated by the calculator scenarios, the garden could be designed with a wormery to compost food waste and produce fertiliser. The garden would also require water, and it could produce food, reducing the need to purchase food from elsewhere. The next scenario introduced rainwater capture to the network, substituting some of the water required for the garden with rain captured from the roofs of the estate buildings. A food-sharing scenario allowed participants to explore the impacts on waste, water and carbon of sharing at different scales within the estate, between households and at community scale. The team invited participant groups to change parameters within different scenarios and use the software to calculate carbon, waste and water impacts.

While exploring options and calculating impacts, the participants were encouraged to discuss the feasibility of the proposed solutions being implemented in the estate. After a round of discussion, the participants voted on the different solutions through a structured voting process (described in Chapter 9). Through this process, the community decided to focus on rainwater capture as an intervention in the WEF nexus on the estate.

The participants gave feedback that the tablet-based LCA calculator was easy to use and the interface intuitive (see Figure 6.5). The participants found that their assumptions were challenged by the calculations of carbon footprints for different solutions. For example, the calculator showed that the introduction of waste compactors did not affect the carbon dioxide emissions as much as expected. The concept of scale that was explored through the calculator was important in the subsequent discussion. The solutions were ultimately assessed more in terms of their viability, informed by the factsheets and concerns from the TRA committee, rather than in terms of their impact on carbon emissions as calculated through the LCA calculator. Nevertheless, the calculator allowed participants to explore the volume of material involved, and in a discussion of implementing a wormery, opened the idea of the estate as a producer of resources, not just as a consumer.

Figure 6.5 Participants discussing possible interventions on the estate using factsheets and the LCA calculator

After workshop 2, an opportunity emerged to install a prototype rainwater-harvesting system on the estate. A start-up firm, KloudKeeper, were looking for a site in London to test a new product designed to allow remote control of rainwater tanks using Internet of Things technology. This technology would enable rainwater harvesting to be used to reduce surface-water run-off into sewers, as well as providing a source of water. As described in Chapter 1, combined sewer overflows arising from surface-water running into London's sewers are a significant environmental problem. The KloudKeeper technology was designed to enable remote control of rainwater-harvesting tanks to help even out the flow of water through London's sewers, reducing combined sewer overflows. The KloudKeeper system was installed on the Meakin Estate, providing residents with the opportunity to observe how rainwater harvesting could work in their community.

Workshop 3: crafting solutions

Workshop 2 showed that rainwater harvesting was the preferred nexus intervention for the Meakin Estate, both in terms of the values of the community members and the practicalities of intervening in the estate's infrastructure. Before workshop 3, the iilab team worked with UCL engineering researchers to develop a second software calculator tool, this time to present more detailed scenarios for rainwater harvesting and calculate the impacts on local water infrastructure in terms of reducing demand for water from the mains supply and reducing combined sewer overflows (described in Chapter 9).

The purpose of workshop 3 was to plan how rainwater capture could be deployed across the estate. Participants in workshop 3 comprised mostly people who had been involved in workshops 1 and 2, including TRA committee members. In this workshop, the focus was more on practical solutions and there was less tension between uncovering residents' aspirations and the practical considerations of implementation.

In the three-hour workshop, the team summarised the previous two workshops, updated participants about the progress made between workshops 2 and 3, and introduced them to the new rainwater calculator. After a general introduction to rainwater harvesting, participants were led through the first two scenarios of the rainwater calculator. These scenarios focused on the amount of water required for different uses and the amount of water prevented from entering the sewers. Participants were shown the KloudKeeper rainwater tank, installed outside the TRA meeting room where the workshop was held. Together, workshop participants

Figure 6.6 On a walk-about to decide locations for further rainwater harvesting tanks

then toured the estate looking for other locations where similar devices could be deployed (see Figure 6.6).

One important consideration was how the water in the water tank would be used. While there was some discussion of using water for gardening, residents pointed out that water could be also made available for car washing. Ultimately this factor was important in the suggested locations for future water tanks emerging from the workshop, with locations close to car parking locations being especially desirable. The residents returned to the meeting room to work with the rainwater calculators to explore the size and location of tanks, based on how much water they needed, where tanks could be installed and how much space was available.

Metadesign of tools for co-designing infrastructure

Many of the tools used in the workshop were developed specifically for Engineering Comes Home. The development of the tools followed the principles of metadesign, described in Chapter 2. Alongside analogue tools such as the Nexy Tokens, photographs and info-sheets, one of the most technically challenging design outcomes for the project was the development of a user-friendly LCA calculator that would allow residents to assess the environmental impact of their design decisions (Borrion *et al.*, 2019). LCA software is typically used by technical experts and is too complex and unwieldy to be used in a community co-design setting. The intention of the Engineering Comes Home team was to develop an intuitive, interactive tool that would allow the participants easy access to the power of LCA.

Workshop 1 provided useful information to the software development team to achieve this. The workshops were recorded in audio, video and photographs, as well as notes, which were used in post-workshop analysis to inform the scope of the LCA database and the requirements for the calculator interface.

Combining the values identified during workshop 1 with the discussion analysis from audio recordings identified opportunities for nexus infrastructure interventions on the estate. The workshop analysis was used to understand the perspective of the participants – the software users – and to predict queries they might have that could be answered by an LCA calculator. These queries informed the first iteration of the project-specific LCA spreadsheet developed by Aiduan to identify data that was likely to be required. The queries also informed the design of the calculator interface by developing the five different scenarios of intervening in the WEF nexus on the Meakin Estate (for more information see Chapter 9), in preparation for its use in workshop 2.

Analysis after workshop 2 required less focus on needs and more focus on technological solutions, as the participants had decided on rainwater capture as their preferred technical solution. The research team produced a second calculator, to analyse rainwater harvesting options. The rainwater calculator built on the methods of representation and the visual language developed for the LCA calculator, introducing seasonality into the timeframes represented to reflect rainfall variation over the year. The rainwater calculator was designed to help facilitate decision-making about deployment of tanks like the KloudKeeper prototype, addressing such variables as tank size, number of rooftops and demand for different types of water use. In every case, the amount of rain released into the London sewage system was reported, to show the impact of the community's decisions on the amount of water flowing into larger scale infrastructure.

Production of an infrastructure co-design toolkit

The Engineering Comes Home team developed a toolkit from the project, designed after consultation with practitioners working on WEF nexus infrastructure. This toolkit, which took the form of a website (Matsushita *et al.*, 2016), organised the tools into six steps, a formulation that was used and adapted when structuring subsequent projects:

1. Setting aims – set aims, expectations and approaches for community engagement.
2. Characterising communities – identify a community partner for your project and understand their needs.
3. Requirements capture – work with your community using innovative tools to collaboratively identify needs and solutions.
4. Evaluating options – work out the scope of different interventions to generate a shortlist.
5. Detailed design – work with the community to create a detailed infrastructure design.
6. Evaluation – how well did you achieve your aims? Were the community members active co-designers?

The first five steps take place sequentially, while evaluation is carried out across the entire project life cycle. A method statement, clarifying the activities undertaken at each step, was included in the toolkit for each step, and a case-study video documentation of the Engineering Comes Home workshops was provided, alongside the tools that were developed for the project. All work was shared under a CC-BY 4.0 licence, allowing the tools to be replicated and used at no cost provided they are correctly attributed, and the code for the calculator tools published under an MPL 2.0 licence, meaning the full code is available for reuse and adaptation (Allix and Matsushita, 2017). To ensure availability beyond the lifetime of the iilab infrastructure, the calculator tools have been archived using the online archiving service of the Way Back Machine (Matsushita *et al.*, 2021).

Practitioner workshops

Two workshops with infrastructure practitioners informed the development of the toolkit. In the first practitioner workshop, held before the first community resident workshop, the iilab team and Sarah gathered information to better understand how they typically delivered WEF-nexus infrastructure projects and what challenges they encountered. Practitioners took part in a series of exercises, reflecting on previous projects to inform the delivery of Engineering Comes Home and help shape the toolkit.

The main themes emerging from the first workshop were that it was perceived as challenging to facilitate informed participation with community members on design of infrastructure. Many of the points raised are familiar from other forms of participatory work. For example, concern about over-commitment and over-engagement at the expense of other issues, and combatting engagement fatigue by ensuring feedback and follow-up with the community (see, e.g., Hecker *et al.*, 2018). Questions were also raised in terms of who constitutes the community for such a project, and how one can build for diverse, sometimes conflicting, interests; questions that can be addressed by stakeholder analysis at the start of a project, proper ethics and risk assessment, and an appropriate facilitation method. Furthermore, and acting as encouragement for this very volume, there was a call from practitioners to create a compelling case for engaging communities in infrastructure design.

The second stakeholder workshop was run before community workshop 2. The team recapped the outcomes of the first workshop and updated the stakeholders as to the progress of the project. The video documentation of workshop 1 was presented, and the team gathered feedback on the materials that had been prepared for workshop 2. The second stakeholder workshop evolved into more of an information-sharing exercise than a co-design session for the toolkit.

Evaluation

Engineering Comes Home proved that it is possible to engage communities in infrastructure design to address complex problems like the WEF nexus. It also provided valuable experience and knowledge about the processes of working with communities. The main insights into infrastructure co-design relate to individual and community dynamics, orientating participants within the co-design process and the methodological limits to engagement.

Individual and community dynamics

The team initially engaged with residents through research in individual households conducted by Charlotte. The transition between this individual interaction and broader community engagement was not always simple. There was a need to preserve anonymity and privacy, which diminished the potential for turning learning from the ethnography into actionable information during the workshop and led to a disparity in knowledge between the community and the research team.

Community dynamics also affected the workshops. Members of the TRA committee attended each workshop, and it was often unclear as to the capacity in which they were participating – were they estate residents or estate managers? Based on previous interactions and existing relationships, there was an established power dynamic between the TRA as an aggregate organisation, represented by individuals, the community and the research team. In addition, the TRA had been brought on board by the research team with a framing that the process would result in a tangible outcome for them.

As the TRA were present and active during the workshops, this framing of practical outcomes and solutions was prevalent and tangibly reduced the level of exploration possible during the first and second workshops. Free ideation, as intended for workshop 1, was sometimes in tension with the very real and practical constraints of managing a housing estate. For this tension to be productive and to lead to ideas that can both be implemented and challenge established structures that are not working, it is vital to have stakeholders in the room and to ensure a safe space for wild ideas to emerge at the beginning of a co-design exercise.

This tension was present throughout the first two workshops. It was difficult to resolve due to the internal power dynamics of the group, especially as the invited facilitator was unfamiliar with the participants. At subsequent workshops, Charlotte facilitated. Alongside stronger facilitation, the dynamics may have benefited by greater specificity in terms of the aims and scope of each of the workshops. These were clearly stated at the start of each workshop, to better orientate the participants as to the expectations for the workshops and how they contribute to the overall aim of the project, with a focus on the outcomes important to the community members.

Orientation

During preparations for the workshops the research team concentrated largely on providing materials that would facilitate the residents' engagement with infrastructure design. Throughout evaluation, it emerged that a similar amount of preparation would have been beneficial in both the elaboration of the co-design process and in the methods that would be used in the workshops. Specifically, at the start of each workshop it would have been beneficial to include an outline of the co-design process in relation to the current stage, including descriptions of the activities that would take place. For instance, in the first workshop it would have been helpful to identify the ideation phase and how this fitted into the overall co-design process. Method steps 3–5 (capturing requirements, evaluating options and crafting solutions) may have provided a structure from which to begin these conversations. Further work was also needed in explaining the workshop aims to overcome preconceptions of the process.

Methodological limitations

As the process of co-design was new to the participants, some of the tools and methods employed were engaged with in surprising ways. For instance, while the research team found it helpful to elicit values from participants at the start of the workshop in order to make design choices for tool development, these values were rarely referred to by the participants themselves.

Similarly, the Nexy tokens were not typically used to make full 'stories' illustrating the participants' relationship with the WEF nexus, but rather as emblems of a particular thing. This may have been because the participants worked in groups rather than individually, due to high participant numbers and limited tokens available. Participants also seemed reluctant to generate stories on their own, and stories were not swapped as originally intended.

During the research team's own reflections and evaluation sessions there was a question within the team over whether this process could be called true co-design. The aim of the project had been to engage the community in the co-design of small-scale technological innovation that enabled them to live more sustainably at the WEF nexus, informed by their lived experiences. Through the delivery of the project, it became apparent that for true co-design of a technological solution to be achievable from the ideation stage of technology design, more time with the community and further tools for engaging with engineering and technology design would be beneficial. However, within the framework of the project it was possible to refine elements of existing solutions and their implementation on the estate itself, as was finally achieved.

Conclusion

Engineering Comes Home demonstrated a method to involve a local community in discussion and design of a technical system to meet WEF resource needs that are typically supplied by large, centralised systems. Discussing options for alternative supply systems provided a unique context for residents to engage with and constructively intervene in these larger systems of provision and their environmental impacts. For instance, participants in the project increased their knowledge of urban drainage and combined sewer overflows through their interest in rainwater harvesting for water supply, finally deciding on an infrastructure intervention that would address both water use and urban water overflows.

Participatory design processes were used in the project to achieve three outcomes:

1. Infrastructure co-designed with the community – The initial infrastructure knowledge and needs within the community were assessed through household-based research with residents. Building on this, a series of workshops were developed to explore the WEF nexus as a design problem, then to focus on one particular issue and finally to co-design a solution. This culminated in the implementation of a prototype rainwater-harvesting system on the estate and a plan for scaling up this implementation.
2. Metadesign of tools for infrastructure co-design – Throughout the project the team developed and refined design tools that were used in participatory design workshops with residents. The development of the tools was informed by the design objectives of the research team along with analysis of the workshop outcomes to align the tools with residents' values, interests and needs.
3. Production of an infrastructure co-design toolkit – Beyond testing the feasibility of community co-design, the project aimed to create a toolkit that could be used by other infrastructure design teams. The toolkit was intended to help structure and formulate the involvement of community members in co-design projects. Two workshops were held with infrastructure professionals to understand the needs of those working in the field, helping to establish the six-step co-design method that was used in other bottom-up infrastructure projects.

The pilot rainwater-harvesting implementation provided a demonstration to residents of the capability of Internet of Things technologies to improve management of smaller-scale technologies, linking data infrastructure to everyday experience of rainwater, car washing and gardening. Through participating in a design process that attended to the specific needs and values of the community, residents developed ideas for improving their neighbourhood, with the added outcome of increased knowledge about infrastructure. The tools and the process tested in Engineering Comes Home provided the basis for the Bottom-Up Infrastructure co-design method (Chapter 4) and was adapted in further projects addressing different urban infrastructure issues – air quality (Chapter 7) and water management (Chapter 8).

7
Collaborating for environmental justice: Somers Town air quality

> **Community voices**
>
> This chapter includes contributions from Slaney Devlin, representing STNF; Donna Turnbull, representing Voluntary Action Camden; and Claire Holman from Brook Cottage Consultants. They were collaborators and clients for the project. The chapter was written three years after the project was completed. Initial discussions with Donna, Slaney and Claire shaped the framing of the chapter, identifying key points to be included. They provided feedback on the draft, alongside sharing documents and materials that were included in the chapter. Donna and Claire also wrote their own reflections, which are presented in Voices 7.1 and 7.2.

The impacts of pollution, climate change and other environmental crises are unevenly distributed. Poor and marginalised communities are more likely to live in polluted places, with limited access to green spaces and higher exposure to environmental risks such as flooding (Bullard, 1993). They are also more likely to be vulnerable to the effects of air pollution due to pre-existing illness. Environmental justice is a form of research and activism that aims to address the connection between social and environmental inequality, discussed in Chapter 2 (Agyeman, 2013; Holifield *et al.*, 2017; Walker, 2012). This chapter presents the Somers Town Air Quality project, which grew out of legal analysis of the environmental injustices experienced by residents of one of London's busiest neighbourhoods.

Somers Town has a rich history of social innovation and community action, but a high degree of social deprivation. It is a residential neighbourhood surrounded by big infrastructure and constant construction. Residents live with some of the city's poorest air quality and have very little access to green space in a highly urbanised environment. As introduced in Chapter 2, Voluntary Action Camden and the Somers Town community convened an inquiry into environmental justice. Supported by UCL Laws and the Environmental Law Foundation, the Somers Town community identified air quality as a major issue of environmental justice, requiring further technical exploration and action. As both a collaborator and client of the Engineering Exchange, the STNF worked with researchers to identify urban planning and monitoring measures, aiming to hold construction contractors and the local council to account in improving air quality (see Figure 7.1).

This chapter begins with the experience of environmental injustice in Somers Town as the motivation for the community engaging with technical analysis of air quality and interventions to reduce pollution. The neighbourhood planning system in the UK is described as a mechanism for the community to influence local infrastructure and housing development. The process of defining and delivering the Somers Town Air Quality project is described, following the six-step bottom-up

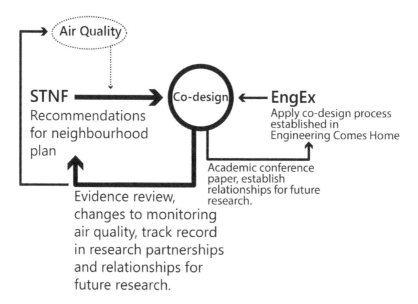

Figure 7.1 Somers Town Air Quality – community as collaborator-client

Table 7.1 Somers Town project summary

Project title	Air quality in Somers Town
Project budget	£30,000
Funder	UCL EPSRC Impact Acceleration Account
Duration	2017–18
Research team (UCL)	Sarah Bell (lead), Ed Manley, Charlotte Johnson Claire Holman
Collaborating groups	Somers Town Neighbourhood Forum
Relationship type	Community as collaborator and client
Outputs (non-academic)	• Technical report • Summary of inputs to neighbourhood plan • Four factsheets • Academic conference presentation
Outcomes	Changes to air quality monitoring in Somers Town
Future developments and collaborations	Research collaborations with UCL and Camden Council
Tools used in this project (refer to Chapter 9)	Factsheets, feedback forms

infrastructure co-design method. The outputs and impacts of the project, including a detailed technical report and recommendations for the neighbourhood plan are summarised, and the chapter ends with reflection on the process, outcomes and community experience. Table 7.1 summarises the inputs, outputs and contributors to the project.

Project initiation

Somers Town is home to about 18,000 people and is in one of the most highly populated wards in the London Borough of Camden, while also being its most highly deprived (Camden Council, 2020, p. 4). The neighbourhood is across the road from UCL, a familiar divide of a world-class university neighbouring a deprived community, with limited and sometimes problematic engagement. The area is also surrounded by large and nationally significant infrastructure. For example, it has three of London's major rail termini, including the international station St Pancras, while its southern border is one of the city's main east-west thoroughfares.

The past 20 years have seen a constant progression of large construction projects as these infrastructures are redeveloped and the area targeted for regeneration. The central location and good transport links means that its neighbours now include the British Library, the Francis Crick Institute (a UK centre for medical research), as well as technology giant Google, in addition to UCL. These institutes now call their shared area the 'Knowledge Quarter' (Knowledge Quarter, 2022). Construction of the UK's second high speed rail line, HS2, is ongoing in the area. Within Somers Town, the residents come from diverse ethnic, socioeconomic and age groups. The population is young by comparison to other wards in Camden, but with the highest rate of unemployment, and one of the lowest rates of life expectancy (Camden Council, 2020). These two urban realities create stark differences in experiences of environmental quality. Residents live with years of construction noise, traffic and airborne pollutants, while new headquarters are built. Once open for business, those visiting or working at these sites tend to enjoy the purified air of the latest heating, ventilation and air-conditioning technology installed in the buildings, while systems vent pollutants into the outdoor air.

The pressure from continuous construction and encroachment onto local green spaces motivated a group of residents, employers and employees to establish the STNF in 2013 (STNF, 2022). The group works to influence the development of their inner-city neighbourhood. In 2017, STNF and Voluntary Action Camden convened an environmental justice inquiry with UCL Laws and the Environmental Law Foundation (ELF). More than 90 individuals and groups from the Euston area got involved in the process, attending events and meetings, and making 'witness statements' about the impact that years of construction and redevelopment have had on their health and wellbeing.

Residents chose priorities for discussion and led roundtable debates at three main events focused on different development sites, chaired by an ELF Queen's Counsel. The resulting report was used to develop an action plan. Local residents' priorities were published and shared, providing guidance and evidence for STNF and other local agencies and groups to use. The report makes for tough reading as residents describe the physical and mental health impacts of the poor air quality, loss of green space and removal of trees (Holder, 2018). The report also indicates a range of procedural flaws that have contributed to residents' loss of trust in the planning system. It reflects a sense among residents that their local council acts as 'developer, landowner and decision-maker' and that residents feel some forms of evidence are overlooked, and decisions are taken with disregard for residents' concerns or the impacts on their lives. Voluntary Action Camden continue to support groups in applying the insights and using the data collected through the inquiry.

The poor air quality of the area and the low levels of green space stood out as issues that could potentially be influenced through STNF's neighbourhood development plan. Neighbourhood forums are the smallest unit in the UK's planning system (GOV.UK, 2020). They can produce neighbourhood development plans that must be taken into account by local planning authorities when assessing applications for developments. The STNF wanted to develop a plan that could address poor air quality and loss of green space, and make recommendations that would limit further degradation from imminent construction projects. Slaney Devlin, the chair of the STNF, had been involved in the legal review. She had also been involved in other initiatives run by UCL to engage with local community groups and act as a 'good neighbour'. Sitting in one of these meetings, Slaney felt that the university could do more to act on the concerns raised by residents in the report. The university was training engineers, environmental designers, urban planners and building physicists. There was clearly the expertise within the university that could be usefully deployed to make Somers Town's neighbourhood plan contain robust requirements that could lead to tangible improvements, or at least slow the rate of environmental degradation affecting residents' lives.

Voice 7.1 Donna Turnbull's reflection on initiating the collaboration with UCL Engineering Exchange

Genuinely resident/community led approaches are important to flag up I think, as they happen so rarely. The concept of co-production has been well illustrated throughout the work – the Environmental Justice Inquiry was very much about putting residents in the driving seat supported by amazing expertise. The collaboration took the work into areas we wouldn't have envisaged at the start. This isn't often allowed to happen as usually other people's agendas are imposed. The more standard approach is for residents to be consulted or 'engaged'/coerced into involvement in things they never wanted to start with. The air quality work with Sarah then continued that process of resident-led engagement. It provided more incredible resources to support a process driven by residents.

Donna Turnbull, community development manager,
Voluntary Action Camden

From the residents' perspective, it felt as if UCL would use Somers Town as a research and student 'resource', while doing nothing in return to support the local community. Consequently, the STNF asked the Engineering Exchange to support their neighbourhood planning process, demanding a more involved contribution from their academic neighbour. The group wanted to compile a list of planning recommendations that could reduce the harmful impacts of the upcoming construction and prioritise the spending of the Community Infrastructure Levy (CIL) (a planning charge paid by developers to local authorities). Again, the application for funding provided the mechanism to set the aims of a project that could be delivered jointly. The STNF and the Engineering Exchange successfully applied for funding from UCL's knowledge exchange and innovation funding to run a co-design process and generate agreed actions for two sections of their neighbourhood plan:

1. Planning recommendations to minimise negative air quality impacts of construction and regeneration projects that are specific to their community.
2. Research commitments to ask of academic partners in the Knowledge Quarter that will improve evidence of local air quality and strategies to improve it.

The funding allowed the team to run a series of workshops to discuss options and commission an independent air quality expert to review recent air quality assessments and the planning decisions that these assessments supported.

Air quality as a focus for neighbourhood planning

Neighbourhood forums were introduced into the UK's planning system in 2010 as part of the Conservative–Liberal Democrat government's localism agenda (Brownill and Bradley, 2017). This form of neighbourhood planning can be situated in a much longer trajectory of shifting boundaries between state and citizen control that have been enacted in the UK by different governments. In this iteration, the Coalition government placed strong emphasis on the idea of 'localism' and empowering local groups. The Localism Act 2011 included provisions for local communities to develop 'neighbourhood plans' to guide and control development. This created a framework for local communities to outline their priorities for their area, but they are not the decision-makers. The local authority is the decision-maker, but their planning decisions must be consistent with the National Planning Policy Framework (in England). A neighbourhood plan cannot introduce a policy that is opposed to a policy higher in the hierarchy. The need for new housing (to meet the local authority housing target) tends to override other considerations, as the planning system must balance a number of factors.

Current guidance explains that 'Neighbourhood planning is not a legal requirement but a right which communities in England can choose to use' (GOV.UK, 2020). Scholarship on neighbourhood forums in England shows an ambivalence over this form of engagement as being either progressive, enabling an alternative form of politics and real potential for self-governance; or regressive, allowing those with the most capacity to shape local developments to their interests, while leaving less well-resourced neighbourhoods behind (Cowie and Davoudi, 2015; Parker, 2017; Wills, 2016).

As well as the construction of nationally significant infrastructure, the local area also has development work driven by local authority priorities of residential densification and the low carbon transition (see Table 7.2). Camden Council runs the Central Somers Town Community Investment Programme, which is designed to deliver new housing. Residents are concerned about losing green space to these new housing developments. This is particularly problematic given concerns that the units will not be genuinely affordable, but are a mechanism for the local authority to generate income as a landowner and developer, rather than

Table 7.2 Recent major construction works in and around Somers Town

Twenty years of major construction works for national infrastructure …	
2001–7	Highspeed Rail 1 and the redevelopment of St Pancras International
2007–11	The redevelopment of King's Cross Railway Station
2011–16	Francis Crick Institute constructed
2018–ongoing	Highspeed Rail 2 and the redevelopment of Euston
Planned	British Library extension
… and local authority works	
2017–19	Redevelopment of Maria Fidelis (secondary school)
2019	Expansion of Phoenix Court Energy Centre
2014–ongoing	Central Somers Town Community Investment Programme

to house local people. The expansion of the Phoenix Court Energy Centre, part of the district energy network developed by Camden Council, raised similar concerns. The local authority plan to remove communal boilers from housing blocks and connect them to a local energy network. While this will remove sources of pollution from estates that join the network, there is concern over the increase in emissions from the energy centre, and concentration of pollutants at this location in close proximity to nurseries and sheltered accommodation.

Air quality is a technically complex issue, but some residents of Somers Town have become experts in environmental quality issues due to the continual construction and development of their area. The residents have organised to protect their neighbourhood. Another outcome of all the redevelopment is that Somers Town has a lot of air quality monitoring, as shown in Figure 7.2. Three of the monitoring points are owned by the local authority (Euston Road automatic monitoring station and two NO_2 diffusion tubes), and the other 10 are owned by developers.

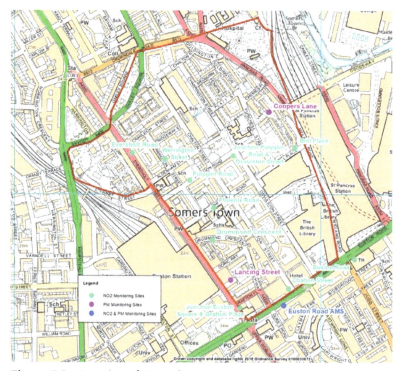

Figure 7.2 Location of air quality monitors in Somers Town

Source: Brooke Cottage Consultants, © Crown copyright Ordnance Survey. All rights reserved

Residents recognise this monitoring as a resource, if they can get access to the data and have the technical support to act on its interpretation. The monitoring could give the STNF a baseline against which they could check the impact on air quality of new developments planned for the area. However, the developers do not typically make the data publicly available. They are also not required to continue monitoring once their construction project has ended. For example, the Cooper's Lane particulate matter monitor (in pink in Figure 7.2) was installed by developers Argent to monitor their redevelopment of Kings Cross, but has since been taken on by Camden Council. The STNF felt that the university could support them with a technical inquiry into local air quality issues.

Supporting community groups with technical expertise was the main objective of the Engineering Exchange. Slaney Devlin, the chair of the STNF, was invited along to an Engineering Exchange meeting on air quality in London. During this meeting she felt frustrated by the lead given to academic partners to direct research. She approached Sarah with her specific need to act on poor air quality in Somers Town. Slaney has lived in the area for years, raising her children in Somers Town. She talked of the conflict she felt about this. On the one hand she felt that she had given her children an excellent start in life, allowing them access to the cultural life of a global city, in contrast to her own rural upbringing. However, this was tempered by her fear that by letting them grow up in such a polluted area she had exposed her children to harm and wiped years off their life expectancy. Slaney also pointed to the number of nurseries and schools in the area, and how young people coming daily into Somers Town required some protection. She spoke about the mental and physical health struggles of those she knew in the local area. Slaney felt that UCL could build on the collaboration with UCL Laws and do more to provide technical expertise on air quality. Slaney worked with Sarah, Charlotte and others at UCL to put in a funding application to UCL's impact fund to enable the STNF to commission some support and technical input into the project.

Defining an air quality project with the community

The Somers Town Air Quality project provided the opportunity to test out the tools and methods developed in Engineering Comes Home (Chapter 6) on a much smaller budget. The grant that Sarah, Slaney and Charlotte had successfully applied for was approximately 10 per cent of the Engineering Comes Home budget (see Tables 6.1 and 7.1).

The project retained and adapted the three-workshop structure developed in the Engineering Comes Home pilot, as part of the six-step bottom-up infrastructure co-design method (Figure 7.3). The capturing requirements workshop was designed to allow STNF members and supporters to debate air quality issues and think broadly about where to intervene locally, within the neighbourhood, and also strategically within the planning and development processes affecting the area. Following this, the research team would provide a synopsis of relevant evidence to support the group in prioritising actions and clarifying further research needs. The analysing options workshop was designed to review the available evidence and run a consensus-building process to agree where technical expertise could be best deployed. The final crafting solutions workshop was designed for the group to interrogate the technical report and discuss recommendations that could be usefully included in their neighbourhood plan.

Setting aims

Slaney and the STNF had two clear requests from the collaboration. The group wanted to be able to make specific recommendations in their neighbourhood plan that could reduce the negative air quality effects of planned developments. They also wanted to prioritise their options for spending income generated through the CIL. This is a fee paid to local authorities by developers. Each local authority can determine whether to use this levy, how much to charge developers and how much to spend on the communities most impacted by the development project (Lord, 2009). Developers in Camden are charged a Camden Council CIL and a GLA CIL, which are used to fund local community works. The group wanted the research project to help them gauge the potential impact of different options for improving local environmental quality.

Characterising the community

One outcome of the smaller budget for this project was to reduce the amount of qualitative research carried out in the characterising communities step. Instead, the research team drew on the significant work that had been done by previous researchers working in and with Somers Town. The environmental justice inquiry by Jane Holder and colleagues was especially useful in providing information to help understand the problems, aspirations and strengths of the community.

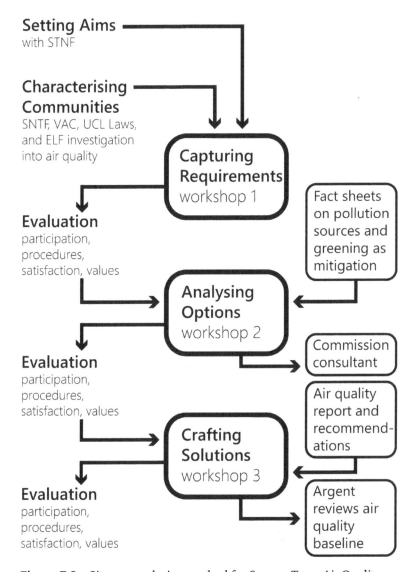

Figure 7.3 Six step co-design method for Somers Town Air Quality

The community organisation and representation by the STNF also reduced the need for detailed, original ethnographic research. The research team relied on the STNF to engage with its members and their knowledge and experience of the community to define the project and inform the co-design process. Located close to a major university, Somers Town had also been the subject of previous social science research, and community members expressed some frustration and 'research fatigue'. Detailed new research characterising the Somers Town community was therefore both unnecessary and inappropriate, and the team used existing research and the knowledge of the STNF as collaborators.

Workshop 1: capturing requirements

The capturing requirements workshop took place in the Living Space (a community centre attached to the Francis Crick Institute), scheduled after working hours to allow residents to come. Slaney Devlin, as STNF chair, compiled the known issues in the area and a series of questions for the group to debate about how to have an impact on issues through the neighbourhood plan. She opened the meeting giving an overview of the current status of air quality in the area, the main sources of pollution and how the group could affect air quality through their plan. Participants split into working groups to debate three issues in detail, which Slaney had identified as the main air quality issues that could be included in the neighbourhood plan. These were traffic; trees and greening; and urban form and street canyons. The STNF had previously identified these as the main air quality issues that could be included in the neighbourhood plan, based on their previous work in developing the plan.

The participants had diverse life experiences, held different aspirations for their neighbourhood and recognised different priorities for the plan. Collectively they had very high levels of expert knowledge and lived experience of the construction impacts on the local area. This included understanding of what a construction project entailed in terms of traffic, non-road mobile machinery (NRMM), noise and particulate matter. The discussions encompassed a wide range of potential solutions that varied in scale (see Table 7.3). People framed air quality issues not only in terms of policies and sector-wide interventions (e.g., changes to energy production and innovations in the transport sector) but also what they could do as individuals. Examples ranged from protecting oneself by staying inside or wearing a mask, to taking direct action such as asking drivers to turn off their idling engines. The group that focused on traffic spoke about tactics that could improve the impact of individual actions, such as having official signs at taxi ranks directing that engines must not idle. They also came up with more radical and longer-term ideas, such as designing a new form of small electric rickshaw to hop passengers between railway stations.

Table 7.3 Ideas from the themed discussion groups at workshop 1

Participants' suggestions from workshop 1	Source of pollution/ mitigation
Code of construction practice – ensure standards are enforced	Construction, traffic, rail
Push for highest regulations on operational emissions for new builds	Buildings
Traffic-management plan	Traffic
Involve Crossrail in an impact assessment of construction traffic	Traffic
Require landlords to minimise operational impacts of buildings or flats	Buildings
Urban form and layout for Somers Town to conserve and enhance the unique layout of each estate	Urban canyons, greening
Collective ideas with High Speed 2, Crossrail, Camden Local Plan	Rail, urban canyons, greening
Extend Central Activities Zone north to cover NRMM pollution	Construction
Car free days/zones (e.g., around schools)	Traffic
Electric vehicles/adding electric chargers	Traffic
Designated delivery drop-off points	Traffic
Finance incentive to replace polluting taxis with electric cars	Traffic
Resident-led campaign to stop idling	Traffic
Car-free new residential developments (with access for services and people with disabilities)	Traffic
Identify areas in residential estate that could be greened	Greening
Support community gardening initiatives and children getting involved in gardening	Greening

The discussion at the 'trees and greening' table was particularly emotive, reflecting the strength of feeling about the natural environment and the impact of seeing local trees cut down. The group recognised the need to strengthen the evidence about the benefits that mature trees provide in dense urban environments, and queried the appropriateness of policies used by the council. Slaney raised the issues of the wording in an existing neighbourhood policy, which asked developers to plant an equivalent numbers of new trees where trees are cut down. The table discussed whether the plan could include a requirement for developers to consider the variety in type and age of tree being replaced and to consider the time frame in which benefits will be achieved. A young tree will take a long time to mature and sequesters a small proportion of carbon compared to a mature tree.

At the 'urban form' table, the discussion focused on how to use existing best practice standards and ensure that they are followed by developers. Some participants were planning professionals or had worked in urban development. They had the capacity to translate proposed developments into tangible impacts, talking, for example, about how walking routes in the neighbourhood would be affected by the planned very tall buildings that could have canyoning impacts, channelling strong winds into narrow walkways. They also raised the requirement for developers to do more during the construction process to improve local air quality, by using electric trucks and machinery rather than diesel ones. The discussion group queried how pressure could be applied to landlords to maintain new builds and ensure that the installed heating and ventilation systems performed as predicted and did not contribute to negative effects once operational.

Overall, the key priorities that emerged through the discussion were to reduce health risks to vulnerable groups, ensure current regulations are enforced, and leverage participation from organisations in the Knowledge Quarter to improve air quality monitoring and provide accurate baselining. The groups came up with a series of ideas that provided the research team with the direction for their evidence review. The main steers were:

- Identify the groups most impacted by different sources of emissions and different interventions;
- Identify wider impacts on Somers Town (e.g., wellbeing, community building, biodiversity); and
- Assess potential for baselining and generating evidence versus interventions to limit or mitigate sources of pollutions.

Following this workshop, the Engineering Exchange team compiled available evidence that would allow a degree of comparison across these different areas and enable a prioritisation activity. The team created a series of factsheets about sources of pollution and the extent to which urban greening was able to mitigate pollution or its effects (Engineering Exchange, 2018). Factsheets are tools, described in Chapter 9. These factsheets provided insight into the specific questions raised during workshop 1,

Table 7.4 Source of emissions in 2013 from LAEI data

Emissions sources	PM$_{2.5}$	PM$_{10}$	NOx
Construction and demolition dust	0.3%	2%	0%
Resuspension (particulate matter lifted back into the air after settling)	2%	**27%**	0%
Other	5.2%	3%	0%
Domestic and commercial other fuels	2.6%	2%	1%
Rail	3.6%	2%	2%
NRMM	**16.2%**	8%	4%
Domestic and commercial gas	8%	4%	**12%**
Road transport	**62.2%**	**53%**	**82%**

while also flagging where the evidence was limited and how additional research could be used to provide more accurate insight into the situation in Somers Town. Data from the Mayor's London Atmospheric Emission Inventory (LAEI) (see Figure 7.4 and Table 7.4) shows that the main source of local emissions is road transport. In the evidence review, the UCL team searched for evidence of strategies that could reduce or mitigate the impact of transport-based emissions locally, finding some evidence on the effectiveness of information campaigns to limit idling, for example. The factsheets also outlined the potential for producing more accurate analysis based on targeted monitoring of local areas rather than relying on modelling. This could be used to identify more specific exposure and harm to the most vulnerable groups, such as children or elderly residents. It could also be used to check that air quality assessments for new developments were using appropriate baselines. For example, the evidence review found that the assessment of the proposed residential skyscraper at Brill Place in the east of Somers Town modelled NOx emissions from the combined heat and power generator installed and found very limited impact. NOx refers to both nitrogen oxide (NO), which is a potent greenhouse gas, and nitrogen dioxide (NO$_2$), which is associated with respiratory ill health. However, the assessment used modelled background levels, rejecting the higher levels detected by monitoring (Vital Energi, 2017).

Workshop 2: analysing options

Once compiled, the evidence review gave the team some content to be used in a decision-making workshop to plan the allocation of the grant

Figure 7.4 LEAI 1 km by 1 km background pollution grid covering Somers Town (yellow indicates the squares covering Somers Town). The map is based on OpenStreetMap® and the base data is available under the Open Database Licence

Table 7.5 Criteria for STNF to assess evidence needs against STNF priorities

	Traffic	Trains	Buildings	Trees and greening
Evidence				
Evidence is clear or has potential to be improved for Somers Town?				
Assess scale of impact				
Impacts on vulnerable groups (young, elderly, other health conditions)?				
Other impacts on Somers Town (e.g., wellbeing, community-building, biodiversity, accessibility/inclusivity)?				
Already being targeted in policy?				
Can STNF make an impact?				
with CIL				
with direct action				
with monitoring or new evidence				
through policy				
Other issues and concerns (e.g., canyoning, overlap with other areas)				

money. The analysing options workshop was held in a local high school in March. The plan was to discuss the evidence and review it against the criteria that the STNF had raised as key priorities in workshop 1 (see Table 7.5). The intention was to collectively identify one issue to work on and then spend some time scoping a project that the UCL team could deliver with the grant money. The UCL team had identified a number of ways that a project could work, with options related to which types of stakeholder group to collaborate with and what level of engagement STNF members would want to have. The workshop activity was designed to prompt discussion specifically on the type of project: whether to focus on baselining and generating evidence or on assessing intervention effectiveness or policies to limit pollution; whether to work independently or with local polluters; and whether to involve residents in generating the evidence or to report back.

The turnout was less than the capturing requirements workshop, as another local meeting was called on the same day and representatives from Network Rail and local developers did not attend. Nonetheless, approximately eight residents came to discuss the evidence and select a research idea that the Engineering Exchange could deliver. During the meeting, groups found it hard to assess the evidence review in the time allocated. The information was briefly summarised at the start of the workshop, but there was a lot of information to read and take in. The group found it easier to discuss the issues rather than read the information sheets and assess the content in the template provided. Instead, the workshop moved into a general discussion of the issues presented. The UCL team steered the group towards defining a project that could be delivered with the grant money. Slaney and STNF members outlined types of project they could see as being useful to their own process of developing a neighbourhood plan. Following the meeting, the research team produced a list of actions that they could take forward, and liaised with the STNF to prioritise these. The STNF agreed to the following list:

- Evaluate the current monitoring of air quality in Somers Town and future needs compared to best practice.
- Review air quality forecasts in the environmental impact assessments for recent developments, compared to current air quality.
- Link with the UCL-Environmental Law Foundation Environmental Justice Inquiry findings on cumulative impacts of development on air quality and health.
- Work with Knowledge Quarter stakeholders and others to reduce congestion from last-mile delivery traffic.
- Support citizen science 'window wipe' testing to identify pollutants.
- Improve data about current street trees and identify optimal locations for tree planting.

The Engineering Exchange team's evaluation meeting following the workshop discussed the challenge of getting participants to focus on the neighbourhood plan and in clearly articulating what UCL researchers could do in terms of providing technical expertise. However, the ranked list did fulfil an objective in terms of enabling the group to commission a bespoke piece of research for the STNF. Air quality expert and UCL senior research associate Claire Holman was commissioned to write a technical report. This would address the first two points by including an evaluation of Somers Town air quality monitoring and a review of the air quality forecast in recent developments' environmental impact assessments.

Research into Somers Town's air quality

Claire worked through the summer on the analysis, liaising with Slaney and the STNF to gain a detailed understanding of the area. This was helpful for the first section of the research, which focused on Somers Town's extensive air quality monitoring. Claire's work details how the local air quality modelling tools are used and how this can lead to optimistic assessments. Specifically, Claire flagged that the background concentrations used by the developers of HS2 for Somers Town could be overestimating the amount of existing pollution and therefore underestimating the impact of the development work.

Claire's report states:

> The HS2 monitoring locations in Somers Town are classified as kerbside and roadside locations where local traffic emissions influence the measured concentrations. Kerbside and roadside are defined in Local Air Quality Management technical guidance as within 1 metre of the kerb, and 1 metre to 5 metres of the kerb respectively. Background sites are those away from the immediate influence of local sources of pollution and are representative of a wide area. The HS2 monitoring sites are close to the local roads, but there is little traffic on many of these roads (in the absence of construction traffic).

Claire argues in the report that while some of the boundary roads are busy and should be classified as roadside or kerbside, roads within Somers Town 'are not busy and are not the normal type of roadside or kerbside locations where NO_2 concentrations are monitored as part of local air quality management. If the HS2 urban background adjustment factor (0.909) had been used concentrations would be 1–7% higher than in the table in Somers Town' (Holman, 2018, p. 22). This means that HS2 would have found that their construction work had had a bigger impact on local air quality than reported. When this was raised, HS2 reissued some of their data.

Claire also carried out a retrospective review of the air quality impact assessments that had been carried out for local developments. The first assessment reviewed was that of the Francis Crick Institute, the biggest single biomedical research laboratory in Europe, which had opened two years earlier in 2016. The assessment included construction impacts (both construction plant and traffic), lab emissions (e.g., formaldehyde and benzene), traffic associated with the institute once operational, the energy plant and the back-up diesel generators. Claire found the assessment to be thorough but flagged that 'it would be useful to find out what energy plant was actually installed (see Phoenix Court Energy Centre), the frequency of the test firing of the diesel generations and their operational use to date' (Holman, 2018, p. 27).

The next assessment was the Phoenix Court Energy Centre (now known as Somers Town Energy), a gas-powered facility built to provide district heating to Camden Council-owned housing estates in the area. The energy centre is located in the car park of a residential building and in close proximity to two nurseries and sheltered accommodation for elderly people. These groups are vulnerable to poor air quality. The energy centre had two air quality assessments carried out – one in December 2013 and an update in 2017. These were ordered by Camden after planning permission had been granted, rather than for use in deciding whether the energy centre should go ahead. Furthermore, Claire's analysis identified a number of inaccuracies and discrepancies between these two assessments, with no transparent explanation. Discrepancies included a change in the chimney stack height and different background concentrations being used in each report. The 'background concentration' refers to the level of air pollution that cannot be attributed to local sources of pollution and is used to understand the impact of introducing new pollution sources. The outcome was that the second air quality assessment found the significance of the impacts to be lower, ranging from negligible to moderate. Claire explains that if the same background concentration had been used in the new air quality assessment, the report would have found 'substantial' impacts at seven of the 13 points used to model the impact. She goes on to observe:

> The fact that the Energy Centre is going to make air quality deteriorate in an area where the AQO [air quality objective: the target] is already exceeded by a wide margin, suggests that it should not have been given planning consent. Whilst is it true that the boilers at the Energy Centre will be more efficient and have lower NOx emissions (in g/kWh) than those it will replace, more emissions will be released in one place possibly resulting in a larger impact on air quality close to the Energy Centre than near the existing boilers. (Holman, 2018, p. 29)

The third air quality assessment reviewed was for the Central Somers Town Community Improvement Plan. This is the council's own regeneration programme for the local area, which includes some building redevelopment. Camden Council had commissioned its own independent review of the assessment, which flagged that the impact of the construction traffic had not been included and should have been. The plan involved the redevelopment of a school and community facilities, as well as the construction of 136 homes within seven new buildings. The estimated construction traffic was expressed as '25 or more HGV [Heavy Goods Vehicle] movements per day' (p. 31) and should have been included.

The fourth air quality assessment reviewed was for the Maria Fidelis Catholic School. Again, this did not include the impact of construction traffic and Claire points out that when building in an area of very poor air quality, the impact of construction traffic can be significant and should be included. Her report also shows that a wide range of background concentrations was used in the assessments, which can make the difference between an air quality objective being met or not.

This highly technical report was the result of a collaboration between Claire and Slaney. Slaney, representing the STNF, was able to provide detailed insight into the nature of the local area and signpost the relevant reports to look for and compare. Together they were able to able to interrogate some of the assumptions underpinning the evidence and relate this to residents' own experiences of poor air quality and their concerns. It was through this collaboration that clear recommendations for a neighbourhood report crystallised. These recommendations covered advice on planning applications, design, planning conditions, enforcement, ideas for local authority funds (e.g., CIL money) and awareness-raising. These recommendations have been produced as a two-page summary available on the STNF website (STNF, 2022). In brief, the recommendations were:

- Planning application summaries – developers should produce two-page summaries written in non-technical language explaining impacts, mitigation measures and assessment methods used.
- Air quality assessments – use conservative background concentrations and justify verification method. Major developments' air quality assessments should include construction-traffic impacts.
- Air quality positive – all major developments should be air quality positive in Somers Town.

The recommendations for planning conditions were:

- Ensure that all major development submits an air quality and dust management plan. Include a ban on construction vehicles during school start and finish times. Adopt Central London NRMM requirements and consider electric construction equipment.

- Require electric charging provision in developments with parking.
- Monitor and revise travel plans annually.
- New schools and extensions should restrict private car access.
- Require details of installed boilers or combined heat and power engines to be submitted for approval prior to first operation or occupation of development.

Workshop 3: crafting solutions

The crafting solutions workshop was held in November 2018 to discuss the findings of the technical review and the recommendations for the neighbourhood plan. Twenty-six residents came. Claire presented her work, opening with an overview of how to think about air quality and recognise that at least 50 per cent of local air pollution stems from background sources that are outside London and include industrial sources such as transport and construction, but also natural sources such as dust from the Sahara desert. She was also keen to point out that the local emissions in London have reduced in recent years and that air quality has improved. This is largely because new, less-polluting car engines are gradually replacing the old, more polluting ones. She also pointed to the achievements of Transport for London in retrofitting particulate filters and improving its bus fleet. She did not, however, shy away from the poor air quality of Euston Road or diminish the impacts of construction and regeneration projects on local air quality. She talked through her analysis, emphasising how it had been enabled and strengthened through the collaboration with the STNF. This combination of technical expertise with local knowledge was key to producing this analysis of the issues that affect residents' lives. She also went through her recommendations for the plan and emphasised how local knowledge is key for good decision-making by local government.

The audience response was diverse. Many expressed an appreciation of the analysis and the tangible recommendations made for the plan. On the other hand, other participants were frustrated by the limited scope of the report, wanting to hear more about the implications of the air quality for their health and general wellbeing. Failing to acknowledge the impact of the loss of green space and the removal of trees was also disappointing for some. There was also scepticism that the report had not adequately conveyed the negative impacts of the demolition and construction on their lives. Claire framed the report as being focused on steps that the group could take to influence future construction, rather

Table 7.6 Results from the feedback form for workshop 3

	Strongly agree	Agree	Disagree	Strongly disagree	Neither
After the workshop(s), I know more about air quality in Somers Town	8	3	0	1	0
After the workshop(s), I know more about how the neighbourhood plan can impact on air quality	3	8	0	0	0
The project report and outcomes are useful for the STNF	6	4	0	1	1
My ideas and concerns have been listened to	4	6	2	0	0
The ideas came mostly from the community	2	7	2	0	1
The workshop(s) helped me to get to know others in the community	2	8	0	0	2

than to go over past impacts. In total 26 members of the STNF turned up to debate the report and the recommendations. Of these, 12 filled out a feedback form and their responses gave a positive impression of the workshop and outcome (see Table 7.6).

Influencing air quality policy and management

With the report in hand, Slaney (representing the STNF) pushed HS2 to improve its air quality assessments and change its bias adjustment factors. Bias adjustment factors are used to model the impact of local pollution above modelled background levels (Department of Environment, Food and Rural Affairs, 2021). A street designated as a 'road side' site is estimated to have a higher background concentration than a 'residential' site. Changing the bias adjustment factors can therefore affect the proportion of the air pollution that is attributed to local sources and can better represent local street conditions.

Slaney also contacted Camden Council to challenge its approval of the Phoenix Court Energy Centre. Slaney outlined the argument that an air quality assessment should have been done before awarding planning permission to the energy centre. Camden Council challenged this, responding that the assessment and approval process was in order, but agreed with Slaney's suggestion about increasing electric heating in the area, rather than automatically looking to connect more existing buildings to the network. The council invited the STNF to join it in a new area of work looking at electrifying heating in the borough.

The Somers Town Air Quality project was one of a number of initiatives that resulted from the initial environmental justice inquiry. Camden Council has collaborated with other UCL academics on air quality; notably, Muki Haklay created the Clean Air Partnership, which ran a 'Clean Air Design Day' and led to the council's 2019 Air Quality Action Plan. This document outlines the council's priorities and strategy, but it also includes the actions that local stakeholders can take. This includes the university and its potential to support monitoring, evaluation and citizen science initiatives.

The STNF also continues to act on local environmental issues. In 2021 it submitted a bid with the council to the GLA's 'Future neighbourhoods 2030' fund to explore local climate change mitigation and adaptation. It was one of two London neighbourhoods chosen to receive funding. The STNF with the Somers Town Community Association will be leading on a neighbourhood strategy.

Evaluation

The Engineering Exchange project with the STNF evolved from a community as collaborator into a community as client mode of operation. The residents' experience of years of construction, regeneration and poor health impacts made them experts on issues not only related to air quality and environmental harms, but also of the planning processes through which there is opportunity to effect change and demand better outcomes. As such, the group could commission a technical review that it could use in political processes to draw attention to failings and rectify oversights.

However, the project also requires reflection on the reality of living with environmental harms and the emotional aspect of engaging. For some residents, minor changes to monitoring were not enough given the experience of watching trees being cut down and green space paved over.

The project also raises the question of how much is demanded of residents who wish to improve local environmental outcomes. Even when the formal structures existing with the planning process for groups to engage, actually achieving this engagement, and doing so on terms that are set by expert bodies, is very hard.

> ## Voice 7.2 Reflection from Dr Claire Holman, director, Brook Cottage Consultants
>
> As an air quality professional working in the planning system I have seen how difficult it is for community groups to effectively influence planning decisions. They need time, the ability to understand technical information and money to pay for professional advice, or preferably all three. Most of the Somers Town residents were simply coping with their day-to-day lives, they certainly did not have the ability to pay consultants. By the time I got involved the Engineering Exchange had already worked with the community and there was a high degree of knowledge on air quality and the planning applications affecting their area. They understood the issues but were frustrated by how little notice Camden Council took of their views. My report set out a number of recommendations to make it easier for them to understand the air quality impacts of any future planning applications, and some simple suggestions for them to lobby their Camden Council. I enjoyed working with the STNF and hope I have contributed in some small way to making Somers Town a better place for the future.
>
> Dr Claire Holman, director, Brook Cottage Consultants

Conclusion

The Somers Town Air Quality project demonstrated that the co-design methods developed in Engineering Comes Home (Chapter 6) could be adapted to support neighbourhood planning for a complex issue in an area shaped by infrastructure development. The project also showed that the methods could be applied with a much smaller budget, and to work with a community with a very high level of technical knowledge about their environment.

The Somers Town project connects to wider movements of citizen science and academic engagement to support environmental justice (Ottinger, 2010; Riesch *et al.*, 2013). The Somers Town community had a long experience of being participants and subjects in research projects and valued the opportunity shape and lead the research questions, direction and outcomes as both client and collaborator. The project reveals how modes of engagement are flexible and can change within a project as the needs and strengths of the partners, and the nature of their relationship evolve.

8
Integrating water and urban greening: the Kipling Garden

Community voices

This chapter includes contributions from Joanna Vignola and Clive Shaw, residents of the Kipling Estate. They were collaborators in the project. Their insights and reflections on the project are included in the chapter in their own writing throughout the text in Voices 8.1–8.4. A visit and tour of the Kipling Estate, led by Joanna and Clive, shaped the narrative of this chapter. They provided text and comments on drafts, alongside sharing their thoughts and insights into wider concepts and issues, around partnership working, raised in this chapter.

The Kipling Garden, which was introduced in Chapter 1, was a collaborative project initiated when community ambitions for a garden coincided with researcher and industry interests in sustainable water management in London. The focus of the collaboration was a large concrete playground built on top of a garage block in a 1960s housing estate. The playground can be seen by residents looking out from their flats in two connecting tower blocks, but has been inaccessible to them since the 1980s due to security concerns. Residents had long wanted to turn the space into a roof garden and worked with researchers from the CAMELLIA project to assess options. The community acted as collaborator with the CAMELLIA researchers (see Figure 8.1).

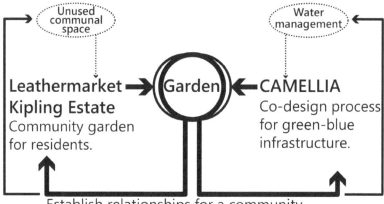

Figure 8.1   Kipling Garden – community as collaborator

Residents participated in a co-design process to outline their garden and its wider benefits. Greening the playground would create high water demand but also reduce storm water run-off. The researchers developed tools that helped communities link urban greening projects to water infrastructure management. Community members and researchers worked together throughout, securing funding, recruiting people to join the project and supporting further work on estate greening. Residents ultimately created the garden in a different location on the estate and the playground remains inaccessible. The chapter presents the tools and processes that can bring water into community decision-making, but also provides insights into the complexities of community-led green-blue infrastructure development. Table 8.1 summarises the inputs, outputs and contributors to the project.

Project initiation

The Kipling Estate is located in central London. It has almost 300 homes, a mix of low-rise buildings and tower blocks. It is managed by the Leathermarket JMB, who also manage the Meakin Estate (Chapter 6). Andy Bates, head of the JMB, knew about residents' ideas of turning

Table 8.1 Kipling project summary

Project title		Kipling Garden
Project budget		Approximately £200,000 (£4,129,083 CAMELLIA total)
Funder		Natural Environment Research Council
Duration		2017–20
Research team	UCL	Sarah Bell (UCL lead), Tse-Hui Teh, Charlotte Johnson, Diala Nour-Eddine (MSc student)
	Imperial	Adrian Butler (CAMELLIA lead)
	British Geological Survey	Carl Watson, Rehan Kaleem, Javid Yousef
Collaborating groups		LB Southwark, Leathermarket JMB, Thames Water
Relationship type		Community as collaborator
Outputs		One successful grant application Kipling calculator Two academic conference presentations
Outcomes		Gardening group established on Kipling Estate Raised beds constructed elsewhere on site
Future developments and collaborations		Generic calculator to support integrated garden and sustainable water design through CAMELLIA
Tools used in this project (refer to Chapter 9)		Archival research, stakeholder interviews, value elicitation, Infrastructure Safari, formulating options, Kipling calculator, infrastructure literacy gauge, feedback forms

the playground into a green space. After working with the UCL research team on the Meakin project, JMB staff showed the area to the team and opened up the possibility of a new collaboration. Converting concrete into green space in the centre of London has environmental benefits that a researcher-resident collaboration could explore and seek to maximise. The work carried out in Meakin Estate (see Chapter 6) had piloted a bottom-up infrastructure co-design process and shown how researchers could work with residents. The Kipling Garden project was an opportunity to take a different starting point; resident initiated rather than researcher led. Setting the aims of the project therefore took the form of a negotiation between residents' representatives, researchers and the management body. The garden idea was included in a funding bid for the CAMELLIA project, led by Adrian Butler, a professor in subsurface hydrology at Imperial College. The bid was shortlisted for interview and two Kipling residents, Joanna Vignola and Jackie Scorer, went with the academics to the funding panel and helped to win the £5 million research grant. CAMELLIA started in 2019, with the Kipling Garden as the project's first case study.

The garden project brought together a number of groups whose members had different priorities and motivations. The main mobilising force was a small group of residents interested in greening the garage roof playground and bringing it back into use. This small group was supported by their management board (Leathermarket JMB) who help their tenants and residents run projects that benefit their housing estate and community. The Leathermarket JMB also wanted to improve their work on sustainability and explore the potential of the playground that they kept in a state of managed decline due to a lack of resources. The JMB assigned a resident liaison officer to support the project.

The CAMELLIA researchers came from different institutions with different areas of expertise and interest. The Imperial team, led by Adrian, was interested in the water benefits and stresses that a new roof garden would create. The British Geological Survey team, led by Carl Watson, was interested in data visualisations that help community groups investigate and make decisions about water impacts of community greening. The UCL team, led by Sarah, was interested in using a co-design process to bring together residents and stakeholders to explore the social and environmental possibilities of the space.

Co-design is a method that enables different groups to work together on an intervention that affects their physical or organisational environment. Co-design can 'enable constituents to coalesce, collaborate and create ideas for their future forms of living' (Teh, 2019). The UCL team felt that this method could align residents' ambitions for a garden with the research team's interest in improving water management in London. The UCL team's intention was to run an exploratory design process that could investigate the possible benefits of greening the roof and identify funding routes for implementation.

Voice 8.1 Clive's reflections on project initiation

Firstly, the feeling of 'finally!' when UCL first appeared at a General (monthly) TRA Meeting in 2018. The ground-level garages/roof-area make up a significant and central space within the estate, but aside from the persistent water ingress affecting car owners, it is curious that it is barely discussed. The constant underlying potential for development looms over it with a feeling that literally anything could replace it at any time. Coupled with the absolute prohibition of access dating from some misremembered accident from the early 1980s, it is a totally neglected jewel that is visibly disintegrating before us. UCL's proposal to base their research on this lost space was more than just welcome, it broke an unspoken barrier that had lasted decades. Along with their detailed case for urgent action on London's water, it was memorable moment in an otherwise workaday meeting. That bright start continued when Kipling was chosen as CAMELLIA's social housing site in Southwark several months later. Sarah, Charlotte and the other researchers then outlined a series of workshops and visits that were both inspiring and empowering. That kick started both the development of the Kipling Community Garden and the total transformation of our TRA. The former into a fully realised and delivered community asset and the latter, a more responsive and accountable group that continues to this day.

Clive Shaw, Kipling Estate resident

London's water problems

The Kipling Estate is a housing estate in the inner-London borough of Southwark. Its location brings a number of issues relevant to community water management. First, the estate is within the area of London's combined sewer system (Dolowitz *et al.*, 2018). This system was developed in the nineteenth century and mixes surface-water drainage with foul-water drainage in one sewer network. It is designed to overflow into the Thames during times of very high rainfall to avoid sewage backing up into homes and streets. Since the construction of the combined sewer, London has grown and densified, increasing the city's impermeable surfaces and leading to more surface run-off with heightened flood risk. The growing population creates a second issue: the stress on the city's drinking-water supplies. London abstracts water from the environment at a faster rate than rainfall can replenish it, and is forecast to have a water deficit by 2030 unless there is significant investment in water infrastructure. Climate change exacerbates these problems, creating more storm events and drought periods. These two infrastructural challenges are exacerbated by a third challenge: London's high land value means pressure to develop on green space is extreme and community-based environmental governance is impacted by political processes beyond their control.

Water governance in the UK is fragmented across central government, local government and industry. However, community engagement is increasingly recognised as essential in addressing the sustainability challenges facing London's water system (Morris and McGuinness, 2019). Water policy and regulation in the UK has recently shifted towards greater end-user and community engagement. This is driven by three wider trends: a catchment-area-based approach; a recognised need for demand management and behaviour change; and the increasing importance of decentralised infrastructure (e.g., sustainable drainage systems such as rain gardens, green roofs and swales). The UK's water regulator Ofwat requires customer engagement from private water companies (Ofwat, 2019), and local authorities recognise the importance of engaging communities in flood-risk management and green infrastructure delivery (Potter and Vilcan, 2020). Local green-blue infrastructure initiatives are increasingly important in London to reduce the frequency of combined sewer overflows, to manage surface-water flood risk and to maintain capacity within the sewers to be able to adapt to climate change and accommodate future development (Mayor of London, 2016). The Kipling Garden was seen by the researchers as an opportunity to align these objectives with the residents' plans for developing a new community garden.

Co-designing a multi-functional garden

Figure 8.2 shows Joanna's view onto the playground above the estate's garages. The space is vast at approximately $1,700m^2$. It is accessed via the first floors of the two tower blocks, through rooms originally designated as 'homework rooms', which are currently being used by the JMB cleaning staff and maintenance teams. The garages beneath are rented out to residents and non-residents. The garage units are small by today's standards and are used largely as storage spaces. The rental income goes to the JMB, but the cost of refurbishing the garages and the playground is too high to be justified by the JMB. The whole structure is kept in a state of managed decline.

Figure 8.2   Joanna's view of the rooftop (image credit Joanna Vignola)

Repurposing the space from grey to green infrastructure opens up the possibility of creating environmental and social benefits. A green roof can contribute to reduced run-off in storm events and improve sewer capacity. A community garden can bring a range of social benefits, and mental and physical health benefits for those doing the gardening, as well as broader environmental benefits (Draper and Freedman, 2010; Guitart *et al.*, 2012; Uwajeh and Ezennia, 2018). However, ensuring that a community garden thrives requires a lot of water to irrigate the space. Sourcing this from rainwater harvesting creates further stormwater capture potential while reducing the use of drinking water. Repurposing the space in this way requires a change in existing access and governance arrangements, and broad-based support from residents and management. It also requires funding.

The Kipling Garden project was conceived to meet the aspirations of the community for a new garden and the research team's objectives to demonstrate community-based, integrated water management in London. The project was led by the UCL team in the CAMELLIA project, building on the co-design process piloted in Engineering Comes Home (Chapter 6). It followed the same six-step format, with activities centred on three workshops (see Figure 8.3).

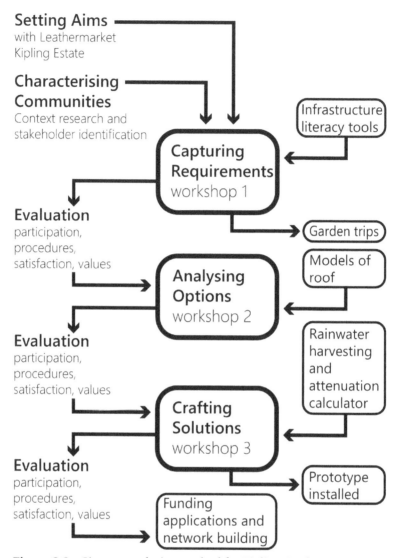

Figure 8.3 Six-step co-design method for Kipling Garden

Setting aims

The Kipling co-design process was intended to:

- bring together stakeholders interested in or impacted by the greening project to develop design options and investigate the benefits and limitations of different aspects; and

- introduce scientific analysis of water impacts into the residents' and stakeholders' design decisions.

The research project became a way for the community to meet their aims of establishing a garden, providing a potential pathway to funding and expertise that otherwise would not have been available. The research team and community aims were complementary but separate.

Characterising communities

Having established broadly the project aims through the process of writing the funding bid, the next stage of the project was to gain some contextual insight about the estate and the garage roof and to identify relevant stakeholders. This characterising communities process involved archival research and qualitative research. Archival research and stakeholder interviews used in this project are described as tools for wider application in Chapter 9. The research team interviewed the two TRA members who had participated in the CAMELLIA funding interview and discussed how the space was currently used, as well as ideas and concerns about changing it into a green space. They spoke to relevant teams at the JMB, including the gardening team, to get their perspective on how this might impact on existing maintenance and gardening responsibilities. In parallel, they asked for relevant local contacts and identified stakeholders who had some power to influence the space. This included local councillors, staff from the flood risk and urban regeneration teams and the wastewater strategy team in the utility company, Thames Water. The research team's assumption was that each of these groups had valuable and complementary knowledge about parts of the infrastructure that they could bring together to co-create capacity. For example, the stakeholders brought with them their knowledge of institutional priorities and programmes. Residents understood the reality of the estate and how its infrastructure worked, as brought to their ideas for repurposing the space. The researchers brought academic expertise on water impacts in a form that was usable by the participants, and they could deploy processes that would elicit different perspectives and bring participants together to design the garden.

Through this research, the team came to learn about residents' aspirations for the space as well as past activity on the roof and some of the existing concerns related to it. Jackie Scorer, the head of the TRA at the time and a director of the JMB, is a long-time resident of the area. She remembers fetes taking place on the roof and it being used by children. She moved to the estate in the late 1980s and by this time the roof had been closed off in response to safety concerns. Jackie explained that large items – furniture and appliances – were thrown from flats' balconies onto the roof space. She felt that this trouble emanated from people with little respect for the estate or its residents. However, it was a temporary issue that resolved as residents moved on. The departure of 'troublemakers' did not entirely get rid of concerns about the safety of being on the roof, and it was kept inaccessible. Residents could apply to use the homework rooms and access the space, but a key-holder would have to accompany any group. Jackie explained that there were security concerns about letting people into the building, and as the only access to the space was through the main door to the tower blocks, residents would want to know that visitors were being appropriately shepherded to avoid any security risks.

Joanna, the other member of the TRA who had supported the CAMELLIA bid, spoke about her interest in creating a green space that could bring residents together to garden and learn. Joanna is a keen gardener and environmentalist who had been attempting to get support for greening the roof for some years. Both Joanna and Jackie felt that existing green spaces in the estate were not used much by residents and that any greening project would need to actively engage people.

The TRA is the formal governance structure that allows residents to feed their ambitions for estate management into the management body. All residents are automatically members, although only some actively engage. The TRA had supported the researchers' funding bid; however, their members held different opinions about the playground. Some wanted it to become a green space, others preferred for it to remain inaccessible to residents due to safety concerns, while some were interested in broader environmental gains beyond the playground that collaborating with a research project could open. Conflicting opinions and contrasting values often occur between members of the same community. This is illustrated within some of the regeneration literature. Andrew McCulloch (2000) explores the role of 'the community' in the decision-making processes of regeneration initiatives, noting how in many cases this actually relies on a member from the local community to represent the views of the wider community. However, the risk is that nominating a representative of the community, or encouraging their emergence, can inadvertently lead to an 'inverse community': without wider engagement processes the decisions or actions may only meet certain interests.

Clive and Joanna reflected on the 'community' created by the estate greening project and the opportunities that were brought about by the co-design process. This gave an opportunity to learn from others by sharing knowledge, resources, experience and expertise – not just through the researcher team, but from visits, from reaching out to the local authority and from involvement of further organisations and stakeholders.

Kipling's green spaces are maintained by the JMB's gardening teams, so the research team was conscious of the additional gardening duties that greening the roof could entail. The lead gardener supported the idea, coming up with ideas for planting that could sustain low rainfall conditions on the roof and could tolerate the wind gusts created by the tower blocks. He spoke about the structure, flagging concerns about getting water and equipment onto the roof and getting leaves and dead matter off the roof. He also raised concern about being left with maintenance responsibilities if residents' enthusiasm waned. He talked about some forms of gardening as being elitist. Vegetable growing, for example, could be done by people who had the time to make things grow and who would then benefit from it. In contrast ornamental planting, he explained, created an environment that could be enjoyed by all residents. The gardeners were also responsible for the Meakin Estate and explained that they did not use the water tank there much as it was always empty in the dry periods when they needed water.

The research team also spoke to the JMB about the condition of the structure and the ability to build on it. The JMB explained that a structural survey had been done 15 years previously that had found that the buildings to be sound but in bad condition, and more recently an assessment had been carried out showing that it was possible to build on the roof space in its current condition. The JMB suggested that funds be included in the implementation budget for the garden to commission a good quality structural survey. The JMB agreed to inform the London Borough of Southwark (the building owners) of the project. The JMB also suggested that a risk assessment about the safety of operating on the site be carried out at the implementation phase.

A number of key factors emerged from these conversations that would need to be addressed through the planned co-design process:

- security of the space and the risk from things being thrown down;
- the load capacity and condition of the roof;
- access to the space;
- health and hygiene; and
- maintenance.

With this understanding of the context, the researchers, together with the JMB liaison officer for the Kipling Estate and some interested TRA members, set about encouraging participation in the co-design process and opening up discussion about what could be done on the roof.

Co-creation workshops

The first step in the co-design process was to gain interest from residents in the estate to participate and to encourage stakeholder organisations to support the process. The team placed a notice in the JMB newsletter, attended TRA meetings to widen awareness, sent out letters and put up posters around the estate. Both Thames Water and Southwark Council's flood-risk team committed to send people to participate in the workshops. The promotion of these workshops tapped into existing groups on the estate, including the Kipling DIY group. The research team devised the workshop activities to bring together the different forms of expertise, encouraged by the monthly Kipling DIY Club, established by resident Robert Beveridge (see Table 8.2).

Workshop 1: capturing requirements

The capturing requirements workshop took place in the TRA hall in April 2019. As people entered the room, they were invited to place stickers on a wall chart, indicating their knowledge of the local water and drainage system. This was intended to show the diverse spread of knowledge, and later to track any gains in this 'infrastructural literacy', a tool described in Chapter 9. After introductions and a brief overview of London's combined sewer system, the first activity started. This was the 'infrastructure safari', as described in Chapter 9. The group of 19 residents, stakeholders and researchers divided into two mixed groups and set off on a walk around the estate. The route had been planned by the research team to allow participants to visit key points of the estate's water system drains, views of neighbouring green roofs and the rooftop playground. The objective was to build an understanding of how water systems and green infrastructure interrelate, but also to allow for this understanding to be produced collectively. The teams were asked to jot on an estate map any points of local flooding or issues, and also to find any downpipes that could be used as a source of rainwater for growing a garden on the roof. Through the safari, the participants from Thames Water and Southwark Council were able to provide insight into how greening such an expanse of concrete could reduce pressure on local sewers at times of intense downfalls by slowing down the journey of the rain into the drain. For some residents this was the first time that they had been able to access the roof space in the centre of their estate. Through the safari it also became clear that all the rainwater pipes were internal to the building, the only exposed ones were inside the garage block under the playground. This meant the research team focused

Table 8.2 Aims, activities and participants in the three workshops

Workshop	Aims	Participants				Activities/tools used
		Residents	Stakeholders	Researchers	Students	
1: Discussing values	Produce a shared understanding of the local water infrastructure system and impacts Explore aspirations and concerns for the space	9	4	4	2	Knowledge gauge, infrastructure safari and value elicitation game
2: Creating solutions	Identify factors that will enable or constrain the garden's implementation and use Identify pathways to realisation that incorporate these factors	7	3	3	1	Macro moves, landed and prioritising
3: Detailed design	Produce outline designs using a water impacts calculator, select a design, outline a process for implementation	7	2	6	1	Measuring the space, group designs, fundraising discussion

the co-design process on opportunities for rainwater harvesting on the playground site, not the broader estate. This focus disappointed some of the residents, particularly those who had hoped to provide water for their own gardens.

Following the safari, the research team led a value elicitation game in which the group discussed their main interests and concerns for the space, detailed in Chapter 9. All the participants were asked to write down things that they wanted to see in the space on green index cards, and things they did not want to see in the space on yellow cards. The cards were then sorted together in a group with everyone identifying commonalities and trends in the hopes and fears for the space. Residents raised similar issues about access and safety that Jackie had flagged. They also showed a diverse range of aspirations. Some wanted safe cycle storage, others wanted opportunities to grow plants and the majority wanted to increase biodiversity. The main concern was 'unrestricted access', which was opposed by six people. The range of desired and undesired factors is shown in Figure 8.4.

The exercise drew attention to the multitude of perspectives and agendas for the space, and importantly that everyone who was 'engaged' in this process did not share the same values, expectations and goals. Conflicting differences between stakeholders are not negatives to be eliminated, but diverse values to be recognised (Hillier, 2003). Within the public policy field, Marilyn Taylor (2011) notes that there is a general unwillingness of many partnership initiatives to engage with 'conflict',

Figure 8.4 Results from the value elicitation

resulting in a failure to accept and work with difference. She highlights that working through this tension is a considerable skill.

Workshop 2: analysing options

The objective for the analysing options workshop, which took place in May 2019, was to think through pathways to implementation and focus on creating solutions. In preparation, the research team created maquettes of the roof garden, which could be used by workshop participants to realise their ideas. The second workshop opened with a brief discussion from Thames Water and Southwark Council on funding and support mechanisms available for community gardens from their organisations. They presented two ends of the funding spectrum. First, diverted regeneration funds that entailed a requirement for public access and possibly commercial use of the space and secondly, utility funding for green infrastructure, which would minimise public access, including the residents. Residents discussed these options with some consensus that a middle option allowing residents' access without requiring full public access was optimal. The tools to formulate options are summarised in Chapter 9.

The first activity was 'macromoves', which is designed to elicit enabling and constraining factors. Similar to the value elicitation task, the group individually listed factors on index cards and then collectively sorted them into themes. The group identified volunteering as key to successful implementation, while management of access was identified as the key limiting factor.

The next activity was 'landed'. Small groups worked together to produce maquettes of the garden and record a narrative about its realisation. Each group was given a scale model of the roof, images related to the wants identified in workshop 1, Lego pieces, pens, paper, scissors and glue. The groups had 30 minutes to develop a garden scenario together and then made a five-minute presentation on how the garden had come to be realised (see Figure 8.5). This explanation was filmed not just to capture it, but also with the aim of making it available to other residents who were interested in the project, but unable to join all the workshops. Two narratives were developed. The first focused on the exposed climate conditions of the roof and had a strategy of using temporary screens and planters to progressively try different arrangements that would protect the planting but also maintain the privacy and security of the flats immediately overlooking the space. The second narrative took a staged approach, progressively building up access and ending with a new ramp connecting the rooftop garden to existing gardens and providing water storage underneath (see Table 8.3).

Figure 8.5 A modelled design for the garden

Table 8.3 Groups' design ideas for the rooftop

Scenario 1: 'a battle of the elements'	Scenario 2: 'a phased approach'
• Start with temporary structures to identify the wind and sun • Create shaded areas, use wind breaks • Locate elements in response to towers, to reduce anti-social behaviour and increase privacy and safety (e.g., green roof near base of towers, beehives in far corner) • Use tall raised beds so no need to kneel or bend over • Access only for residents of the towers, and selected groups (e.g., the new pensioners' group)	• Start with greening the walls and providing seating • Access only for residents of the towers and voluntary management committee at start • Over time get funding for additional ramp access with water storage tank underneath

Common across both scenarios were the following:

- phase the garden to get greenery in quickly and to trial access, usage and interest;

- manage security through phased access, using green roof in vulnerable areas, and netting;
- create opportunities for water storage (tanks or green roof); and
- cover the perimeter walls and ventilation shaft walls early.

Following these presentations, the participants had a discussion on how each scenario had addressed the five main areas of concern (funding; safety and security; water management; community; and environmental impacts) and identified the ideas that they wanted to take into the detailed design phase.

Between the workshops

In between the second and third workshops the research team organised two garden visits, installed a rainwater-harvesting prototype and developed a water impacts calculator to be used in the detailed design workshop. Group visits are a tool described in Chapter 9. The intention behind the garden visits was to provide residents with some inspiration about what could be possible and hear from others what is required to create and run community gardens. The first visit was to Golden Lane Estate, a similarly modernist housing estate where residents had successfully fundraised for mini allotments and a communal courtyard. The second visit was to a community group piloting a micro-anaerobic digestor and exploring how their garden could create a circular economy. The trips were also intended to help residents to get to know each other outside of the context of a TRA meeting and support them in developing a governance group specific to the garden, rather than relying on the TRA or the JMB. The research team wrote up a blog of the trips, which was posted on the JMB website to continue to raise awareness about the project.

> ## Voice 8.2 Clive's reflections on the garden trip to Golden Lane Estate
>
> In meeting other groups, recognising similar interests and familiar stories meant these interactions had a huge impact on residents. Also realising that gardening isn't a specialised skill that people living on estates can't grasp or quickly learn was a big step for many of the residents. This early link to the 'Golden Baggers' helped the Kipling develop their membership policies and other groups, near and far, have given the Kipling gardeners advice, plants, seeds,
>
> *(Continued)*

> support and their time. The most active members then grasped the nettle of the whole project with this encouragement and moved quickly to consolidate and to recruit others. This leap of faith sustains the momentum to this day.
>
> Clive Shaw, Kipling Estate resident

Rainwater-harvesting prototype

Installing a rainwater-harvesting prototype was intended to bring to light other governance issues and raise awareness in a more direct way. Its purpose was to give residents a chance to see what a rainwater-harvesting system looked like; how big it was, how it fitted by the garage. However, it was also a way to identify all the parties within the JMB that would be required to allow a system to be installed and commit to maintain it. Connecting a water tank to one of the downpipes involved negotiating access to the individual garage unit that was rented to someone outside the JMB estate. The research team negotiated access to this space and received permission from the garage user and the JMB maintenance team to cut the cast-iron pipe and put in a connection to divert rainwater. The team moved the water tank that was not being used at the Meakin Estate to a position just next to the garage (it could not be placed inside the garage as all the corner units were rented out). Robert Beveridge, a resident and qualified plumber, took on the plumbing work (see Figure 8.6). The research team commissioned a local community energy group to add a solar photovoltaic unit and solar powered pump to pump rainwater from the ground to the rooftop where a smaller tank was also installed. The system was commissioned by the community energy group. Due to the COVID-19 pandemic, a more public demonstration and hand over of the pump was delayed.

In contrast to the inspiration provided by the gardening trips, the water tank has proved to be more of a liability. It was vandalised soon after installation when the straps securing it were cut. Later the pipe connections were chewed through by foxes. With changes to the garden implementation, the system is currently functionless. The research team aims to move the pilot to a more useful site for the current gardeners.

Kipling calculator

The third activity that took place between workshops 2 and 3 was the design of the Kipling calculator. This was developed to support the

Figure 8.6 The water tank being installed by Robert

detailed design work that would be done by workshop participants, in a similar way to the LCA calculator and rainwater calculator in Engineering Comes Home (Chapter 6). The idea for the workshop was to come up with a design brief for the rooftop, but to make design decisions with an understanding of the water impacts of these decisions. The team summarised the function of the calculator as 'bringing scientific calculations into the community's decision-making'.

The research team worked with the British Geological Survey (BGS) to develop a web-based calculator that would allow residents to instantly see the water impacts of any designs. The calculator needed to focus on the water demand created by planting arrangements, as well as the reductions in surface-water run-off achieved. The UCL team came up with a simple idea based on three garden design elements discussed by workshop participants. The first element was a planter that could be used to grow food and ornamental planting. This was the residents' main aspiration for the garden. This element created demand for water. The second element was an extensive green roof. 'Extensive green roof' refers to a type that uses sedum and is designed not to require watering. By contrast, 'intensive green roof' refers to planting that requires water. Extensive green roof does not create water demand, but it does still help attenuate surface-water run-off. This element aligned with Thames Water's interpretation of most effective use of the space. Extensive green roof was also recognised by the participants as delivering environmental positives such as increased biodiversity, but less able to deliver the social benefits of community gardening. The third element was water storage: tanks that could be used to capture rainwater and provide a source of water for the planters. This element would help a garden to serve a dual purpose of enabling community gardening, with reduced negative water systems impacts. The calculator was a simple drag-and-drop tool that instantly showed the water impacts of any element added. The calculator showed the concrete playground divided into a seven-by-seven grid, each unit being a square, 6 metres (m) by 6 m. Adding a unit of planters shows the amount of water needed, prompting the addition of water tanks to meet this demand. Adding a unit of extensive green roof makes the attenuation score (the amount of water run-off avoided) increase. The attenuation impacts are displayed as a percentage score with theoretical 100 per cent achievable if the whole roof area was given over to extensive green roof. The intention behind this was to prompt workshop participants to reflect on the trade-offs made alongside design decisions. A 100 per cent attenuation score may deliver an optimal outcome for the local water system, but fall short on delivering on residents' ambitions for the space. The BGS team designed the interface and developed the tool and the Imperial team provided the water impacts calculations.

In preparation for the final workshop, the UCL team tried to broaden interest across the estate, producing updates, attending TRA meetings and running a stall at the JMB fun day handing out seedlings that had been donated by a local community gardening organisation to interested residents. The team also took a group of residents to buy some plants, planters and soil just before the third workshop. These were part of the pilot system, designed to create something visible on the roof that residents could see, as well as create a very tiny bit of gardening that could be done by residents.

Workshop 3: crafting solutions

The crafting solutions workshop was held in September 2019, in the early evening, at the TRA hall. The objective for this meeting was to develop a design brief that could be used to start fundraising for implementation. The workshop was also seen by the research team as the point at which the researchers moved from leading the co-design process to supporting residents in taking forward the outcomes. Joanna and Clive agreed to lead the final discussion activities of the workshop and therefore progress the garden plan beyond the co-design process. The researchers would be able to support the gardeners at least for the duration of the CAMELLIA research project (a further three years).

The plan for the workshop included:

- mapping activity – using string/chalk to map out the garden onto the roof space;
- calculation activity – what are the impacts of our design on the water system;
- decision activity – which elements do we want;
- discussion – how to move forward on funding (led by Joanna); and
- discussion – how to move forward on project realisation (led by Clive).

Many of the residents had been to one or two of the previous workshops, although for some, like Gaye, it was the first workshop that they had joined. The meeting started with a recapped discussion around funding mechanisms led by the JMB staff. Then, as the autumn sun was setting, the group (which included the BGS calculator developers) went up to the roof, carrying the new planters, plants and soil. One of the participants' children was with the team. This trip marked her first time going on the roof and when she stepped out onto the space she broke into a run. It was a moment that illustrated the capacity of this huge, vacant, inaccessible space to inspire engagement and encourage play.

On the roof, the group measured out grid squares, 6 m by 6 m, that corresponded to the unit size of the elements in the calculator (see Figure 8.7). After gaining this sense of scale and discussing ideas, the participants moved back into the TRA hall and gathered around iPads to use the calculators. Some participants immediately understood the

Figure 8.7 Measuring the roof in workshop 3

concept of the calculator (see Figure 8.8). 'Feel the love' remarked Clive, adding some green roof units and seeing his attenuation score leap up. Others struggled with the calculator, not being confident computer users. Some found the noise in the TRA hall clouded their comprehension of the explanations being offered by the research team. The design activity did not therefore lead to a discrete set of designs and a voting activity for residents to select their most preferred option as we had planned. However, the group did move into a resident-led discussion about next

Figure 8.8 Using the rainwater and attenuation calculator in workshop 3

steps. A core group formed discussing the potential to submit an application to Southwark Council's Cleaner, Greener, Safer fund, and the GLA's Greener City fund. The residents encouraged the research team to pack up. The researchers and stakeholders left, with the CAMELLIA team assuring the residents they would be available to support any funding bids or future resident-led activity in the space.

Fund raising for the garden

The residents submitted the two funding applications. They asked for support in budgeting the garden from the research team as well as in describing the intended benefits. The research team outlined the potential water benefits of greening the concrete roof. The residents created their own design and the UCL team used the calculator to gauge the water impacts. The residents' design included:

- $784m^2$ raised beds;
- $555m^2$ extensive green roof; and
- $24m^3$ water storage.

The calculated estimated the attenuation capacity of the design as a 38 per cent reduction in peak flow.

The gardening group was invited to pitch the idea to Southwark Council in December 2019 with a very short 'Dragon's Den' presentation to the three ward councillors who make the decisions based on council officers' assessments. The residents felt well briefed by Sarah, and Andy was there to support the group. The residents left hopeful, but the bid was rejected.

The funding application to the GLA's Greener City fund was successful and the residents received £19,990 in early 2020 to begin implementing their greening plans. Joanna led and signed the grant application. When the grant was announced, the JMB commissioned a short structural survey and an appraisal of the drainage. Both surveys showed the need for remedial works. Tenants and residents continued to debate whether to allow to access onto the roof and ultimately opposition was too strong. In order to progress with the gardening idea and make use of the grant money, the gardeners found a new site on an existing green space in the estate. Clive led a project to create raised beds and Joanna led a project to develop an orchard and wild meadow area on a green space joining the raised beds. Joanna reflects on this process and provides an update on where things are at the time of publication in Voice 8.3.

Voice 8.3 Joanna's reflections

With invaluable input from Charlotte as well as Rachel Brain from JMB, I wrote the application to the Mayor's Greener City fund and we were awarded a grant of £19,990, £10 under the maximum, which was hugely exciting. I signed the award agreement.

I then handed over my continued running of the project in August 2020 to Kipling TRA (as soon Clive was elected chair), as until then I had experienced very scant support and felt that all of our and UCL's work together was in danger of falling apart. I felt also for the project to be created by a community team rather than be perceived as a 'niche' idea, thus giving ownership to all residents, was very important.

Due to insurmountable issues of residents' access to the roof and logistics (that is increasing costs of material and delivery) we became concerned about Greener City's deadlines, looking for a solution which suddenly appeared early this year [2021]. The big green space where we now have our garden had been left in very poor shape by the people hired by JMS to renew heating in our homes, we stepped in and with JMS's agreement took it over for the growing area. At the same time, I found an area along the edge of the site measuring exactly that of the water attenuation meadow that we had planned on the roof, so I bagged that for the meadow. This move enabled both wildflower meadow and fruit orchard of up to two dozen trees planted on it at ground level as well as saving us a lot of money. We were able to build many more grow boxes as well, up to 23 now.

We're in the final stage now of allocating the grant, I've got a few more trees to order and we will buy polytunnel which we'll place in the next-door secluded green space. The next chunk of work will be to skim off the turf from the meadow area, mark out the tree placings, dig planting holes and plan planting days. Good timing will be essential as the trees are bare-rooted and can't wait long. I'll wait until early next year to sow the flowers.

I'm very keen to replicate the solar-powered pump arrangement on low-rise roofs as well as the existing garage roof.

Joanna Vignola, Kipling Estate resident

Since receiving the initial grant, the TRA have successfully bid for funding from Southwark Council to further develop the community garden. The 'Dragon's Den' format prevailed (via Zoom, due to pandemic lockdown) and Clive pitched the idea on his own. He had met the panel several times in the intervening year and felt far more confident in his ability to deliver this new scheme.

The new community garden on the estate delivers the social value that the residents wanted to achieve. Clive knocked on every door of the estate to introduce neighbours to the community garden and has involved residents in the project who were not previously engaged in estate activities or the TRA. Furthermore, over the course of the project, the members of the TRA have become more confident within decision-making, with certain members taking on roles to get the group constituted and to get a bank account. The group have created 23 allotments on a previously inaccessible green space. Clive explains that the estate looks so much better and there is a better 'feeling' on the estate that he ascribes to an increased sense of community cohesion as residents come together to use what was a locked green space. It is hoped that through the gardening project, people have a greater sense of pride in where they live, and an improved sense of community.

The new site for the community garden has meant less impact on the water system. The new site was already a green space, and therefore has not increased the attenuation capacity of the area. The garden has an outdoor tap and the allotments are watered with drinking water. However, the research team have recently been invited by the group to consider how rainwater harvesting might be used within the new site to reduce use of tap water.

Evaluation

The co-design process run by the researchers had two aims: bring together stakeholders to develop design options; and add scientific analysis of water impacts into the group's design decisions. The researchers hoped this would support residents in changing the playground from grey to green infrastructure. The process delivered on both the aims, but it was unable to support a change in use or make a positive impact on the local water system. Reflecting on the outcomes of this collaborative piece of work, it is helpful to consider the outcomes for the research team and the outcomes for the residents, and then reflect on the process of collaborating and how this could have been improved.

Research team perspectives

The Kipling Garden allowed the research team to pilot a co-design process and develop a new set of tools to be used in community-university collaboration. The research team evaluated the co-design process as it was being implemented. Its main focus was on the useability of the tools, the success of the process in engaging stakeholders and in supporting residents' ambitions.

First, the tools. The team made assumptions around levels and types of literacy and assumed ability to participate in writing activities and computer tasks. In the event, some people were unable to participate in the activities, such as the value elicitation game, which required them to write their own ideas on cards. Some found it hard to understand or use the calculator. The residents did recognise the value of considering the water impacts of their design. They found these calculations useful for logistics; planning the source and amount of water needed. They also recognised the intrinsic value of re-using the rainwater. However, some found the tool itself hard to use and asked the research team to add the elements and interpret the outcomes on their behalf. The team is continuing to develop the calculator to be useful outside of a co-design process.

Second, residents' participation in the process. The research team took the decision to progress the project with a small group of dedicated residents with the hope that they would gain additional support from other residents. The research team tried to increase participation and took all opportunities to advertise and inform residents about the project, but broad-based support remained elusive. The role of the JMB to mobilise residents was unclear and it was later felt that the team could have done more to support broader engagement. The TRA also felt that it could have done more to motivate and mobilise the estate (see Clive's Voice 8.4). However, the process did result in successful outcomes, driven by this small and incredibly dedicated team of residents. They successfully fundraised and delivered a beautiful and thriving community garden for the estate.

Third, the role of the stakeholders. The intention behind involving the stakeholders such as Thames Water and Southwark Council was to provide them with insight into the residents' motivations and aspirations. Unlike the research team, the stakeholders had access to resources that could be used to implement the designs. The research team felt that by involving these stakeholders at the start of the co-design process and helping the understand residents' priorities, they would be more willing to fund any designs that resulted from the process. For example, the research team wanted to know if increasing Thames Water's understanding of the co-benefits of the green space would make it more amenable to facilitating the creation of these co-benefits. However, in practice, Thames Water went through an administrative change that meant it stepped back from directly supporting community-based projects. Similarly, there were complexities with Southwark Council's involvement. While the flood-risk team advocated the benefits of greening the garage and was fully supportive of the process and the residents, this did not influence Southwark as a landowner to invest in a change of use. The high land value means that there is significant pressure to develop the site, rather than allow it to become greenspace. The research team's ambition had been for the co-design process to align stakeholders' interest in improving environmental outcomes with residents' plans. Ultimately the complexities of the site and broader institutional priorities meant this alignment was not achieved. This gives cause for concern about the possibilities of community-led green-blue infrastructure and points to the need for strong institutional and political support for the value of such projects.

Residents' perspectives

The research team spoke to four of the residents involved in the co-design process shortly after the GLA award had been announced. At this point, the residents were positive about the research collaboration, feeling that it had allowed the group to progress their plan for a community garden. The residents attributed this to different reasons. One explained that the research team's presence had elevated the idea of a rooftop garden from the usual TRA discussions, making her feel it was a more serious and feasible proposition that encouraged her to get involved. However, another participant explained there was a lack of clarity about the role of the university. He had had a sense the university were going to develop the roof.

In the intervening 18 months the residents had to manage the grant, respond to problems with creating a garden on the roof and design and implement a new garden on a different site. In Voice 8.4, Clive reflects on the extent to which the collaborative process was a support, miscommunication on the role of the research team and how these processes could be improved in future iterations.

Voice 8.4 Clive's reflections on the research team's engagement

On the arrival, involvement and departure of the CAMELLIA team, that bright start was presaged by the mention of figure of £5 million. A figure that gave the team credibility, but also a power that many residents either viewed suspiciously or with some lofty expectation. At no point was this figure offered to the estate, but an implication remained throughout that something exceptional would somehow be delivered. The training and visits were both invigorating and involving but could have been publicised better and more thoroughly to reach those residents who remained sceptical. To be fair, the TRA didn't seek additional resources to help with that outreach. I can't comment on why, but many complained they knew little to nothing until it was too late. I found the entire process fascinating while others found it jargon-laden, impenetrable and ambiguous.

The bigger issue for me followed the departure of the CAMELLIA team. It felt like little had been delivered except a prototype water system that only a handful of residents and JMB staff could access or understand. Again, no more was actually promised but expectations were raised that the team would be there to assist us following the receipt of our grant (£19,990 from the GLA). However, once the irrigation prototype was switched on, the team left the project to the freshly recruited residents. There was some follow up but, and despite COVID, continued presence would have been welcome, and we could have really benefited from the expertise. This feeling of loss was compounded by other factors like the JMB moving the siting of the Community Garden away from the roof space and with the rejection of further funding (£5,000 from the Cleaner Greener Safer fund) that was the next step in the phased project.

The CAMELLIA team have now responded to residents and hopefully with help the Community Garden can soon utilise rainfall from the roof as envisioned. However there remains a feeling that there has been a shortfall in the academic origins of CAMELLIA in delivering to complex urban estates, whose residents are often guarded, suspicious or even resentful of outside assistance. This may be down to many historical, social, political and economic factors but CAMELLIA and other well-intentioned projects need to be prepared to pause before beginning any work and be clear and patient with local groups. In person the CAMELLIA team were all those things, but perception is crucial, and hearts and minds operations need to be extremely mindful of local feelings. I have lived on this estate for over 15 years and am now the Chair of our TRA, but I'm still sometimes viewed as a newcomer. Practice makes perfect, but if research projects are to be trusted and to offer benefits, they need to avoid the view they are parachuting in and out of troubled areas. For months after its installation the pilot model water tank was vandalised and eventually the JMB had to spend money to protect it and its piping. It was a common complaint that nobody understood what it was or who had placed it there. It wasn't loved, but the aims of CAMELLIA were to draw attention to a situation that will increasingly affect every Londoner. We must all find solutions to our problems that people can value – it's the hard part, but the lasting proof of a project's success.

Clive Shaw, Kipling Estate resident

Writing the chapter

Writing the chapter has allowed the research team to revisit Kipling and reconnect with residents since their development of the garden. It has been a process that has made different perspectives apparent. The same values, expectations and goals are not shared by everyone engaged in a co-design process. Differences in values and aspirations were evident within the co-design process and have continued through the writing of the chapter. We have tried to keep this diversity within the text.

This multi-authored narrative shows the very different starting points of the research team and the residents. The research team was focused on whether a garden could be designed in a way that produced water system impacts in a densely populated combined sewer area. The residents wanted to see social and environmental benefits realised within their estate. The research team used a co-design process to draw in stakeholders who are responsible for the water system impacts of the built environment: the planning authority, landowner, water utility and estate management body. The aspiration was that this process would deliver broad-based support for the residents' plans and open up a path towards implementation. While this process generated initial implementation funding, broader support did not materialise, and in its absence, the small groups of residents worked to create their community garden alone. With hindsight, the residents feel the co-design process did not deliver much, because it did not unlock the needed support and the research team lacked the resources and power to act without this support.

Writing the chapter has also revealed areas of miscommunication and opacity around decision-making. For example, the CAMELLIA research funding was misinterpreted as being available for implementation. The reasons for relocating the garden from the roof to an existing green space are unclear: it was a combination of residents' concerns over allowing access, management concerns about the load-bearing capacity and possibly council aspirations to redevelop the garage site into housing. One clear signal, however, was that demonstrating the potential water system benefits was not enough to mobilise support and achieve a change in use. The case study therefore demonstrates more broadly the challenges for community-led water management through gardens and green infrastructure.

Conclusion

This multi-voice narrative highlights the complexity of bringing about change and the numerous experiences, both positive and negative, within the production and reproduction of infrastructure projects. The Kipling garage roof remains unused, which is disappointing for the residents and the research team. Ultimately the space was too contested. To be converted from a state of managed decline into a usable area, the required level of financial investment needs to be justified. One of the most certain forms of investment currently in London is in housing. Future income from a new build would likely cover the costs of removing the garage. But this would add pressure on the drainage and flooding risk in the area. It would also be a huge loss for the residents. This illustrates the systemic problem with creating a liveable London: the low value placed on green infrastructure.

9
Tools for co-design

In co-designing infrastructures, the projects worked with communities at various stages of the infrastructure life cycle, as described in Chapter 3 (see Figure 3.1). The process of delivering the projects, developed, and iterated upon, various tools that help address the complexities of infrastructure design involving various stakeholders.

Tools for bottom-up infrastructure co-design span from software, through hardware, to factsheets and legal documents. Tools for engaging with a community always need to be adapted to a specific context. However, the tools presented here give an overview of what has been found to be useful, and sometimes necessary, based on the delivery of the case study projects reported in Chapters 6–8.

An overview is presented for each of the six steps for the Bottom-Up Infrastructure co-design method, with examples of various tools that have been developed for projects discussed in previous chapters. Listed under Tools in Action, these are by no means a complete set of what is needed for infrastructure co-design. Rather, this chapter is a practical guide to tool development, elaborated on through various examples, exploring how the context of their intended use affected their design, co-design and development, and, most importantly, how they might be adapted for other contexts. Many of the tools discussed here can be found at the Bottom-Up Infrastructure website (Bottom-Up Infrastructure, 2022)

Participation finds its place across multiple points in the course of developing these tools. Often the tools developed for the projects reported here are not co-designed themselves but rather metadesign tools (introduced in Chapter 2), designed for a specific community to inform and facilitate collaborative infrastructure design decisions. They are designed in response to having garnered knowledge of the community's values and needs through ethnography and infrastructure co-design workshops.

165

Setting aims

Aims are set at the start of any project. When working with others it is good practice to set these aims collaboratively, taking time to consider the level of engagement and levels of change that are required for the project. Setting aims also allows those involved to plan how to evaluate the outcomes of the work.

Setting aims should be done in three parts: defining aims; determining the approach; and setting expectations with all stakeholders. Often, this step in infrastructure co-design takes place with the core team and representatives of partner organisations who have a close relationship with the community, rather than directly with the community themselves. In some circumstances, such as the community as client model, aims are set entirely by the community stakeholders. In every case, it is important for the project management team to think about what needs to be communicated and when, so that participants are fully informed when working with the project.

Projects often evolve away from these initial plans, which can be important for the progress of the project. It is key to find a balance between what is needed for the project, the community and other stakeholders, including continuing to meet obligations relating to funding or evaluation strategies. In the best case scenario, the project and its support structures will be put in place to explicitly accommodate some degree of adjustment to the project aims during the subsequent phases. Whenever changes are made to these initial aims and plans, it is important to communicate clearly with all participants, and to collaboratively refresh the project's aims as necessary.

Tools in action

Partnership agreements

Partnership agreements are a way of formalising the expectations and expected outcomes from a project. In discussing these agreements, partners come to a better understanding of how the project might progress, clarify roles and responsibilities, and agree the minimum and maximum expected outcomes from the collaboration. When preparing a partnership agreement, project teams should check with a legal expert to what extent they are legally binding in their respective legal jurisdiction.

Risk assessment logs

It is important to carry out a risk assessment and identify mitigation strategies to give the project the best chance of a satisfactory conclusion for all stakeholders. In the case of working with community members on infrastructure design, it is important to include the risk to participants. This can be physical (e.g., using a ladder, falling into a reservoir), emotional (e.g., over-committing to the project) or personal (e.g., if the issue is highly contentious or involves powerful stakeholders with conflicting interests). Once these risks have been assessed, mitigation strategies can be put in place to minimise risk and to address problems should they arise.

Project-specific communication tools

A well-planned and sustained communication strategy ensures that all stakeholders have the opportunity to engage with the project at multiple junctures. Developing a communication strategy at the start of the project while setting aims allows for a co-ordinated approach to communication. This increases the impact of the outreach and ensures clarity and congruity in communication materials. This helps with recognisability of the project, and also supports mutual understanding of what can be expected from the delivery and outcomes of the collaboration.

Characterising communities

Communities are complex assemblages of individuals, with multiple and often conflicting characteristics. As discussed in Chapter 2, communities arise or come together in different ways. In Bottom-Up Infrastructure projects, who is part of the community is affected by both the design process and infrastructure problem to be addressed. Getting to know the community is an important step in the co-design process.

Characterising communities can be carried out with some overlap with *Setting Aims*, but the focus here is to really get to know the aspects of the community that are crucial to the context of infrastructure co-design. The methods employed, and how much characterisation is required, depends on the relationships between the infrastructure designers and the communities involved. For instance, if the community is well-established and has developed a coherent set of principles by which to operate, or if the character of the community is not relevant to the project outcome, then less depth of research is required to characterise the community. However, if the experiences of the community members are highly pertinent to the outcomes of the project, the first step is to identify stakeholders in the project and then to recruit participants from relevant stakeholder groups. Then individuals or their households should be characterised in the context of the specific infrastructure design problems to be addressed. Characterisation can take the form of observation and research such as visits, structured interviews and diary-keeping, alongside access to materials from the community that detail their position or values.

Tools in action

Diaries

One way to gather information about the variety of ways that people interact with infrastructure in their homes is structured self-reporting through diaries (Wilhite and Wilk, 1987). Diary templates, which are left with residents and later collected and discussed, can help people to record and reflect on their activities in a way that can feed into the infrastructure design process. The diary templates developed for Engineering Comes Home (Chapter 6) covered 6am to midnight each day in 10-minute intervals, with sections for main activity, subsidiary activities, appliances used and who else was there. The diaries also contained a schematic of the dwelling that could be filled in with the person's movements and the time frame indicated. In designing the diary, elements such as time frame, granularity of time intervals and the dwelling schematic should be adjusted as appropriate to reflect as accurately as possible the participants' lives.

While allowing for the collection of fine-grained and time-based data, diary-keeping requires effort for the person in the home. The amount and regularity of information recorded depends on the person's enthusiasm for completing the diary. This should be taken into account, both in terms of the expectations of all stakeholders and in terms of managing risks to data quality and completeness.

Home tour

The home tour data collection sheet developed for Engineering Comes Home (Chapter 6) addressed each dwelling in terms of the appliances and infrastructure used, with a separate section for kitchen, focusing on food as a resource. Hot water, heating, lighting and entertainment were also listed. Data was collected for all categories in terms of the age and origin of the appliance or infrastructure, the patterns of use and the perceived performance.

In Engineering Comes Home, the home tour, gathering together data needed to complete the sheet, prompted discussions that offered insights into the participants' lived experience of interacting with the nexus in their homes. It was easier to arrange and provided more complete data than the diary templates for this project.

Archival research

Another approach to collecting relevant information about the local context is to carry out archival research on the buildings and infrastructure used by the local community. This provides insight into the original design decisions for the built environment and systems installed as well as the financing and governance. This provides a useful basis from which to understand the changes that have happened since. For example, in the Kipling Garden (Chapter 8) the archival research revealed that the original building layout had been designed to have small units (one or two bedrooms) to accommodate elderly households rather than families. This continued to influence the demographics of the resident population. It also showed the estate buildings and garages that had since been knocked down and replaced with new blocks of flats, providing the researchers with an understanding of some residents' memories of how the estate used to look. The archival research into the Kipling Garden (Chapter 8) also produced the original plans and technical drawings for the drainage infrastructure. This was used to develop tools for the co-design workshops.

Stakeholder interviews

When characterising the context in which the co-design process occurs it is important to be aware of the different perspectives held by different members of the community. One way of eliciting these different perspectives is to run semi-structured interviews with a range of people. This approach was taken in Engineering Comes Home (Chapter 6) and Kipling Garden (Chapter 8). The research team used a snowball approach to identify the different groups that had an understanding of the local context and could influence or be affected by the co-design. For example, this included the maintenance and resident liaison teams from the housing management body, residents leading the tenants association, as well as residents not involved in the formal governance systems. The recruitment of the stakeholders and the use of the information that they provide must be managed sensitively and in line with data protection best practice.

Capturing requirements

An openly framed requirements-capture process brings together community members and other stakeholders to collaboratively decide on the design problem to be addressed. This stage works well as a workshop facilitated by someone external to the project. Key at this stage is to bring all stakeholders to a shared level of understanding of both the process and the problem, which ensures everyone can actively participate. Well-designed tools for use in these workshops convey necessary information or are designed to facilitate engagement with the infrastructure design space. An understanding of existing dynamics between the stakeholders involved will help a facilitator in guiding the workshop.

The outcomes of the requirements-capture stage should be identification of the values underpinning the community's engagement with the project and the challenges that the community faces in terms of their lived experience of infrastructure.

Tools in action

Nexy tokens

The Nexy tokens were made for Engineering Comes Home (Chapter 6). They were designed to feel good in the hand and to be visually simple. The tokens needed to have multiple connecting points that could represent various nodes in the interconnecting problem space of resource management at the water-energy-food nexus. Figure 9.1 shows a Nexy token depicting a house using energy during an Engineering Comes Home workshop. The token contains a magnet mounted in the back, so that it can be used in conjunction with a metal presentation board, allowing participants to display their stories once they are completed.

The hexagonal design and visual language of the icons aim to provide prompts for flexibility and creativity in the generation of 'stories' of resource-use at the nexus of water, energy, food and waste. The hexagonal blocks were cut from re-purposed acrylic and were substantial enough to handle easily. The icons for the stamps, selected from pre-existing icons sourced from the Noun Project (a web-based repository of design icons), were chosen to be easily understandable representations of infrastructural elements, such as rainwater capture, composting, solar panels and energy use, among others. The tokens were designed to be as low impact in terms of material as possible, with images that can be wiped off and replaced as necessary. The icons were stamped on the

Figure 9.1 Nexy token

tokens using re-usable rubber stamps and non-permanent ink, so that the tokens could be re-purposed as necessary.

Story creation

Nexy tokens combined with other materials, such as photographs and whiteboards, were used in the process of story creation, which allows the workshop participants to identify design or problem spaces and to generate descriptions of these spaces. Figure 9.2 shows the tools used in Engineering Comes Home (Chapter 6) for story creation. Figure 9.3 shows the Nexy tokens and other tools in use to tell stories about resource use in Engineering Comes Home.

Value elicitation

The tool for value elicitation in Engineering Comes Home (Chapter 6) was adapted from the value methods in the DecarboNet toolkit developed by the Waag Society (Waag Society, 2014), combined with a 2–4-8 prioritisation model to facilitate group allocation of priorities to different values. The procedure is:

1. Short introduction to 2–4-8 method by facilitator (one minute).
2. Community members work in pairs to generate five shared values (three minutes).
3. Pairs join to form groups of four (one minute).

4. In fours, community members generate a new list of five shared values, using previous values to inform (three minutes).
5. Fours join to create groups of eight (one minute).
6. Eights generate a new list of five shared values (three minutes).
7. Feedback from groups on values (five minutes).

Figure 9.2 Engineering Comes Home tool table

Figure 9.3 Using the Nexy tokens to create resource stories

A slightly different process was used by the research team running the Kipling Garden process (Chapter 8). The 2–4-8 structure builds a consensus of shared values as a group. The Kipling Garden process simplified this process by asking participants to individually think about their hopes and expectations for the garden and write or draw each idea on an index card. The group then collectively sorted these cards into themed piles. This allowed the group to see that they held values and aspirations in common, as well as to gauge how many people held the same view. This allowed for an element of anonymity – people were invited to say which they had written, although they did not have to. However, it also places the requirement on everyone to write down their thoughts. At least one member of the Kipling Group was uncomfortable with writing. This process was repeated with a different question, asking participants to write what circumstances would enable or prevent their hopes and expectations from being realised.

When devising the appropriate value elicitation methods, it is important to reflect on the type of interactions you want to support (individual reflections or jointly generated and prioritised values), as well as to gauge the appropriate literacy levels. Some find talking easier than writing, others find writing easier than talking and others find drawing easier than talking or writing.

Infrastructure Safari

The Infrastructure Safari was designed for the Kipling Garden project (Chapter 8). Using the technical plans from the archives combined with visual evidence of leaks, local flooding and drainage issues, and existing green spaces, the research team devised a route around the Kipling Estate that offered up points of discussion and prompts to think about how the water infrastructure worked. The Infrastructure Safari took place at the start of the first workshop (see Chapter 8 for a full description) and groups walked round the estate, noting down their interests on a copy of the technical plan. The safari proved very effective in building a shared understanding of the water infrastructure on the site and the possibilities for intervention, but it also proved to be useful in helping the group to interact, get to know each other and build trust. Safaris can be easily tailored to other contexts and other types of infrastructure.

Analysing options

At this point the ground has been prepared with the community, and the design problem and the values that are important to the community have been collaboratively defined. It may be that participants have collectively come up with a few ideas of design interventions, or maybe the design team has done that in response to the community's prompts. At this stage the participants take a deeper look together at different infrastructure design options to see which ones fit the bill.

Involving the community members in this process is crucial to ensure they have agency in the decision-making process. As with capturing requirements, engaging in this stage through workshops using bespoke tools offers great opportunities for discussion and dynamic feedback.

Tools in action

LCA calculator

The aim of the life cycle assessment (LCA) calculator was to provide an intuitive and interactive tool that allowed community members to make well-informed decisions underpinned by LCA data (Figure 9.4). This calculator was developed for Engineering Comes Home (Chapter 6) after

Figure 9.4 Participants using the LCA calculator in the Engineering Comes Home project

workshop 1, a scoping workshop where implicit and explicit values were elicited while discussing the water-energy-food problem space in the Meakin Estate (see Chapter 6).

The LCA calculator was built on top of a database. This database – in the form of a spreadsheet – described the system that was being studied and calculated the resources used, and the carbon footprint generated from the use of different technologies. In this case, the system was the Meakin Estate in the context of the water-energy-food nexus. An initial version of this spreadsheet was developed in parallel with working with communities once aims had been set in Engineering Comes Home. This was further iterated on in light of the outcomes of the first workshop with the community (Borrion *et al.*, 2019).

Opportunities for interventions were identified from the workshop analysis (see Table 6.2), and these were developed into five different potential interventions to be presented through the calculator interface: composting, waste compacting, urban food-growing, rainwater harvesting and food sharing. In designing the calculator for public use, it was important to ensure not only usability of the interface, but that the calculator would be able to answer questions relevant to its users in their lived experience. To meet this need, it was necessary to take a user perspective: to define the questions users might pose of the calculator about a system, translate them as input parameters to the model and determine how to interact with models and present answers. The workshop analysis was used to understand the perspective of the participants – the would-be users of the device – and to predict potential queries they might have that could be answered by an LCA calculator. These queries were matched against the existing LCA spreadsheet to identify additional information that was likely to be required, which was then sought out and provided.

As part of the iterative development of the LCA spreadsheet, a 'materials flow summary sheet' was developed, which conceptualised the LCA data around a flow of materials through the system of the estate. Having the material flows as the main representation of what is happening with each of the scenarios helped facilitate communication about quantities related to these options – such as amount of waste generated – which allowed the team to introduce the less obvious material impacts, such as emissions.

The queries also informed the design of the calculator interface. The interface consists of process nodes connected by flow arrows. Nodes can be boundary objects (e.g., system inputs and outputs such as food shopping or waste-disposal trucks), transformative processes (e.g., cooking, composting) or productive processes (e.g., solar panels, rainwater

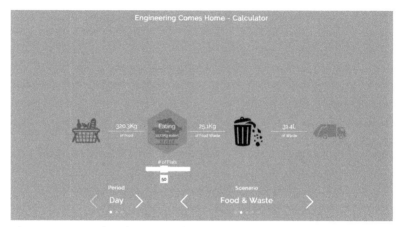

Figure 9.5 Food and waste in the LCA calculator

harvesting). Each node can be clicked or tapped to reveal input parameters when they exist, or more detailed information (e.g., environmental impact data on waste management processes). Flow arrows display quantities with their units.

The scenarios allow users of the tool – the community co-designing infrastructure at the water-energy-food nexus in the Meakin Estate – to explore the practicality of different design choices, and how they affect the overall CO_2 output from the estate. They start from a baseline scenario of 'buy food in shops → cook → dispose of food waste in bin', and increase in complexity through to scenarios including rainwater capture and wormeries or food sharing. This sequence of increasing complexity (with more nodes and arrows) allows users to be progressively introduced to additional parameters and richer systems. Figure 9.5 shows the food and waste scenario in the LCA calculator, with values calculated for 50 flats.

Both the LCA calculator and the rainwater calculator allowed users to see how the impact of different solutions scaled over time, as well as with variation in the uptake of the solutions by the community. Users could scroll between timescales of 'a day' through to an entire year for the LCA calculator. With the rainwater calculator, seasonality was introduced, reflecting variations in average rainfall throughout the year in London.

Factsheets

The background knowledge in communities can be very diverse. While it is important to first introduce the different options through presentation or discussion, providing printed factsheets can be a useful way of ensuring everyone can assess infrastructure design options by having pertinent factors at their fingertips during discussions. The factsheets were key in the Demolition or Refurbishment project (Chapter 5) and Somers Town project (Chapter 7) because these projects dealt with highly technical as well as highly political issues. The factsheets on air quality (Chapter 7) and estate refurbishment and demolition (Chapter 5) were designed to cover the range of issues that the community were concerned about. They were produced explicitly to create access to academic and technical information that is often behind paywalls and written for expert audiences only. In addition, air quality lacks a materiality that participants can engage with. It is difficult to present options for air quality interventions in a way that is as easy to visualise as a rainwater tank or a compost bin. Factsheets are therefore a key enabling tool in allowing community groups to engage with an infrastructure co-design process as equal partners with technical experts.

Factsheets should compile relevant information about the different options and:

- be written clearly and in simple language, avoiding jargon;
- include information that relates to the values expressed in previous stages;
- adhere to the visual language established in previous communications; and
- be broken into clear sections including:
  o a brief description of the option;
  o a list of costs and benefits;
  o a list of local-scale and wider impacts; and
  o an idea of the long-term maintenance, if relevant.

Formulating options

When the group of participants have established their common values, hopes, expectations, opportunities and limitations they are ready to think about practical solutions to achieve their goals. If the goal is to alter space or other physical changes, such as in the Kipling Garden (Chapter 8), then playing with models of the space can enable nuanced conversations about how these changes would occur in real life. For the Kipling Garden, two different models were developed. One was a physical cardboard and paper model of the rooftop to help formulate garden options. The second was a digital model of the water impacts of the garden to help craft solutions. Participants were asked to work in groups to design a garden in line with their shared values and expectations, and in response to their assumed enabling and preventing circumstances. This was a very quick process. Participants were given 30 minutes to design their garden, and five minutes to present their design to the other participants. The narrative of the design told the story of what was already there; why those elements were there; what circumstances enabled it to be there; and what might result because of these changes happening. Following the presentations there was a discussion about the commonalities, the unique points and what parts might be complementary.

Group visits

Introduced by the research team in the co-design process for the Kipling Garden project (Chapter 8), the group visits to existing community garden groups were designed to allow the participants to see what options are possible, but also what is required to make the option a reality. The group visits also play a useful role in helping the participants get to know one another more, outside of a workshop setting. Visiting local projects or relevant infrastructure sites can therefore be a good way to help groups appraise options by considering not only the material impacts (what does it look like, smell like, sound like) but also in terms of governance (how much work is required to run and maintain it, who can do this, what sort of funding or support is available).

Crafting solutions

Deciding on the type of intervention for a design problem is only the beginning. There are multiple different variables – everything from the size of a rainwater butt to the types of worm in a wormery – that must be considered in order to fine tune the infrastructure design to the particular location, situation and/or community. This can be a daunting task for design teams and community alike. It is a good idea to address detailed design with the community in a workshop focused on the pragmatic aspects of realising the intervention, supported by specific tools that aid the discussion and decision-making.

Tools in action

Rainwater harvesting calculator
The rainwater harvesting calculator was the second calculator to come out of the Engineering Comes Home project (Chapter 6), in response to

the selection of rainwater harvesting as the direction in which the community wished to move after the second co-design workshop.

Using the same visual language as the scoping calculator, the rainwater harvesting calculator links the collection and use of rainwater on the Meakin Estate with the wider impact of affecting the rate of rainwater run-off on the city's waterways. The calculator takes the user stepwise through three scenarios of increasing complexity: the effect of installing rainwater collection tanks in general on run-off into the city; this effect when the rainwater is used to irrigate and clean; and a scenario specific to the Meakin Estate allowing users to design adding rainwater harvesting to the roofs of blocks on the estate.

In each case, the calculator reveals the amount of water flowing from the estate into the city's water infrastructure as run-off, allowing for seasonal variability and giving an average per day, week or year. Using the calculator allows the user to gain a sense of how much water runs off from the estate under baseline conditions, and how the implementation of rainwater harvesting tanks affects this. Furthermore, it quantifies how that water can be used and allows the community members to gain a real idea of how much water would be available for gardening and cleaning. Unexpectedly, during the third workshop, the focus was mainly on using water for cleaning, particularly for cleaning vehicles. Once the calculator had given the participants an idea of how many rainwater butts they would like to install (in the range of 3 or 4), the estate was toured and locations for the butts were discussed, with a prioritisation of their being placed near areas where it was possible to park cars.

The calculator development reached a beta version for the workshop. The data used in the back end of the calculator, as with the LCA for the scoping calculator, is site-specific to the Meakin Estate. The design of the interface, however, which echoes the visual language of the Nexy tokens and the Engineering Comes Home scoping calculator, lends itself to being re-purposed for other locations with an alternative database in the back end.

Kipling calculator

The Kipling calculator was designed for a specific scenario with a clearly defined user, as described in Chapter 8. The calculator was developed by the British Geological Survey within the context of the Kipling Garden project (Chapter 8). The aim of the project was to co-design a community garden as part of CAMELLIA in partnership with Leathermarket JMB.

The Kipling calculator was a digital model that calculated the water needed for the plants in the garden and how much water they could store to help London alleviate flooding and combined sewer overflows. It allowed participants to find out how much water would need to be collected and stored if they wanted their plants to survive a 20-day drought. The calculator allows the user to change elements of the design of a rooftop garden that has the dimensions and starting parameters – in this case, a non-permeable, flat roof with two entry-ways – of the rooftop above garages on the Kipling Estate, a prospective site for a rooftop garden. The calculator user has the option to add raised beds, green roof elements, sheds and rainwater harvesting tanks. Based on the elements chosen by the user, the tool calculates the balance of water throughput, that is the amount of water required for, and captured by, the different elements, and the consequences for the flow of water through London.

The team had engaged with residents and local stakeholders through two workshops: a scoping workshop and a design workshop where the participants built models to showcase their ideas for the garden space. The plan for the third workshop was to allow participants to produce detailed designs for the space and understand the water impacts of their proposed gardens. This was both to bring to light the question of how the garden could be practically maintained in terms of water needed for growing, but also to indicate the potential positive impact on rainwater attenuation that greening a concrete space could have. The CAMELLIA team developed a simple drag and drop graphical interface that showed the impacts of adding different garden elements in terms of rainwater attenuation and the volume of water needed to keep the plants growing. Figure 9.6 shows a possible design in the Kipling calculator for

Figure 9.6   The Kipling calculator

the roof that reduces run-off and allows for storage of sufficient water to meet the garden's needs.

The calculator was used in the third workshop, engaging participants with the water impacts of their design. The output of the calculator (volume of water stored, percentage reduction in rainwater flow) was used by the residents' gardening group in their funding applications to the local authority and the GLA to make a case for the garden's impact on rainwater attenuation and its potential to contribute to water management on a city scale. The calculator outputs were also used by the CAMELLIA team to budget the garden design for the grant application. The calculator shows an area of raised beds, an area of extensive green roof, as well as water tanks required. The costs of these elements could be integrated into the tool. The additional load created could also be added to the calculator. Additional load was a key consideration in this case, as the intended location for the garden was a garage rooftop on the Kipling Estate. As rainwater collection and green infrastructure would increase the load on the structure of the garages, calculating the maximum expected load at each point of the rooftop would be useful.

Evaluation

Evaluation is a vital process within community infrastructure projects. Evaluation is integral to project management: it should be valuable and lead to action. Good evaluation should support learning for understanding, improvement and, ultimately, help bring about change. Although evaluation should be integral to project activities, and take place throughout the life of a project, there is no one-size-fits-all approach: evaluation needs to be designed, implemented and shared in relation to its context and purpose. Evaluation must be:

- critical – providing evidence of what works well and not so well;
- reflective – encouraging reflection, and points to feed in learning to improve; and
- collaborative – involving a range of partners, stakeholders and contributors.

The project can be evaluated against its expected aims, which have been set at the start of the project, as well as other bars for evaluation that emerge during the course of the project. Furthermore, the co-design process itself can be evaluated in terms of equality and quality of participation, the effectiveness of procedures, satisfaction of the stakeholders involved and value persistence – that is, whether the values elicited at the start of the project, and the needs that they represent, are carried forward into the final design. It is advisable to consider the amount of time and effort required from volunteers to participate in evaluation activities, and if you plan to gather feedback from project participants or other stakeholders, it is best to alert them prior to their engagement with the project that this will be the case. Furthermore, in evaluation, as in other aspects of the project, it is vitally important that participants' data are managed appropriately, ensuring that anonymity is preserved where necessary and that personal data is collected and stored according to the relevant standards.

Tools in action

Fieldnotes template
The fieldnotes template provides a structure for recording anonymised attendance at workshops, to record observations and notes related to the progression through the workshop plan. Best used during the workshop itself by one or more observers, gathering these immediate impressions of the complex dynamics within a workshop environment helps to add an important and influential depth to post-workshop analysis.

Infrastructure literacy gauge
It can be useful to gauge the levels of 'infrastructure literacy' held by the group and how these change over time. In the Kipling Garden process the researchers invited workshop participants to put a sticker on a gauge showing how much knowledge they felt they had about urban drainage; at the end of the workshop this was repeated, allowing the team to evaluate whether the workshop had raised the knowledge of the participants (see Chapter 8 for a full description). This process could be done at the start and end of the whole process if a key outcome for the project team is to raise the participating group's understanding of the issues.

Feedback forms
Used in most projects, these can be designed to generate quantitative or qualitative data about what the participants felt about the project, what they gained through the process and any improvement they think should be made. This data is useful for the research team to evaluate the project overall and reflect on future iterations of the tools and processes used.

Toolkits

In addition to the tools, two online toolkits have been built. These toolkits, in the form of websites, structure the methods and resources developed to facilitate bottom-up infrastructure engineering. The target users for these toolkits are infrastructure engineers with some interest in engaging in co-design of infrastructure solutions with community stakeholders.

Engineering Comes Home toolkit

The Engineering Comes Home toolkit is structured around the same six method steps that structure this chapter, a framework that emerged from the analysis of the Engineering Comes Home project (Chapter 6). Using the same visual identity as established in the Engineering Comes Home workshops, the toolkit describes and provides links to the tools developed during the project as well as the workshop outlines. Documentary videos of the workshops and publications from the project are also available for context.

Bottom-Up Infrastructure toolkit

More complex and far-reaching, the Bottom-Up Infrastructure toolkit synthesises the tools and experiences of several case studies, providing multiple points of entry depending on the user's interest and role. The information about tools and case studies are orientated around and categorised the six method steps of infrastructure co-design as well as being located at various stages on the infrastructure life cycle.

For each project case study, information on the timing, duration and funding is provided along with a brief synopsis. The tools related to the project are listed, as are the project's publications. Similarly, all methods list the projects and tools related to them. The tools search can be refined by tool type, method step or stage in the infrastructure life cycle. A visual identity was established for the tool types that corresponded with the overall design for the website, created by The Bureau London web design agency.

Crucially, the website also provides an overview of bottom-up infrastructure as a method, engaging up-front with questions about its applicability and ethics. Thus, the site provides an introduction and framing for the key elements of working with communities to co-design infrastructure.

Conclusions

Throughout the projects reported here, the focus has been on the development or adaptation of tools to fit very specific circumstances. In these projects and their associated tools, technical expertise and local knowledge have come together to create something more helpful than a generic tool that would be shoe-horned into the process.

While this is beneficial to the outcome of the infrastructure co-design process, the result is that a significant amount of resources has been put into the development of bespoke tools that cannot be re-used without context-specific adaptation. This is the case for both the digital tools and many of the analogue ones. Where it has been possible, a balance has been struck between usability for the project and re-useability across projects. For instance, the Nexy tokens were specifically designed so that they could be easily re-purposed beyond the Meakin Estate and the water-energy-food nexus focus of the Engineering Comes Home project. Written materials, such as factsheets and agreements are developed along a general structure, but the focus of the information provided should be informed by the needs of the community.

The development and adaptation of digital tools is particularly complex and often expensive. The tools reported here were developed in a well-resourced research environment, yet nevertheless reached only a basic level of development. The Kipling calculator, developed for an extremely specific situation, leaves some pragmatic design questions unanswered. Likewise, the two calculators from Engineering Comes Home, ambitious in design, were released in beta version. The code was published under a Mozilla Public License Version 2.0 to allow for its further development by the open-source community and for diverse use-cases, should there be sufficient interest.

What would be required to adapt these calculators for other uses and users? The Kipling calculator has already been redeveloped as a more generic tool that prompts community gardeners to think through the water impacts of their designs. This version will be made available through a portal developed by CAMELLIA to put all the project tools in the public domain and support community management of water. From the Engineering Comes Home calculators, the structure can be re-used and the underlying LCA database values would need to be adapted to the new use-case. However, should the possibilities for interventions be different, the logic behind the querying of the database by the users would also need to be revisited.

The digital tools have been released into a highly competitive environment in terms of software and apps. When further development is complex and costly, there is a significant potential that the work and the applications get lost in the vast array of digital tools available online.

While it is clear that software development for digital tools must be a social process, finding a big enough demand to justify the resource-intensive development of a bespoke application is challenging. The solution must be to make the tools easier to adapt, and to consolidate the workflow for these adaptations – as far as this is possible. One option is to build the tools from the outset in a more modular manner, which might make their adaptation to new use-cases easier. This must be combined with excellent documentation – another resource-intensive component – to allow developers and researchers to maintain accuracy both in terms of the software development and data gathering, and in terms of methods to match the community members' needs to the tools' design.

Wong-Parodi *et al.* (2020) revealed some key insights to support meaningful integration of relevant tools (into policies for environmental decisions). They suggest six characteristics should be taken into account in the development of decision support tools to enhance stakeholders' ability to make 'high-quality' decisions: to define the decision that needs to be made; to identify alternatives; to obtain relevant information and evidence; to articulate values linked to the decision; to evaluate alternatives; and to monitor outcomes. Used within the six-step co-design method, the tools generated through the Bottom-Up Infrastructure projects work across these six characteristics to bring the lived experience of community members into the design of infrastructure.

All the tools that support co-design processes are mechanisms for collaboration that should allow for participants' different experiences, perspectives and priorities to be brought together. From the initial setting aims to the final feedback and reflection activities, all the tools require careful consideration of the context in which they are being deployed and the process that they are supporting. This chapter shows how tools can be developed and tailored in the context of specific projects. It has also shown that there are common stages and issues that reoccur within and across projects allowing existing tools to be picked up and adapted.

10
Conclusions

'Take more, please. They'll only go to waste.'

It's the end of another workshop. The chairs are being stacked, pens and post-it notes shoved in plastic carrier bags, computers stashed in backpacks. The streetlight shines outside the door. The negotiations over the sandwiches are nearing conclusion. Everyone will soon go their separate ways.

There are always too many sandwiches. Sandwiches of all kinds: posh ones on focaccia for a report launch at the university, white sliced bread with cheese for a Saturday afternoon workshop, wrapped in cellophane and cardboard for a team meeting. The ritualised division of the leftover sandwiches marks the end of time spent together, a small act of care as folk leave this work in community and head back to their private lives. The sandwiches feed children, partners, housemates and students, as well as the co-designers they were catering for. The sharing of food, time and knowledge extends beyond these fleetingly short hours together, but once the sandwiches are divided up, the day's work is done.

Community action holds much promise as a site to reconstitute the world, to create viable, sustainable ways of living in cities in the face of multiple, intersecting global and local crises. Infrastructures shape what is possible in cities, and mediate urban impacts on the natural world and far-away people and places. This book has been about a programme of research to put the power of science, engineering and design into the hands of those with otherwise no extraordinary power, as they grapple with these vast, complex urban systems. The cases here reveal complexities beyond the romantic ideal of community power, political ideology of self-reliance and technical promise of decentralisation.

Communities have their own histories, dynamics and trajectories, as do the bigger cities they are part of. Projects like those in this book are moments in time. Community struggles and action existed before and persist afterwards. Isolated workshops and projects are unlikely to be world-changing in their brief existence, but if they go well, they can bring new perspectives and some modest shift in power to communities. Going back to talk to communities, as the team tried to do for this book, is nerve-wracking, revealing different narratives of success, failure to fulfil expectations and mixed feelings. After the sandwiches, community goes on.

This final chapter looks back on the four projects together: Demolition or Refurbishment, Engineering Comes Home, Somers Town Air Quality and the Kipling Garden. It revisits the six steps of the Bottom-Up Infrastructure co-design method and reflects on three modes of community in co-design research and practice: client, contributor and collaborator. The chapter considers the constraints and possibilities of co-design within the powerful socio-technical systems of urban infra-structures and the implications for communities in responding to com-plex local and global crises. The book concludes with thoughts about how this work might be replicated, adapted and shared, to reconstitute worlds beyond these small efforts in London.

Four small projects

The case studies in this book had their own successes and limitations, and together show the evolution of a way of working, learning through doing and listening, and going back and listening again. The Demolition or Refurbishment project felt like ancient history to Richard and Pat when Gemma and Charlotte returned to hear from them in 2021, yet the distance helped to put the project in the context of a longer arc of action and impact. Engineering Comes Home was a stepping-off point for experiments in co-design, activating a community for the project, rather than responding to a defined need. It was a proof of concept that was then applied in Somers Town with the neighbourhood planning forum, and the start of a relationship with Andy and the Leathermarket JMB that led to the collaboration with the Kipling gardeners. The project in Somers Town was an intervention in a long struggle by Slaney and her neighbours for a clean environment for some of the most deprived Londoners. It provided critical data and analysis, and a new way for the community to work with universities. The Kipling Garden project gave a boost to Joanna, Clive and others with an interest in greening their neighbourhood, with unintended positive outcomes as well as unfulfilled expectations.

The Demolition or Refurbishment project, in Chapter 5, provided proof of concept for the Engineering Exchange, modelling community as client in a professional consulting relationship. The outcomes of the work were conceptual, instrumental and capacity building. It changed how communities, policy-makers and professionals thought about demolition of social housing, and it helped to raise the profile of the issue in London. It demonstrated that working with communities can be an indirect means for university-based researchers to provide evidence for policy change. It also gave the community groups a new pattern for working with researchers, with implications for future collaborations.

Engineering Comes Home, in Chapter 6, was instigated by the research team, with the community as contributor. The outcomes and impacts reflect this origin, with the major learning relating to the methods, tools and processes, rather than the community. This was the only project where participants were paid for their time, reflecting the value that they added to the research without expectation of a direct benefit from the research outcomes. The research team learned the importance of orientating participants to the overall co-design process, for co-designers to be able to see how the pieces fitted together, and where they were headed. Perhaps unsurprisingly, the team also learned that people will use tools in ways that make sense to them and are useful for them, not always as the designer intended. The importance of community dynamics and community experience was also evident, shaping what was possible and resisting external, privileged encouragement to keep ideas open and think beyond constraints. The project provided proof of concept that communities could be engaged in infrastructure design, albeit on a small scale. It also provided the team with experience of meta-designing and 'setting free' tools to support the process.

Somers Town is a community with a long history of urban innovation as well as deprivation. In Chapter 7, the neighbourhood forum worked as both 'client' and 'collaborator' in the project on air quality with the Engineering Exchange. This was the first adaptation of the co-design process developed from the Engineering Comes Home project, with 10 per cent of the budget. The three-stage process followed the essential co-design method and helped the community and researchers to define the scope of a technical project. The technical report provided by Claire helped Somers Town residents to hold powerful interests to account – changing how air quality was monitored and challenging the quality of decision-making in recent developments. The Somers Town community has a strong history of organising, and a high level of knowledge about urban politics and environments, despite low socio-economic status. The project did not fulfil everyone's expectations. The intervention of the Engineering Exchange team and the technical evidence they produced was just one moment in a long struggle for environmental justice.

The Kipling Garden project was conceived with the intention of the community as collaborator, as presented in Chapter 8. Residents initiated the idea of a garden and asked for technical support, as 'clients', and were opportunistically enrolled in a large research proposal. They started out wanting advice on how to irrigate a garden they hoped to build and ended up involved in a multi-million-pound research and innovation consortium. The project did not fulfil its initial objectives from either the researchers' goal of diverting water from London's sewers, or the community's aim of a rooftop garden. Yet it would be too simplistic to designate this as a failure. The experience of the co-design process helped to convene the community and prompt community organisation around the idea of estate greening and climate change action. The Kipling Garden, through the writing of Clive and Joanna, shows the many different viewpoints on collaboration, and the power of community persistence beyond short-term engagement with science, engineering and design.

Six stages of co-design

Co-designing is a complicated task in any context. Working with urban infrastructure adds further layers of complexity, with multiple stakeholders, power dynamics, visions and consequences, entangled with interdependent technical systems. In every case, preparing by developing relationships with community members, communicating clearly and setting expectations is a fundamental starting point. 'Setting aims' as the first stage of co-design came from different starting points, but was always negotiated between the research team, community and other participants, and revisited throughout the projects.

In the projects in this book the implications of the outcomes varied greatly for the participants. What is at stake for these different stakeholders is vastly different. For the researchers, the projects were relatively short term and part of their paid employment and career paths. For community members, the outcomes affected their quality of life, their relationships with their neighbours and the long-term shape of their neighbourhoods. For local governments and agencies, the projects were potentially risky, opening up their decisions and policies to deeper scrutiny, while providing opportunities and resources for citizen-led urban change. For utilities, developers, engineering and design firms, the projects provided an interesting set of experiments at the margins of their core business, with potentially useful methods for engaging customers and communities in new ways.

The communities in these projects had the most at stake. Understanding community needs, strengths and dynamics is therefore of vital importance. Where the community was relatively early in its involvement in the issues of interest (Engineering Comes Home and Kipling Garden), the work of characterising communities relied strongly on the research traditions of anthropology and ethnography. Where the community group was more established (Demolition or Refurbishment and Somers Town), this knowledge of the community and the issues came from trusted, established leaders and representatives.

The three-workshop structure for capturing requirements, analysing options and crafting solutions formed the recognisable 'design' activity within the overall process. Post-it notes, pens, flip-chart paper, site tours, cardboard models, bespoke software, prototypes, factsheets and technical demonstrations are the stuff and business of design and collaboration. The excitement of working together, the buzz of creating something new and the terror that it might all fall apart, happen during these events. These are the moments when co-design feels like it is happening, but the workshops are possible only because of the many hidden hours of in-between work. The meta-design of tools to support collaboration, the specification, coding and testing of software, the selection of games and activities, the analysis of outputs and checking back against aims and values are the less visible, though eminently important, labour of co-design.

Evaluation occurred through the projects, to continuously check how the project was meeting its objectives, to find the things that were not working and to keep adapting the tools and methods to the community and context. Evaluation involves tools and methods like interviews, surveys and polls, to check the effects of activities before and after, to measure the impact. Evaluation is more than the application of tools: ideally, it is a process of critical reflection, one that integrates learning. Most importantly, evaluation thinking requires listening and observing. Working as a team provides many ears and eyes to check for different perspectives, and debriefing workshops are invaluable for interpreting and sense-making.

Evaluation often means gathering evidence of success, but it is perhaps more important to be able to recognise when things go wrong. The unexpected, unpredicted and experiences of failure and confusion are all part of the evaluation process. The project team witnessed conflict within communities, and the projects and activities were themselves sometimes the source of direct conflict. Miscommunication was inevitable, requiring patience and humility. Sometimes the research teams got things wrong. Conflict and confusion are part of creative processes and of community life. It is unethical to instigate or enflame conflict in communities without clear commitment to resolution, and irresponsible to avoid or supress conflict in the interests of a clean, rational, predetermined method or presumed higher order of expertise. Sustained partnership with communities requires the capacity to admit errors and ignorance, and a reciprocal responsibility to continue to learn and adapt together. Evaluation should lead to action – building upon the learning to make decisions, shift approaches and move forward.

The six stages of the Bottom-Up Infrastructure Co-design method, and the tools presented in Chapter 9 and deployed in each project, evolved as the research team learned from experience, and adapted to new circumstances. The team also learned to respond to opportunities as they emerged, whether from previous work or community networks or from funding agencies. Repurposing the resources of universities and their funders, and adapting the tools and methods of science, engineering and design, to support community action, is itself a set of skills and expertise.

The projects were funded by universities and research councils, mostly paying for people's time to do the work, analyse it and write about it. Directing research funding to community-based research reflects its small but growing importance. These are well-resourced research projects. The intention was to create tools and methods that others can replicate and adapt in resource constrained settings, but that is not an easy task.

It has proven much harder to fund implementation of the project outcomes or to fund community work and development. This raises stark contrasts between funding for large institutions and funding for on-the-ground change. As Clive notes in Chapter 8, the £5 million available for the CAMELLIA research consortium left very little trace on the ground where he lives. Kipling was just one small element of a large programme of research and innovation, working with water companies, government and a range of other water management stakeholders in London. The Kipling gardeners were left with greater knowledge about the potential benefits of their plans for London's water system, but the hard work of securing rights to the rooftop space and to pay to build and maintain the garden remained to be achieved.

Three roles for community

The original model for the Engineering Exchange was to provide *pro bono* research and consultancy services to community-based clients. The Demolition or Refurbishment project proved the value of this mode of working. To enable the research team to develop and test infrastructure co-design methods, the residents of the Meakin Estate acted as contributors to the Engineering Comes Home project. The Somers Town community acted at different times as clients and collaborators to the research team, as relationships, objectives and resources changed. The Kipling gardeners were collaborators in a research project, which evolved from a request for technical advice into a case study within a large consortium.

To act as a client the community must be aware of the problems it wants to solve, who or what is responsible for the problem and the types of knowledge that would help them find and deliver solutions. When lacking the capacity to create or access specialist, technical knowledge, the community works with researchers to fill a defined gap. Community as client requires a high level of capacity and awareness of the structures that they operate within. Providing professional, if *pro bono*, consultancy services enhances community capacity to participate in knowledge democracy and influence powerful, knowledge-based institutions.

When the community is a contributor, the project outcome for them is of a more limited scope. Despite the co-design process, the water tank that was installed at the Meakin Estate was utilised only temporarily and fell into disrepair because it was not consistently used by people who cared that it was maintained. Community as contributors can activate communities, but mostly provides opportunities for researchers to learn from them and their experiences, and to test out methods and hypotheses.

The collaborator model of working with communities more actively recognises an intersection of interests, although these are never completely aligned. Power imbalances may be addressed in the practice of the project, but readily reappear in implementation and outcomes. As people engage and disengage, the relationship keeps evolving because there is no pre-eminence of deliverables from either side. In collaboration both sides create and share knowledge, and each achieve beneficial outcomes, shared and separate.

The Three Cs (client, contributor, collaborator) are not a hierarchy. The Engineering Exchange journey began with community as client, with a future ideal in mind to progress towards community as collaborator via experiments with community as contributor. Beginning with

Arnstein's ladder, movements in public participation, citizen science and community engagement either explicitly or implicitly promote two-way collaboration, co-production and co-design as preferred models, empowering communities in knowledge production (Arnstein, 1969; Haklay, 2013; Strasser *et al.*, 2019). However, the experience of co-designing infrastructure and the Engineering Exchange shows that projects and partnerships can shift between collaborator, contributor and client, each bringing benefits and challenges.

Infrastructures and communities

Infrastructure is the focus of much action in recognition of the role that it plays in producing and mitigating the climate and biodiversity crises (Anand *et al.*, 2018; Waage *et al.*, 2015). The recognition that these crises require societal change alongside technical transitions draws attention to the role that citizens, consumers and communities play. This contributes to calls by policy-makers to democratise infrastructure, with more active roles for end-users in the provision and management of services and resources (Cowell and Devine-Wright, 2018; van Oost *et al.*, 2009; van Vliet *et al.*, 2005). The experiences of the case study projects in this book, which were actively trying to rework infrastructure for communities that want to achieve environmental benefits, show the challenges and expose the politics behind the rhetoric. The cases demonstrate success that groups can have when they take the knowledge produced through collaborations into political processes, to support policy and practical change in infrastructure planning and delivery. We also see the challenges that are experienced when groups attempt to make physical interventions in complex infrastructures and find themselves constrained. Incumbent knowledge and power structures are robust, and these experiments in bottom-up infrastructure exist within a world that remains structured to enforce long-standing power relations (Anand *et al.*, 2018; Marvin and Graham, 2001).

The case studies worked with communities of place, brought together for a specific purpose, and drew on shared values and interests. They demonstrated elements of descriptive, normative and instrumental communities, as defined by Marilyn Taylor, demonstrating the complexity and fluidity of communities beyond conventional policy framings (Taylor, 2011). The communities involved in these projects changed and evolved. This was partly through the experience of working with the scientists, engineers and designers, and partly by working with each other in new ways. Co-design as a form of urban practice contributes to forming and shaping community, within much longer and deeper dynamics of relationships (Blokland, 2017).

Communities of infrastructure become apparent when the black boxes of urban socio-technical systems opened. Infrastructures provide connections between people in cities, the corporations and governments that operate utilities and services, and the biophysical and built environment. Infrastructures are forms of relationship (Edwards, 2003; Star, 1999). Understanding the relationships between people connected to the same infrastructures as 'community' draws attention to shared values, purpose and identity. Communities of infrastructure are more than individual users or customers of a big corporate or government utility provider. They share an interest in finding new ways to configure the socio-technical systems that underpin urban life and its connection to the wider environment and resources that support it.

Community co-design holds the potential to disrupt powerful institutional definitions of the role and nature of community by changing how communities access, use and contribute to technical knowledge and methods (Wylie *et al.*, 2014). Opening science, design and engineering to communities is a small step towards reorientating power and knowledge hierarchies embedded within long-standing urban infrastructures (Edwards, 2003; Hall and Tandon, 2017; Star, 1999). The methods and projects in this book show that local communities without specialist technical training are capable of meaningfully contributing to the co-design of infrastructures and of using the outcomes to enact change.

Reconstitute the world

The scale of transformation required to address global crises is vast, and the scale of the projects in this book are tiny. Each project made some difference to the communities involved, as clients, contributors or collaborators. Communities who worked on these projects gained technical evidence and analysis to hold governments and developers to account, and to change policy and practice, on issues of importance to them. Working with researchers and designers through the Engineering Exchange and Bottom-Up Infrastructure programmes provided energy and resources to enhance local organisation and action. Communities were formed and strengthened in their resolve and capacity to improve their neighbourhood and city. Connecting communities with no extraordinary power to powerful methods, tools and knowledge of science, engineering and design, is a small step in reconstituting the world towards sustainability, resilience and justice.

The projects also had an impact on the researchers and the universities. The Engineering Exchange demonstrated not only the feasibility of working with communities as clients, collaborators and contributors, but also the value in doing so. The Engineering Exchange acted as beacon within the university, growing the network of scholars from different disciplines, at different stages of their careers and with different capacities to contribute, providing them with opportunities to engage and support grassroots action. These projects have been presented at international conferences, written about in high-ranking journals, talked about in the press and engaged with the growing interest across universities in how the academy can support action on climate, biodiversity and local environments.

These are indeed small steps. In the face of rapid environmental, social and economic crises, they might seem inconsequential. Rapid change is needed, deep within the socio-technical systems that connect cities to the natural world and structure interactions between people, governments and corporations. The rapid change needed can feel at odds with the speed of building trust and the formation of relationships needed for partnerships to work. The co-design methods and collaborative approaches developed and tested in this book may be of value in 'scaling-up', enabling citizen engagement in the transformation of cities, regions, nations and the international systems. Citizen assemblies, citizen juries and other deliberative processes are examples of how this is already being done, but they serve a different purpose and different constituents.

Rather than 'scaling-up', infrastructure co-design holds greater potential through replication. The 'new ways of doing' can be replicated, embedding the outputs and outcomes of infrastructure co-design to influence beyond the 'small steps'. Enabling more communities, in more cities and countries, to participate meaningfully in the infrastructures of their neighbourhoods, and the policies that govern them, provides a complementary pathway to achieving the changes needed. It does not replace the need for change in larger structures of governance and operation of infrastructure. The struggles to implement bottom-up change can reveal where top-down reform is most needed. It is through replication that change can filter into the other structures hold existing socio-technical systems in place. These other structures include local planning protocols; national policies; financing; land tenure; ownership of assets; responsibilities of utilities, authorities and regulators; and social expectations between different groups of people. All these may be called into question when communities are provided with opportunities, tools and resources to create change.

Replication of infrastructure co-design requires adaptation of tools and methods for particular communities, contexts and issues. The tools and methods used in the co-designing infrastructures case studies were adapted from other contexts, such as engineering analysis, community development, user-centred design and anthropology. In turn, they are intended to be flexible, so others can modify them for their own use. The six-stage process provides a core structure to connect activities and provide an overall rhythm and pattern for the work. It also links the work to methods that are recognisable to scientists, engineers and designers; but it is a guiding frame, not an immutable recipe. The core purpose of placing the knowledge, methods and tools of science, engineering and design into the hands of the communities most affected will be achieved through constant reformulation and sharing of experiences.

As the sandwiches are shared out, this moment of *Co-designing Infrastructures* comes to a close. The projects have left humble legacies in the communities that hosted them. As a body of work, they provide experiences, methods and tools for others to take away, reformulate and make new. Reconstituting the world, with and without extraordinary power, remains ever more urgent, yet never more possible.

References

ADB, and RISE. 2021. *Co-design of Water-Sensitive Settlement Upgrading*. Asian Development Bank and Monash University.

Adeyemi, A. Y., S. O. Ojo, O. O. Aina and E. A. Olanipekun. 2006. 'Empirical evidence of women under-representation in the construction industry in Nigeria', *Women in Management Review*, 21(7), 567–77. https://doi.org/10.1108/09649420610692516 (last accessed 1 October 2022).

Agyeman, J. 2013. *Introducing Just Sustainabilities: policy, planning and practice*. London: Zed Books Ltd.

Aldrich, D.P., and M. A. Meyer. 2015. 'Social capital and community resilience', *American Behavioural Science*, 59, 254–69. https://doi.org/10.1177/0002764214550299 (last accessed 1 October 2022).

Allix, P., and J. Matsushita. 2017. ECH Calculator, GitHub. https://github.com/pallix/ech-calculator (last accessed 1 October 2022).

Analitis, A., B. Barratt, D. Green, A. Beddows, E. Samoli, J. Schwartz and K. Katsouyanni. 2020. 'Prediction of PM2.5 concentrations at the locations of monitoring sites measuring PM10 and NOx, using generalized additive models and machine learning methods: a case study in London', *Atmospheric Environment*, 240, 117757. https://doi.org/10.1016/j.atmosenv.2020.117757 (last accessed 1 October 2022).

Anand, N., A. Gupta and H. Appel. 2018. *The Promise of Infrastructure*. Durham NC: Duke University Press.

Anderson, J. 2012. 'Managing trade-offs in "ecotopia": becoming green at the Centre for Alternative Technology', *Transactions of the Institute of British Geographers*, 37, 212–25. https://www.jstor.org/stable/41427942 (last accessed 10 October 2022).

Architects' Journal. 2022. 'RetroFirst – a campaign by the *Architects' Journal*', *Architects' Journal*. https://www.architectsjournal.co.uk/news/retrofirst. https://www.architectsjournal.co.uk/news/retrofirst (last accessed 8 December 2022).

Arnstein, S. R. 1969. 'A ladder of citizen participation', *Journal of the American Institute of Planners*, 35, 216–24. https://doi.org/10.1080/01944366908977225 (last accessed 1 October 2022).

Aschauer, D. A. 1989. 'Does public capital crowd out private capital?', *Journal of Monetary Economics*, 24(2), 171–88. https://doi.org/10.1016/0304-3932(89)90002-0 (last accessed 1 October 2022).

Atkinson, R., and S. Cope 1997. 'Community participation and urban regeneration in Britain'. In *Contested Communities*, edited by P. Hoggett, 201–21. Bristol: Policy Press.

Austen, Hölker. 2022. 'White Paper of Science Innovation through Citizen Science'. https://doi.org/10.5281/ZENODO.6008115 (last accessed 1 October 2022).

Bal, M., D. Bryde, D. Fearon and E. Ochieng. 2013. 'Stakeholder engagement: achieving sustainability in the construction sector', *Sustainability*, 5(2), 695–710. https://doi.org/10.3390/su5020695 (last accessed 1 October 2022).

Bell, S. 2015. 'Renegotiating urban water', *Progress in Planning*, 96, 1–28. https://doi.org/10.1016/j.progress.2013.09.001 (last accessed 1 October 2022).

Bell, S., A. Borrion, C. Johnson, J. Matsushita, R. Comber and P. Melville-Shreeve. 2017. 'Engineering Comes Home: co-designing nexus infrastructure from the bottom-up, in ISNGI Conference Proceedings', *International Symposium for Next Generation Infrastructure*. https://s16652.pcdn.co/wp-content/uploads/sites/12/ISNGI-Paper-Bell-et-al-Final.pdf (last accessed 10 October 2022).

Bell, S., R. Lee, D. Fitzpatrick and S. Mahtani. 2021. 'Co-producing a community university knowledge strategy', *Frontiers in Sustainability*, 2, 48. https://doi.org/10.3389/frsus.2021.661572 (last accessed 1 October 2022).

Bockman, J. 2013. 'Neoliberalism', *Contexts*, 12(3), 14–15. https://doi.org/10.1177/1536504213499873 (last accessed 1 October 2022).

Blokland, T. 2017. 'Community as urban practice'. In *Urban Futures Series*. Cambridge: Polity Press.

Bom, P. R. D., and J. E. Ligthart. 2014. 'What Have we learned from three decades of research on the productivity of public capital?', *Journal of Economic Surveys*, 28(5), 889–916. https://doi.org/10.1111/joes.12037 (last accessed 1 October 2022).

Bonney, R., H. Ballard, R. Jordan, E. McCallie, T. Phillips, J. Shirk and C. C. Wilderman. 2009. 'Public Participation in Scientific Research: defining the field and assessing its potential for informal science education', *A CAISE Inquiry Group Report*. Online submission.

Bookchin, M. 2005. *The Ecology of Freedom: the emergence and dissolution of hierarchy*. Oakland CA: AK Press.

Borenstein, S. 2014. 'A microeconomic framework for evaluating energy efficiency rebound and some implications', *The Energy Journal*, 36(1). https://doi.org/10.5547/01956574.36.1.1 (last accessed 1 October 2022).

Borrion, A., J. Matsushita, K. Austen, C. Johnson and S. Bell. 2019. 'Development of LCA calculator to support community infrastructure co-design', *International Journal of Life Cycle Assessment*, 24(7). https://doi.org/10.1007/s11367-018-1492-2 (last accessed 10 October 2022).

Boser, S. 2006. 'Ethics and power in community-campus partnerships for research', *Action Research*, 4, 9–21. https://doi.org/10.1177/1476750306060538 (last accessed 1 October 2022).

Bottom-Up Infrastructure. 2022. 'Bottom-up Infrastructure'. https://www.bottomupinfrastructure.org (last accessed 1 October 2022).

Boughton, J. 2018. *Municipal Dreams: the rise and fall of council housing*. London: Verso Books.

Bowes, M. J., L. K. Armstrong, S. A. Harman, H. D. Wickham, D. J. E. Nicholls, P. M. Scarlett, C. Roberts, H. P. Jarvie, G. H. Old, E. Gozzard, N. Bachiller-Jareno and D. S. Read. 2018. 'Weekly water quality monitoring data for the River Thames (UK) and its major tributaries (2009–2013): the Thames Initiative research platform', *Earth System Science Data*, 10, 1637–53. https://doi.org/10.5194/essd-10-1637-2018 (last accessed 1 October 2022).

Brady, J. 1985. 'Uncertainty in demand forecasting and its consequences in water resource planning: the Teeside experience', *Proceedings of the Institution of Civil Engineers*, 78(6), 1383–401. https://doi.org/10.1680/iicep.1985.1059 (last accessed 1 October 2022).

Brigg, M., and M. Graham. 2020. 'The relevance of Aboriginal political concepts: relationalism, not sovereignty', *UQ eSpace*. https://www.abc.net.au/religion/aboriginal-political-philosophy-relationalism/12954274 (last accessed 1 October 2022).

Brownill, S., and Q. Bradley (eds). 2017. *Localism and Neighbourhood Planning: power to the people?*, 1st edn. Bristol: Bristol University Press. https://doi.org/10.2307/j.ctt1t89h5j (last accessed 1 October 2022).

Bullard, R. 1993. 'Anatomy of environmental racism and the environmental justice movement'. In *Confronting Environmental Racism: voices from the grassroots*, edited by R. Bullard, 15–40. Boston MA: South End Press.

Bullard, R. D. 2008. *Dumping in Dixie: race, class, and environmental quality*, 3rd edn. Boulder CO: Westview Press.

Camden Council. 2020. 'Ward Profile Jan-2020 St Pancras and Somers Town Ward'. https://opendata.camden.gov.uk/People-Places/Ward-Profile-Jan-2020-St-Pancras-and-Somers-Town-w/gvty-8p38 (last accessed 1 October 2022).

Charlton, M. B., and N. W. Arnell. 2011. 'Adapting to climate change impacts on water resources in England: an assessment of draft water resources management plans', *Global Environmental Change*, 21, 238–48. https://doi.org/10.1016/j.gloenvcha.2010.07.012 (last accessed 1 October 2022).

Churchman, C. W. 1967. 'Guest editorial: wicked problems', *Management Science*, 14(4), B141–2.

Clarke, L., T. Costello, J. Mason and M. Thomas. 1977. 'Somers Town history workshop', *History Workshop Journal*, 4, 249–50. https://doi.org/10.1093/hwj/4.1.249 (last accessed 1 October 2022).

Close, R., and M. Loosemore 2014. 'Breaking down the site hoardings: attitudes and approaches to community consultation during construction', *Construction Management and Economics*, 32, 816–28. https://doi.org/10.1080/01446193.2013.879195 (last accessed 1 October 2022).

Cole, L. W., and S. R. Foster. 2000. *From the Ground Up: environmental racism and the rise of the environmental justice movement*. New York: New York University Press. https://www.jstor.org/stable/j.ctt9qgj6v (last accessed 10 October 2022).

Colomb, C. 2007. 'Unpacking new labour's "Urban Renaissance" agenda: towards a socially sustainable reurbanization of British cities?', *Planning Practice & Research*, 22, 1–24. https://doi.org/10.1080/02697450701455249 (last accessed 1 October 2022).

Coolsaet, B. 2020. *Environmental Justice: key issues*. Abingdon: Routledge.

Costanza-Chock, S. 2020. *Design Justice: community-led practices to build the worlds we need*. Cambridge MA: MIT Press.

Cowell, R., G. Bristow and M. Munday. 2011. 'Acceptance, acceptability and environmental justice: the role of community benefits in wind energy development', *Journal of Environmental Planning and Management*, 54(4), 539–57. https://doi.org/10.1080/09640568.2010.521047 (last accessed 1 October 2022).

Cowell, R., and P. Devine-Wright. 2018. 'A "delivery-democracy dilemma"? Mapping and explaining policy change for public engagement with energy infrastructure', *Journal of Environmental Policy & Planning*, 20(4), 499–517. https://doi.org/10.1080/1523908X.2018.1443005 (last accessed 1 October 2022).

Cowie, P., and S. Davoudi. 2015. 'Is small really beautiful? The legitimacy of neighbourhood planning'. In *Reconsidering Localism*, edited by Simin Davoudi and Ali Madanipour. New York: Routledge. https://www.taylorfrancis.com/chapters/edit/10.4324/9781315818863-9/small-really-beautiful-legitimacy-neighbourhood-planning-paul-cowie-simin-davoudi (last accessed 1 October 2022).

Crawford, C., S. Bell, F. Davies, C. Johnson, S. Joo, S. Hayward and R. Lee. 2016. 'Hacking London's demolition decisions: a new collaboration to scrutinise the technical justifications for retrofit, refurbishment and demolition'. In *Engaged Urbanism*, edited by B. Campkin and G. Duijzings, 77–82. London: I. B. Tauris.

Crawford, K., C. Johnson, F. Davies, J. Sunyoung and S. Bell. 2014. 'Demolition or Refurbishment of Social Housing? A review of the evidence', *UCL Engineering Exchange*, London.

Cutter, S. L., K. D. Ash, C. T. Emrich. 2014. 'The geographies of community disaster resilience', *Global Environmental Change*, 29, 65–77. https://doi.org/10.1016/j.gloenvcha.2014.08.005 (last accessed 1 October 2022).

Cutter, S. L., L. Barnes, M. Berry, C. Burton, E. Evans, E. Tate and J. Webb. 2008. 'A place-based model for understanding community resilience to natural disasters', *Global Environmental Change*, Special issue: Local evidence on vulnerabilities and adaptations to global environmental change, 18(4), 598–606. https://doi.org/10.1016/j.gloenvcha.2008.07.013 (last accessed 1 October 2022).

Davis, M. 1998. *Thinking Like an Engineer: a collection of addresses and essays*. Oxford: Oxford University Press.

Delanty, G. 2003. 'Ideologies of the knowledge society and the cultural contradictions of higher education', *Policy Future Education*, 1, 71–82. https://doi.org/10.2304/pfie.2003.1.1.9 (last accessed 1 October 2022).

Della Croce, R. 2011. 'Pension Funds Investment in Infrastructure: policy actions', *OECD Working Papers on Finance, Insurance and Private Pensions*, 13. Paris: OECD Publishing. https://doi.org/10.1787/5kg272f9bnmx-en (last accessed 1 October 2022).

Della Croce, R., and S. Gatti. 2014. 'Financing infrastructure – international trends', *OECD Journal: Financial Market Trends*, 2014(1), 123–38. https://doi.org/10.1787/fmt-2014-5jxvpb4jfrf1 (last accessed 1 October 2022).

Department of Environment, Food and Rural Affairs. 2021. 'National Bias Adjustment Factors'. https://laqm.defra.gov.uk/air-quality/air-quality-assessment/national-bias/ (last accessed 1 October 2022).

Dolowitz, D. P., S. Bell and M. Keeley. 2018. 'Retrofitting urban drainage infrastructure: green or grey?', *Urban Water Journal*, 15, 83–91. https://doi.org/10.1080/1573062X.2017.1396352 (last accessed 1 October 2022).

Dove, M. R. 2006. 'Indigenous people and environmental politics', *Annual Review Anthropology*, 35, 191–208. https://doi.org/10.1146/annurev.anthro.35.081705.123235 (last accessed 1 October 2022).

Draper, C., and D. Freedman. 2010. 'Review and analysis of the benefits, purposes, and motivations associated with community gardening in the United States', *Journal of Community Practice*, 18(4), 458–92. https://doi.org/10.1080/10705422.2010.519682 (last accessed 1 October 2022).

Draper, N. 2013. *The Price of Emancipation: slave-ownership, compensation and British society at the end of slavery*. Cambridge: Cambridge University Press.

Durose, C., L. Richardson and B. Perry. 2018. 'Craft metrics to value co-production', *Nature*, 562, 32–3. https://doi.org/10.1038/d41586-018-06860-w (last accessed 1 October 2022).

Edwards, P. 2003. 'Infrastructure and modernity: force, time and social organization in the history of sociotechnial systems'. In *Modernity and Technology*, edited by T. Misa, P. Brey and A. Feenberg. Cambridge MA: MIT Press.

Egert, B., T. J. Kozluk and D. Sutherland. 2009. 'Infrastructure and growth: empirical evidence', *SSRN Electronic Journal*. https://doi.org/10.2139/ssrn.1360784 (last accessed 1 October 2022).

Engineering Exchange. 2018. 'Somers Town Air Quality Factsheets'. https://www.ucl.ac.uk/engineering-exchange/sites/engineering-exchange/files/somers_town_aq_factsheets.pdf (last accessed 1 October 2022).

EPSRC. 2014. 'Design the Future Expression of Interest Call'. https://webarchive.nationalarchives.gov.uk/ukgwa/20210302201321/https://epsrc.ukri.org/files/funding/calls/2014/engineeringdesignauditioncall/ (last accessed 10 October 2022).

Estate Watch. 2022. 'Estate Watch'. https://estatewatch.london/ (last accessed 1 October 2022).

Feenberg, A. 2012. *Questioning Technology*. London: Routledge.

Foucault, M., and C. Gordon. (1980). *Power/Knowledge: selected interviews and other writings, 1972–1977*, 1st US edn. New York: Pantheon Books.

Fuad-Luke, A. 2009. *Design Activism: beautiful strangeness for a sustainable world*. London: Earthscan.

Funtowicz, S., and J. Ravetz. 1991. 'A new scientific methodology for global environmental issues'. In *Ecological Economics: the science and management of sustainability*, 137. New York: Colombia University Press.

Furlong, K. 2020. 'Geographies of infrastructure 1: economies', *Progress in Human Geography*, 44(3), 572–82. https://doi.org/10.1177/0309132519850913 (last accessed 1 October 2022).

Gibbons, M. 1999. 'Science's new social contract with society', *Nature*, 402, C81–C84. https://doi.org/10.1038/35011576 (last accessed 1 October 2022).

Gilroy, P. 1993. *The Black Atlantic: modernity and double consciousness*. London: Verso Books.

Glass, J., and M. Simmonds. 2007. '"Considerate construction": case studies of current practice', *Engineering, Construction and Architectural Management*, 14(2), 131–49. https://doi.org/10.1108/09699980710731263 (last accessed 1 October 2022).

GOV.UK. 2020. 'Neighbourhood Planning'. https://www.gov.uk/guidance/neighbourhood-planning--2 (last accessed 1 October 2022).

Graham, S. 2009. 'When infrastructures fail'. In *Disrupted Cities: when infrastructure fails*, 1–26. New York: Routledge.

Graham, S., and C. McFarlane (eds). 2014. *Infrastructural Lives*, 1st edn. London: Routledge. https://doi.org/10.4324/9781315775098 (last accessed 1 October 2022).

Greater London Authority. 2018. *Better Homes for Local People – the Mayor's good practice guide to estate regeneration*. London: Greater London Authority.

Guitart, D., C. Pickering and J. Byrne. 2012. 'Past results and future directions in urban community gardens research', *Urban Forestry & Urban Greening*, 11(4), 364–73. https://doi.org/10.1016/j.ufug.2012.06.007 (last accessed 1 October 2022).

Haklay, M. 2013. 'Citizen science and volunteered geographic information: overview and typology of participation'. In *Crowdsourcing Geographic Knowledge: volunteered geographic information (VGI) in theory and practice*, edited by D. Sui, S. Elwood and M. Goodchild, 105–22. New York: Springer. https://doi.org/10.1007/978-94-007-4587-2_7 (last accessed 1 October 2022).

Hall, B. L., and R. Tandon. 2017. 'Participatory research: where have we been, where are we going? A dialogue', *Journal of Service Research*, 1(2), 365–74. https://doi.org/10.18546/RFA.01.2.12 (last accessed 2 October 2022).

Halliday, S. 1999. *The Great Stink of London*. Stroud: Sutton Publishing.

Hanson, J. 2000. 'Urban transformations: a history of design ideas', *URBAN Design International*, 5, 97–122. https://doi.org/10.1057/palgrave.udi.9000011 (last accessed 2 October 2022).

Healey, P. 2006. *Urban Complexity and Spatial Strategies: towards a relational planning for our times*. London: Routledge. https://doi.org/10.4324/9780203099414 (last accessed 2 October 2022).

Hecker, S., M. Haklay, A. Bowser, Z. Makuch, J. Vogel and A. Bonn (eds). 2018. *Citizen Science: innovation in open science, society and policy*. London: UCL Press. https://doi.org/10.14324/111.9781787352339 (last accessed 2 October 2022).

Helm, D., and T. Tindall. 2009. 'The evolution of infrastructure and utility ownership and its implications', *Oxford Review of Economic Policy*, 25(3), 411–34. https://doi.org/10.1093/oxrep/grp025 (last accessed 2 October 2022).

Herr, K., and G. Anderson. 2005. *The Action Research Dissertation: a guide for students and faculty*. Thousand Oaks CA: SAGE.

Hewitt, R. J., N. Bradley, A. Baggio Compagnucci, C. Barlagne, A. Ceglarz, R. Cremades, M. McKeen, I. M. Otto and B. Slee. 2019. 'Social innovation in community energy in Europe: a review of the evidence'. *Frontiers in Energy Research*, 7, 31. https://doi.org/10.3389/fenrg.2019.00031 (last accessed 2 October 2022).

Hillier, J. 2003. 'Agon'izing over consensus: why Habermasian ideals cannot be "real"', *Planning Theory*, 2(1), 37–59. https://doi.org/10.1177/1473095203002001005 (last accessed 2 October 2022).

Hoff, H. 2011. 'Understanding the Nexus. Background paper for the Bonn 2011 conference: The Water, Energy and Food Security Nexus', Stockholm Environment Institute. https://www.scribd.com/document/318464767/Understanding-the-Nexus (last accessed 2 October 2022).

Holden, A., and K. Iveson. 2003. 'Designs on the urban: New Labour's urban renaissance and the spaces of citizenship', *City*, 7, 57–72. https://doi.org/10.1080/13604810302221 (last accessed 2 October 2022).

Holder, J. 2018. 'Environmental Justice in Somers Town and the Euston Area'. Joint report by Voluntary Action Camden, Somers Town Neighbourhood Forum, Environmental Law Foundation and UCL, London. https://www.ucl.ac.uk/laws/sites/laws/files/eji_web_environmental_justice_inquiry_in_the_euston_area_0.pdf (last accessed 2 October 2022).

Holifield, R., J. Chakraborty and G. Walker. 2017. 'Introduction: the worlds of environmental justice'. In *The Routledge Handbook of Environmental Justice*. Abingdon: Routledge.

Holling, C. S. 1996. 'Engineering resilience versus ecological resilience'. In *Engineering Within Ecological Constraints*, 31–44. Washington DC: National Academy of Engineering.

Holman, C. 2018. 'Somers Town Neighbourhood Plan: air quality (no. 1861)', Brook Cottage Consultants. https://somerstownplan.info/wp-content/uploads/2018/12/1861-_STNF_03December2018.pdf (last accessed 2 October 2022).

Holm, I. 2006. *Ideas and Beliefs in Architecture and Industrial Design: how attitudes, orientations, and underlying assumptions shape the built environment*. Oslo: Arkitektur- og designhøgskolen i Oslo.

Hommels, A. 2008. *Unbuilding Cities: obduracy in urban sociotechnical change*. Cambridge MA: MIT Press.

Hughes, T. P. 1993. *Networks of Power: electrification in Western society, 1880–1930*, new edn. Baltimore MD: Johns Hopkins University Press.

Hymel, K. M., K. A. Small and K. V. Dender. 2010. 'Induced demand and rebound effects in road transport', *Transportation Research Part B: Methodological*, 44(10), 1220–41. https://doi.org/10.1016/j.trb.2010.02.007 (last accessed 2 October 2022).

Imrie, R. 1996. 'Equity, social justice, and planning for access and disabled people: an international perspective', *International Planning Studies*, 1, 17–34. https://doi.org/10.1080/13563479608721641 (last accessed 2 October 2022).

Imrie, R., S. Pinch and M. Boyle. 1996. 'Identities, citizenship and power in the cities', *Urban Studies*, 33, 1255–61. https://doi.org/10.1080/0042098966637.

Institution of Civil Engineers. 2017. 'ICE Code of Professional Conduct'. https://myice.ice.org.uk/ICEDevelopmentWebPortal/media/Documents/About%20Us/ice-code-of-professional-conduct.pdf (last accessed 8 December 2022).

Iphofen, R., and M. Tolich. 2018. *The SAGE Handbook of Qualitative Research Ethics*. London: SAGE.

Irwin, A. 2002. *Citizen Science: a study of people, expertise and sustainable development*. London: Routledge. https://doi.org/10.4324/9780203202395 (last accessed 2 October 2022).

Israel, M., and I. Hay. 2006. *Research Ethics for Social Scientists*. London: SAGE.

Jansson, P. M., and R. A. Michelfelder. 2008. 'Integrating renewables into the U.S. grid: is it sustainable?', *The Electricity Journal*, 21(6), 9–21. https://doi.org/10.1016/j.tej.2008.07.005 (last accessed 2 October 2022).

Jevons, W. 1906. *The Coal Question; an inquiry concerning the progress of the nation and the probable exhaustion of our coal-mines*, 3rd edn (revised). London: Macmillan and Co. Ltd.

Johnson, C., S. Bell, A. Borrion and R. Comber. 2020. 'Working with infrastructural communities: a material participation approach to urban retrofit', *Science, Technology, & Human Values*, 46(2). https://doi.org/10.1177/0162243920916235 (last accessed 2 October 2022).

Just Space. 2018. 'Research Protocol'. https://justspace.org.uk/history/research-protocol/ (last accessed 2 October 2022).

Just Space. 2022. 'Community Groups Supporting Each Other on London Planning'. https://justspace.org.uk/ (last accessed 2 October 2022).

Kaika, M. 2017. '"Don't call me resilient again!": the New Urban Agenda as immunology ... or ... what happens when communities refuse to be vaccinated with "smart cities" and indicators', *Environment and Urbanisation*, 29, 89–102. https://doi.org/10.1177/0956247816684763 (last accessed 2 October 2022).

Kirk, A. 2001. 'Appropriating technology: the *Whole Earth Catalog* and counterculture environmental politics', *Environmental History*, 6, 374–94. https://doi.org/10.2307/3985660 (last accessed 2 October 2022).

Klein, M. U. 2012. 'Infrastructure policy: basic design options' (SSRN Scholarly Paper No. ID 2193774), *Social Science Research Network*. https://doi.org/10.2139/ssrn.2193774 (last accessed 2 October 2022).

Knowledge Quarter. 2022. 'Knowledge Quarter – King's Cross, St Pancras, Euston, Bloomsbury'. https://www.knowledgequarter.london/ (last accessed 2 October 2022).

Kurian, M. 2017. 'The water-energy-food nexus', *Environmental Science & Policy*, 68, 97–106. https://doi.org/10.1016/j.envsci.2016.11.006 (last accessed 2 October 2022).

Larkin, B. 2013. 'The politics and poetics of infrastructure', *Annual Review of Anthropology*, 42(1), 327–43. https://doi.org/10.1146/annurev-anthro-092412-155522 (last accessed 2 October 2022).

Leathermarket JMB. 2015. 'Our Homes'. https://leathermarketjmb.org.uk/estates/ (last accessed 10 October 2022).

Leck, H., D. Conway, M. Bradshaw and J. Rees. 2015. 'Tracing the water–energy–food nexus: description, theory and practice', *Geography Compass*, 9(8), 445–60. https://doi.org/10.1111/gec3.12222 (last accessed 2 October 2022).

Liberatore, A., and S. Funtowicz. 2003. '"Democratising" expertise, "expertising" democracy: what does this mean, and why bother?', *Science and Public Policy*, 30, 146–50. https://doi.org/10.3152/147154303781780551 (last accessed 2 October 2022).

Liboiron, M. 2021a. *Pollution is Colonialism*. Durham NC: Duke University Press.

Liboiron, M. 2021b. 'Decolonizing geoscience requires more than equity and inclusion'. *Nature Geoscience*, 14, 876–7. https://doi.org/10.1038/s41561-021-00861-7 (last accessed 2 October 2022).

Linnerud, K., T. K. Mideksa and G. S. Eskeland. 2011. 'The impact of climate change on nuclear power supply', *The Energy Journal*, 32(1). https://doi.org/10.5547/ISSN0195-6574-EJ-Vol32-No1-6 (last accessed 2 October 2022).

Little, R. G. 2002. 'Controlling cascading failure: understanding the vulnerabilities of interconnected infrastructures', *Journal of Urban Technology*, 9(1), 109–23. https://doi.org/10.1080/106307302317379855 (last accessed 2 October 2022).

Loftus, A., H. March and T. F. Purcell. 2019. 'The political economy of water infrastructure: an introduction to financialization', *WIREs Water*, 6(1), e1326. https://doi.org/10.1002/wat2.1326 (last accessed 2 October 2022).

London Assembly. 2015. 'Knock It Down or Do It Up?', London City Hall. https://www.london.gov.uk//about-us/london-assembly/london-assembly-publications/knock-it-down-or-do-it (last accessed 2 October 2022).

London Assembly. 2022. 'Whole Life-Cycle Carbon Assessments Guidance', London City Hall. https://www.london.gov.uk//what-we-do/planning/implementing-london-plan/london-plan-guidance/whole-life-cycle-carbon-assessments-guidance (last accessed 2 October 2022).

Lord, A. 2009. 'The community infrastructure levy: an information economics approach to understanding infrastructure provision under England's reformed spatial planning system', *Planning Theory & Practice*, 10(3), 333–49. https://doi.org/10.1080/14649350903229778 (last accessed 2 October 2022).

Lowe, M., S. Bell, J. Briggs, E. McMillan, M. Morley, M. Grenfell, D. Sweeting, A. Whitten and N. Jordan. 2021. 'Urban Resilience for Local Government: concepts, definitions and qualities', Melbourne Sustainable Society Institute. https://sustainable.unimelb.edu.au/publications/issues-papers/urban-resilience-for-local-government-concepts,-definitions-and-qualities (last accessed 2 October 2022).

McCauley, D., and R. Heffron. 2018. 'Just transition: integrating climate, energy and environmental justice', *Energy Policy*, 119, 1–7. https://doi.org/10.1016/j.enpol.2018.04.014 (last accessed 2 October 2022).

McCulloch, A. 2000. 'Evaluations of a community regeneration project: case studies of Cruddas Park Development Trust, Newcastle upon Tyne', *Journal of Social Policy*, 29(3), 397–419. https://doi.org/10.1017/S0047279400006000 (last accessed 2 October 2022).

McInroy, N. 2000. 'Urban regeneration and public space: the story of an urban park', *Space Polity*, 4, 23–40. https://doi.org/10.1080/713697747 (last accessed 2 October 2022).

Marres, N. 2016. *Material Participation: technology, the environment and everyday publics.* London: Palgrave Macmillan.

Marvin, S., and S. Graham. 2001. *Splintering Urbanism*. London: Routledge.

Matsushita, J., P. Allix and K. Austen. 2021. 'ECH Rainwater Harvesting Calculator Interactive, Rainwater Harvesting Calculator'. https://web.archive.org/web/20210928161121/https://calculator.iilab.org/rwh/ (last accessed 2 October 2022).

Matushita, J., K. Austen and P. Allix. 2016. 'Engineering Comes Home'. https://web.archive.org/web/20210928161013/https://ech.iilab.org/ (last accessed 10 October 2022).

Mayor of London. 2016. 'London Sustainable Drainage Action Plan', City Hall. https://www.london.gov.uk//what-we-do/environment/climate-change/surface-water/london-sustainable-drainage-action-plan (last accessed 2 October 2022).

Melosi, M. V. 2001. *Effluent America: cities, industry, energy and the environment.* Pittsburgh PA: University of Pittsburgh Press.

Mies, M. and V. Shiva. 1993. *Ecofeminism*. Melbourne: Spinifex.

Morris, J., and M. McGuinness. 2019. 'Liberalisation of the English water industry: what implications for consumer engagement, environmental protection, and water security?', *Utilities Policy*, 60, 100939. https://doi.org/10.1016/j.jup.2019.100939 (last accessed 6 October 2022).

Mutale, E., and M. Edwards. 2002. 'The London Development Agency and local regeneration Issues: an overview of urban regeneration management', *Local Economy*, 17, 25–34. https://doi.org/10.1080/02690940110079868 (last accessed 6 October 2022).

Ness, K. 2012. 'Constructing masculinity in the building trades: "most jobs in the construction industry can be done by women"', *Gender, Work & Organization*, 19(6), 654–76. https://doi.org/10.1111/j.1468-0432.2010.00551.x (last accessed 6 October 2022).

OECD. 2021. 'Unlocking Infrastructure Investment: innovative funding and financing in regions and cities', OECD Report for the G20 Infrastructure Working Group. https://www.oecd-ilibrary.org/docserver/9152902b-en.pdf?expires=1643275045&id=id&accname=guest&checksum=4873F6BBAA787FF7ED0F2E2F131540C2 (last accessed 6 October 2022).

O'Fallon, L. R., and A. Dearry. 2002. 'Community-based participatory research as a tool to advance environmental health sciences', *Environmental Health Perspectives*, 110, 155–9. https://doi.org/10.1289/ehp.02110s2155 (last accessed 6 October 2022).

Ofwat. 2019. 'Time to Act Together: Ofwat's strategy', Crown Copyright. https://www.ofwat.gov.uk/wp-content/uploads/2019/10/Time-to-act-together-Ofwats-strategy-1.pdf (last accessed 6 October 2022).

Olson, M. 2008. *The Rise and Decline of Nations: economic growth, stagflation, and social rigidities.* New Haven CT: Yale University Press.

Ottinger, G. 2013. *Refining Expertise: how responsible engineers subvert environmental justice challenges, refining expertise.* New York: New York University Press. https://www.jstor.org/stable/j.ctt9qgg5g (last accessed 10 October 2022).

Ottinger, G. 2010. 'Buckets of resistance: standards and the effectiveness of citizen science', *Science, Technology & Human Values*, 35, 244–70. https://doi.org/10.1177/0162243909337121 (last accessed 6 October 2022).

Pahl, R. 2005. 'Are all communities communities in the mind?', *The Sociological Review*, 53, 621–40. https://doi.org/10.1111/j.1467-954X.2005.00587.x (last accessed 6 October 2022).

Parker, G. 2017. 'The uneven geographies of neighbourhood planning in England'. In *Localism and Neighbourhood Planning: power to the people?*, 1st edn, edited by S. Brownill and Q. Bradley. Bristol: Bristol University Press. https://doi.org/10.2307/j.ctt1t89h5j (last accessed 6 October 2022).

Parker, E. A., B. A. Israel, M. Williams, W. Brakefield-Caldwell, T.C. Lewis, T. Robins, E. Ramirez, Z. Rowe and G. Keeler. 2003. 'Community action against asthma', *Journal of General Internal Medicine*, 18, 558–67. https://doi.org/10.1046/j.1525-1497.2003.20322.x (last accessed 6 October 2022).

Patel, R. L., and D. J. Pitroda. 2016. 'The role of women in construction industry: an Indian perspective', *Indian Journal of Technical Education*, 17–23.

Peck, J. 2012. 'Austerity urbanism: American cities under extreme economy', *City*, 16(6), 626–55. https://doi.org/10.1080/13604813.2012.734071 (last accessed 6 October 2022).

Penner, B. 2014. *Bathroom*. London: Reaktion Books.

Perez, C. C. 2019. *Invisible Women: data bias in a world designed for men*. New York: Harry N. Abrams.

Petrovic-Lazarevic, S. 2008. 'The development of corporate social responsibility in the Australian construction industry', *Construction Management and Economics*, 26, 93–101. https://doi.org/10.1080/01446190701819079 (last accessed 6 October 2022).

Pickerill, J. 2018. 'Black and green: the future of Indigenous-environmentalist relations in Australia', *Environmental Politics*, 27, 1122–45. https://doi.org/10.1080/09644016.2018.1466464 (last accessed 6 October 2022).

Pickerill, J. 2020. 'Eco-communities as insurgent climate urbanism: radical urban socio-material transformations', *URBAN Geography*, 738–43. https://doi.org/10.1080/02723638.2020.1850618 (last accessed 6 October 2022).

Pimple, K. D. 2002. 'Six domains of research ethics', *Science Engineering & Ethics*, 8, 191–205. https://doi.org/10.1007/s11948-002-0018-1 (last accessed 6 October 2022).

Plumwood, V. 1993. *Feminism and the Mastery of Nature*. London: Routledge.

Potter, K., and T. Vilcan. 2020. 'Managing urban flood resilience through the English planning system: insights from the "SuDS-face"', *Philosophical Transactions of the Royal Society A: Mathematical, Physical and Engineering Sciences*, 378(2168), 20190206. https://doi.org/10.1098/rsta.2019.0206 (last accessed 6 October 2022).

Public Lab. 2022. 'Public Lab: a DIY environmental science community'. https://publiclab.org/ (last accessed 6 October 2022).

Raco, M., and J. Flint. 2001. 'Communities, places and institutional relations: assessing the role of area-based community representation in local governance', *Political Geography*, 20, 585–612. https://doi.org/10.1016/S0962-6298(01)00012-9 (last accessed 6 October 2022).

Ranganathan, M., and C. Balazs. 2015. 'Water marginalization at the urban fringe: environmental justice and urban political ecology across the north-south divide', *Urban Geography*, 36(3), 403–23. https://doi.org/10.1080/02723638.2015.1005414 (last accessed 6 October 2022).

Ravetz, J., and S. Funtowicz. 2015. 'Post-normal science'. In *Ethics of Science in the Research for Sustainable Development*, 99–112. Baden-Baden: Nomos Verlagsgesellschaft mbH & Co. KG. https://doi.org/10.5771/9783845258430-99 (last accessed 6 October 2022).

Raworth, K. 2017. *Doughnut Economics: seven ways to think like a 21st-century economist*. London: Random House.

Reed, M. S. 2008. 'Stakeholder participation for environmental management: a literature review', *Biological Conservation*, 141(10), 2417–31. https://doi.org/10.1016/j.biocon.2008.07.014 (last accessed 6 October 2022).

Rey-Mazón, P., H. Keysar, S. Dosemagen, C. D'Ignazio and D. Blair. 2018. 'Public Lab: community-based approaches to urban and environmental health and justice', *Science and Engineering Ethics*, 24(3), 971–97. https://doi.org/10.1007/s11948-018-0059-8 (last accessed 6 October 2022).

RIBA. 2020. *Greener Homes*. London: Royal Institute of British Architects.

Rich, A. 2018. 'Natural resources'. In *The Dream of a Common Language: Poems 1974–1977*. New York: W. W. Norton and Company.

Riesch, H., C. Potter and L. Davies. 2013. 'Combining citizen science and public engagement: the Open Air Laboratories Programme', *Journal of Science Communication*, 12(3), A03. https://doi.org/10.22323/2.12030203 (last accessed 6 October 2022).

Rioja, F. 2013. 'What is the value of infrastructure maintenance? A survey', *Infrastructure and Land Policies*, 13, 347–65.

Rith, C., and H. Dubberly. 2007. 'Why Horst W. J. Rittel matters', *Design Issues*, 23, 72–74.

Romp, W. E., and J. de Haan. 2005. 'Public capital and economic growth: a critical survey', *EIB Papers*, 10(1), 41–70.

Sage, A. P., and W. B. Rouse. 2014. *Handbook of Systems Engineering and Management*. Hoboken NJ: John Wiley & Sons.

Sager, T. 2011. 'Neo-liberal urban planning policies: a literature survey 1990–2010', *Progress in Planning*, 76(4), 147–99. https://doi.org/10.1016/j.progress.2011.09.001 (last accessed 6 October 2022).

Schlierf, K., and M. Meyer. 2013. 'Situating knowledge intermediation: insights from science shops and knowledge brokers', *Science Public Policy*, 40, 430–41. https://doi.org/10.1093/scipol/sct 034 (last accessed 6 October 2022).

Schlosberg, D., and L. B. Collins. 2014. 'From environmental to climate justice: climate change and the discourse of environmental justice', *WIREs Climate Change*, 5, 359–74. https://doi.org/10.1002/wcc.275 (last accessed 6 October 2022).

Schumacher, E. F. 1973. *Small is Beautiful: a study of economics as if people mattered*. London: ABACUS.

Shirk, J. L., H. L. Ballard, C. C. Wilderman, T. Phillips, A. Wiggins, R. Jordan, E. McCallie, M. Minarchek, B. V. Lewenstein, M. E. Krasny and R. Bonney. 2012. 'Public participation in scientific research: a framework for deliberate design', *Ecological Society*, 17, 29. https://doi.org/10.5751/ES-04705-170229 (last accessed 6 October 2022).

Shove, E. 2004. *Comfort, Cleanliness and Convenience: the social organization of normality*. Oxford: Berg Publishers.

Shove, E., F. Trentman and M. Watson. 2018. 'Introduction'. In *Infrastructures in Practice. The dynamics of demand in networked societies*. Abingdon: Routledge.

Smith, A. 2005. 'The alternative technology movement: an analysis of its framing and negotiation of technology development', *Human Ecological Review*, 12, 14.

Smith, D. A. 2004. 'An R&D Lab for Utopia? Alternative technology centres in the UK', presented at *The Politics of Utopia: Intentional Communities as Social Science Microcosms*, Uppsala, Sweden, 19.

Smith, P. L. T. 2021. *Decolonizing Methodologies: research and indigenous peoples*. London: Zed Books Ltd.

Sofoulis, Z. 2005. 'Big water, everyday water: a sociotechnical perspective', *Continuum: Journal of Media & Cultural Studies*, 19(4), 445–63. https://doi.org/10.1080/10304310500322685 (last accessed 6 October 2022).

Star, S. L. 1999. 'The ethnography of infrastructure', *American Behavioral Scientist*, 43(3), 377–91. https://doi.org/10.1177/00027649921955326 (last accessed 6 October 2022).

Star, S. L., and K. Ruhleder. 1996. 'Steps toward an ecology of infrastructure: design and access for large information spaces', *Information Systems Research*, 7(1), 111–34. https://doi.org/10.1287/isre.7.1.111 (last accessed 6 October 2022).

Stevens, M., M. Vitos, J. Altenbuchner, G. Conquest, J. Lewis and M. Haklay. 2014. 'Taking participatory citizen science to extremes', *IEEE Pervasive Computing*, 13, 20–9. https://doi.org/10.1109/MPRV.2014.37 (last accessed 6 October 2022).

STNF. 2022. 'Somers Town Neighbourhood Forum – our local forum'. https://somerstownplan.info/ (last accessed 6 October 2022).

Stovin, V. R., S. L. Moore, M. Wall and R. M. Ashley. 2013. 'The potential to retrofit sustainable drainage systems to address combined sewer overflow discharges in the Thames Tideway catchment', *Water Environment Research*, 27, 216–28. https://doi.org/10.1111/j.1747-6593.2012.00353.x (last accessed 6 October 2022).

Strasser, B., J. Baudry, G. Sanchez and É. Tancoigne (eds). 2019. '"Citizen science"? Rethinking science and public participation', *Science and Technology Studies*, 32(2). https://doi.org/10.23987/sts.60425 (last accessed 6 October 2022).

Streeck, W. 2014. 'The politics of public debt: neoliberalism, capitalist development and the restructuring of the state', *German Economic Review*, 15(1), 143–65. https://doi.org/10.1111/geer.12032 (last accessed 6 October 2022).

Symonds, P., J. Milner, N. Mohajeri, J. Aplin, J. Hale, S. J. Lloyd, H. Fremont, S. Younkin, C. Shrubsole, L. Robertson, J. Taylor, N. Zimmermann, P. Wilkinson and M. Davies. 2021. 'A tool for assessing the climate change mitigation and health impacts of environmental policies: the Cities Rapid Assessment Framework for Transformation (CRAFT)', *Wellcome Open Research*, 5, 269. https://doi.org/10.12688/wellcomeopenres.16345.2 (last accessed 6 October 2022).

Taylor, M. 2011. *Public Policy in the Community*. London: Macmillan International Higher Education.

Teh, T.-H. 2019. 'Playing for the future: using codesign games to explore alternative sanitation systems in London', *Urban Planning*, 4(4), 126. https://doi.org/10.17645/up.v4i4.2338 (last accessed 6 October 2022).

Teo, M. M. M., and M. Loosemore. 2010. 'Community-based protest against construction projects: the social determinants of protest movement continuity', *International Journal of Managing Projects in Business*, 3(2), 216–35. https://doi.org/10.1108/17538371011036554 (last accessed 6 October 2022).

Thacker, S., D. Adshead, M. Fay, S. Hallegatte, M. Harvey, H. Meller, N. O'Regan, J. Rozenberg, G. Watkins and J. W. Hall. 2019. 'Infrastructure for sustainable development', *Nature Sustainability*, 2(4), 324–31. https://doi.org/10.1038/s41893-019-0256-8 (last accessed 6 October 2022).

Tonnies, F., and C. P. Loomis. 2002. *Community and Society*. North Chelmsford MA: Courier Corporation.

United Nations. 2015. 'Transforming Our World: the 2030 agenda for sustainable development' [Preprint].

United Nations. 2022. 'The 17 Goals: sustainable development'. https://sdgs.un.org/goals (last accessed 6 October 2022).

Uwajeh, P. C., and I. S. Ezennia. 2018. 'The socio-cultural and ecological perspectives on landscape and gardening in urban environment: a narrative review', *Journal of Contemporary Urban Affairs*, 2(2), 78–89. https://doi.org/10.25034/ijcua.2018.4673 (last accessed 6 October 2022).

Van Oost, E., S. Verhaegh and N. Oudshoorn. 2009. 'From innovation community to community innovation: user-initiated innovation in wireless Leiden', *Science, Technology, & Human Values*, 34(2), 182–205. https://doi.org/10.1177/0162243907311556 (last accessed 6 October 2022).

Van Vliet, B. 2016. 'Innovation in urban networks: co-evolving consumer roles'. In *Retrofitting Cities: priorities, governance and experimentation*, edited by M. Hodson and S. Marvin. London: Earthscan.

Van Vliet, B., E. Shove and H. Chappells. 2005. *Infrastructures of Consumption: environmental innovation in the utility industries*. London: Earthscan.

Vassão, C. A. 2017. 'Design and politics: metadesign for social change', *Strategic Design Research Journal*, 10(2), 144–55. https://doi.org/10.4013/sdrj.2017.102.07 (last accessed 6 October 2022).

Villarroel Walker, R., M. Beck, J. Hall, R. Dawson and O. Heidrich. 2014. 'The energy-water-food nexus: strategic analysis of technologies for transforming the urban metabolism', *Journal of Environmental Management*, 141, 104–15. https://doi.org/10.1016/j.jenvman.2014.01.054 (last accessed 10 October 2022).

Vital Energi. 2017. 'Addendum to support an update to the previously discharged condition No. 4 of planning application 2013/0884/P 1'.

Volland, B. 2016. 'Efficiency in Domestic Space Heating: an estimation of the direct rebound effect for domestic heating in the U.S.' (Working Paper No. 16–01), *IRENE Working Paper*. https://www.econstor.eu/handle/10419/191481 (last accessed 6 October 2022).

Waag Society. 2014. 'DecarboNet Utility Toolkit'. https://www.decarbonet.eu/2014/10/10/utility-toolkit/ (last accessed 6 October 2022).

Waage, J., C. Yap, S. Bell, C. Levy, G. Mace, T. Pegram, E. Unterhalter, N. Dasandi, D. Hudson, R. Kock, S. Mayhew, C. Marx and N. Poole. 2015. 'Governing the UN Sustainable Development Goals: interactions, infrastructures, and institutions', *The Lancet Global Health*, 3(5), e251–e252. https://doi.org/10.1016/S2214-109X(15)70112-9 (last accessed 6 October 2022).

Wachelder, J. 2003. 'Democratizing science: various routes and visions of Dutch science shops', *Science, Technology, & Human Values*, 28(2), 244–73. https://doi.org/10.1177/016224390 2250906 (last accessed 6 October 2022).

Wajcman, J. 1991. *Feminism Confronts Technology*. University Park PA: Penn State University Press.

Walker, G. 2012. *Environmental Justice: concepts, evidence and politics*. Abingdon: Routledge.

Walton, H., D. Dajnak, S. Beevers, M. Williams, P. Watkiss and A. Hunt. 2015. 'Understanding the Health Impacts of Air Pollution in London', 129. https://www.london.gov.uk/sites/default/files/hiainlondon_kingsreport_14072015_final.pdf (last accessed 6 October 2022).

Warren, K. J. 1990. 'The power and the promise of ecological feminism', *Environmental Ethics*, 12, 125–46.

Whyte, K. 2016. 'Indigenous experience, environmental justice and settler colonialism', SSRN Scholarly Paper No. ID 2770058), *Social Science Research Network*. https://doi.org/10.2139/ssrn.2770058 (last accessed 6 October 2022).

Wilhite, H. L., and R. Wilk. 1987. 'A method for self-recording household energy-use behavior', *Energy and Buildings*, 10, 73–9. https://doi.org/10.1016/0378-7788(87)90007-7 (last accessed 6 October 2022).

Wills, J. 2016. 'Emerging geographies of English localism: the case of neighbourhood planning', *Political Geography*, 53, 43–53. https://doi.org/10.1016/j.polgeo.2016.02.001 (last accessed 6 October 2022).

Wilson, E. 1992. *The Sphinx in the City: urban life, the control of disorder, and women*. Berkeley CA: University of California Press.

Winner, L. 1988. *The Whale and the Reactor: a search for limits in an age of high technology*, new edn. Chicago IL: University of Chicago Press.

Wood, J. 2013. 'Meta-designing paradigm change: an ecomimetic, language-centred approach'. In *The Handbook of Design for Sustainability*, edited by H. L. Walker, J. Giard and S. Walker, 428–45. London: Bloomsbury Publishing.

Wong-Parodi, G., K. J. Mach, K. Jagannathan and K. D. Sjostrom. 2020. 'Insights for developing effective decision support tools for environmental sustainability', *Current Opinion in Environmental Sustainability*, 42, 52–9. https://doi.org/10.1016/j.cosust.2020.01.005 (last accessed 6 October 2022).

Wylie, S. A., K. Jalbert, S. Dosemagen and M. Ratto. 2014. 'Institutions for civic technoscience: how critical making is transforming environmental research', *The Information Society*, 30, 116–26. https://doi.org/10.1080/01972243.2014.875783 (last accessed 6 October 2022).

Yunkaporta, T. 2019. *Sand Talk: how indigenous thinking can save the world*. Melbourne: Text Publishing.

Zahedieh, N. 2010. *The Capital and the Colonies: London and the Atlantic economy 1660–1700*. Cambridge: Cambridge University Press.

Index

academic institutions, responsibilities of 68
academic research 15, 56–7, 67, 143
access management 47, 149, 158
active participation 21
activism 27, 48
affordable housing 75
aim-setting 63, 118, 166–7, 189
air quality 4, 8, 17, 109–13, 116–22, 126–32
  projects on 109–11, 23, 32, 117, 119
'appropriate technology' movement 27
Arnstein, Sherry 21
assessment, continuous 63
Austen, Kat 9
Australia 25
authorship of the present book 9, 14–16
automation 39–40
autonomous communities 24

'back-to-basics' 27
Bartlett School of Planning 73
basic provision 34, 47
Basil Jellicoe Hall 17–18
Bates, Andy 86, 92, 136–7, 157, 187
bathwater 33–5
Bell, Sarah 2, 9, 13–14, 55, 60–1, 73–4, 85, 92–3, 96, 104, 117, 139, 157
Bermondsey 92
bespoke tools 184–5
best interest of clients 53
best practice 122
Beveridge, Robert 146
big projects 5, 41
black spots 49
Blokland, TaIja 22
Bookchin, Murray 24
bottom-up approaches 3–7, 27, 52, 60–2, 69, 81, 88, 108, 167, 183, 187, 191–5
'bucket brigades' 28
budget deficits 42
Butler, Adrian 137–8

calculators 100–3, 152–6, 160, 179–81
Camden Council 18, 111, 128–9, 132–3
CAMELLIA *see* Community Water
  Management
canyoning 122
capital markets, access to 42
carbon emissions 4, 24, 78, 100
Carpenters Estate 51–5, 70, 81
case studies 8, 15, 69, 187, 193, 196
centralised and decentralised systems 27, 49
change, speed of 195

circumstances 20
cities learning from disaster 22–3
citizen science 28–30, 55, 134
civil society 21
civil technoscience 29
climate change 18, 46, 139–40
climate crisis 28, 32–5
climate justice 24
coal consumption 44
co-authoring 15
co-creation 95–105, 143, 146
co-design process 5–8, 14, 41, 35, 59, 61–9, 85, 88, 96, 102, 106, 114, 119, 136, 138, 141–8, 159–60, 163, 167, 189–96
cohesion of communities 159
collaborative work 8–15, 31–2, 109, 135, 137, 192
Colman, Claire 126–8
'combined' sewers 2
communication infrastructure 34, 167
communities 18–20, 32, 186, 190, 193–4
Community Action Against Asthma
  project 28
community-based action 6, 21, 25
community-based research 18, 29
community benefits funding 48
'community of communities' 20
Community Infrastructure Levy (CIL) 114, 118, 129
community involvement in projects 174
community partners 14–15
Community University Knowledge Strategy 57
Community Water Management for a Liveable
  London (CAMELLIA) project 8, 59, 94, 135, 141, 155, 157, 164, 180, 184, 191
construction of systems 18–39
construction traffic, impact of 128–9
consultimg, commercial 54–5
Cooper's Lane 117
council house sales 74–5
COVID-19 pandemic 4
Crawford, Kate 74
crowdsourcing 29
cycling 35

data visualisation 138
Davies, Felicity 74
debate, public 56
decision-making 21, 27, 38, 48, 53, 71–4, 78–81, 123, 174
decommissioning 40
demolition of houses 53, 74–83

209

Demolition or Refurbishment project 7, 58, 69, 71–3, 81–5, 187–92
deprivation 8
design of systems 6, 38
Detroit 47–8
Devlin, Slaney 109, 113, 117–21, 126–32
diary-keeping 168–9, 84–5
disaster, learning from 22–3
disconnection 49
disruptions to service 39
distribution networks 43
drinking water 36, 139
Durose, Catherine 83
dynamics 63, 105–6

Earth Summit (Rio de Janeiro, 1992) 25–6
eco-communities 27
ecological crisis 27
effectiveness of procedures 66
efficiency 42–3
electricity grid 46
embedding of researchers 61
embodied carbon 83–4
emotional harm 67
Employment Law Foundation (ELF) 112
end users 30
energy infrastructure 34, 49
energy needs 45
engagement 52–5, 60–1, 66, 81, 88, 105, 140, 144, 155, 167
'Engineering Comes Home' project 7, 9, 33, 45, 57–9, 68–9, 87–96, 133, 102–8, 141, 168–72, 175, 183–4, 187–90
'Engineering Exchange' project 6–7, 29, 52, 55–61, 69, 76–7, 81–2, 85, 89–91, 132–3, 168–72, 175, 183–4, 187–90
environmental impact 45
environmental justice 4–7, 17, 23–4, 28, 31–2, 38, 47, 109–112, 134
Environmental Law Foundation (ELF) 110, 112
environmentalism 6, 25, 27
ethics 67–8, 191
Euston 17–18, 23, 31
evaluation process 64–8, 81–5, 181–2
everyday needs and experiences 50
everyday technologies 30
experience, learning from 191; see also lived experience
experts and expertise 38, l 143
'extensive green roof' 153

facilitators 96
factsheets 79–80, 122–3, 176–7
feedback, explicit and implicit 66
feedback forms 182
feminism, ecological 24
fieldnotes template 182
fixed assets 46
flooding 24, 109, 139–40
food sharing 99
food waste 99
Francis Crick Institute 127–8
free use of infrastructure 41
funding and fundraising 149, 155, 157, 160, 163–4, 191

Gemeinschaft and Gesellschaft 19
gender issues 48
Geological Survey, British 138
Gibbons, Michael 83
global financial crisis (2008) 47
government
    eventual transfer of assets back to 43
    ownerhip of and spending on 41
Graham, Mary 25
green-blue infrastructure 136, 140, 161
greenhouse gases 78

Haklay, Muki 29
Healey, Patsy 20
health inequalities 77–8
heating, efficiency of 44
high speed train (HS2) 112, 127, 131
Holman, Claire 109, 130, 133
horizon-scanning technology 98
housing 48
housing associations 73
Hurricane Katrina 24
hydrology 138

ideation stage of technology design 107
indigenous knowledge and knowledge systems 25
individual actions 120
'infrastructural literacy' 146
infrastructure, social and community aspecs of 40–50
infrastructure companies 42–3
infrastructure providers 39
infrastructure 'safari' 146, 173
intelligence 29
interactions, human 22
interdependence of infrastructure 45–6
'intermediate technology' 27
investment in infrastructure 42
involvement 36, 38, 94, 161
Irwin, Alan 28

Jevons, William 44
Johnson, Boris 80
Johnson, Charlotte 9–12, 15, 33, 74, 92–6, 105–6, 117, 139, 187
Just Space 7, 57, 70–85
Just Transition movement 40

Khan, Sadiq 80
Kipling calculator 152–4, 179–81, 184
Kipling Garden project 1–4, 8–9, 15–16, 69, 92, 135–42, 145, 160–4, 171, 187–91
Kipling Tenants and Residens Association (TRA) 2–3
KloudKeeper (company) 101, 103
knowledge democracy 54–6, 69
knowledge as distinct from opinion 48
Knowledge Quarter 122

'ladder' of participation 21–2
land values 140
LCA calculator 174–6
learning with communities 15–16
Leathermarket Joint Management Board (JMB) 2, 92, 94, 98, 137–40, 143, 145, 187

life cycle assessment (LCA) 91, 98–103
life cycles, infrastructural 6, 53, 37–40
literacy gauge for infrastructure 182
literature, academic 79
lived experience 29, 73, 107, 120, 175
lnitiation of cycles 37
local authorities 73, 145
local communities 24m 38–9
local environments 27
local knowledge 139
localism and Localism Act 114
lockdowns 4
lock-in 46–7
London 2–4, 7–8, 15–16, 34–54, 69, 72–3, 135, 139–40, 164, 187
  problems faced by 4, 139–20
London Assembly Housing Committee 73–4, 80–1
London Tenants Association (LTA) 7
London Tenants Federation (LTF) 7, 55

McCulloch, Andrew 144
maintenance
  of council housing 75
  of infrastructure 39–40, 47–8
marginalised communities 7, 109
Maria Fidelis Catholic School 129
Marres, Nortje 30
Mayor of London's guidance 80–3
Meakin Estate 7, 9, 58–9, 68, 86–8, 92–7, 101, 103, 136–7, 145, 175–6, 192
measurement of success 63
metadesign 31, 102–3, 165, 188
monopolies, natural 43
Moore, Gemma 9–10, 15, 70, 187

National Planning Policy Framework 115
National (US) Institute for Environmental Health Sciences 29
National (US) Science Foundation 28
needs, fulfilment of 66–7
neighborhood forums 114; see also under Somers Town
neighborhood planning 110, 115, 126
neoliberalism 18, 23, 42–3
New York 46–7
Newcomen engine 44
Newham, Borough 51–4
Nexy tokens 97, 107, 170–2, 184

Ofwat 140
Olympic Games 51–2
organisational processes 71
over-commitment and over-engagement 105
overflow 2, 107, 139–40
ownership of infrastructure, *public* or *private* 41–3

participant satisfaction 66
participation 28–32, 48–9, 108, 136
partnership agreements 166–7
payment of research participants 188
Peck, Jamie 47
peer review 78–9
Phoenix Court Energy Centre 128
planning processes 38, 74, 112–15, 133

policy and political issues 21–2
political processes 140
pollution 4–7, 27, 40, 109, 116–17, 120–5, 128–31
positionality 15
poverty 7, 24
power stations 46
power structures 193
prioritisation 122
private ownership and investment 40, 42
privatisation 43, 74–5
problems of design 24, 28–32, 43–50, 70
professional standards 56
'prosumers' 49
protocol for research collaboration 82–3
prototype solutions 65, 95, 101, 152
public health 36
'Public Lab' 28
public transport 21, 37, 46

race and racism 4, 23
railway services 47
rainfall 46
rainwater capture/harvesting 99–103, 107–8, 149–60, 178–9
rates 41
Raworth, Kate 84
rebound effect 44
reconstituting the world 3–4, 196
recycling of building materials 78
refurbishment costs 68, 76–80
regeneration programmes 7, 20, 51–5, 70–1, 74, 77–84, 112, 128, 144, 149
  social and community impacts and benefits of 70–1
Regents Park 18
regulation 43
rehousing 53
renewable energy 40, 78
rents of council houses 75
representativeness 66, 144
repurposing 141, 143, 191
reputational risk 67
requirements, capturing of 170–3
research in action 68–9
research councils 55, 60
research fellowships 61
research relationships 73
researchers and research teams 15, 59–60, 63–4, 68–9, 160–4, 173, 188, 191–2
residents' garden away from Kipling Estate 3
residents' perspectives 146, 161
residents wishing to improve local environment 133
resilience 23, 35, 61, 72
resource use 44–5
retrofitting 76, 78, 83
reviews of progress 56
Rich, Adrienne 1–4
'right to buy' 74–5
risk assessment 167
roads 47
roles of clients, contributors and collaborators 4–6, 58–60, 82, 192
Royal Institution of Brtish Architects (RIBA) 83
run-off 154

safety concerns 144
science, engineering and design 4–6, 27, 29
Scorer, Jackie 138, 143–4, 148
service to and management by the
    community 49
sewer system and sewerage 1–2, 33, 36, 46,
    103–9, 141, 146
shared values 63, 194
Shaw, Clive 135, 144, 151–2, 155–62, 187–91
Shirk, Jennifer 29, 58
Shove, Elizabeth 44
slavery 4
'small is beautiful' 26–7
'smart' metering 49
social barriers to travel47
social design and benefits 94, 141
social distancing 4
social divisions 24–5
social houaing 55, 72–81, 139
social movements 27
social needs 52
social values 46–7
sociotechnical systems 36, 49
solutions, crafting of 65, 178–81
Somers Town 7–8, 18, 69, 110–20, 124–7,
    132–4, 187–90, 117–19
    Neghbourhood Forum (STNF) 8, 68,
    112–14, 117–20, 125–33
Southwark Council 2, 139, 145–6, 149, 157–9
space, use of 143
stakeholders 37, 71, 105–6, 142–5, 148,
    168–9, 189–90
story creation 97, 171
streaming services 43–4
sustainability 21–2, 53, 25–6, 140
Sustainable Development Goals (SDGs)
    36, 41, 47

talking preferred to writing 173
Tate Modern 40
Taylor, Marilyn 19–20, 148–9, 193
technical assessments of refurbishment
    costs 76–7
technological horizon scanning 98
Teh, Tse-Hui 9, 12–13
Tenants and Residents Association (TRA) 2–3
tenants' rights 80
Thames Water 143, 146, 149, 154
Thames, River 1, 4, 139
tools for co-design of bottom-up infra-
    structure 8, 31, 61, 64, 80, 90–1, 96–7,
    103–4, 107, 165–71, 174–9, 182–5,
    188, 196
top-down initiatives 4–6, 195
touring of individual homes 168–9
traffic congestion 37, 44–5
transformation, scale of 194
transittions 24
transport fares 41–2

Transport for London 130
tree replacement 121–2
Tuhiwai Smith, Linda 25 ???
Turnbull, Donna 109, 113
Turnbull, Pat 70

United Nations *see* Sustainable
    Development Goals
United States 46–7
university-based researchers 188, 191, 195
University College London (UCL) 6, 8, 51–2,
    55–7, 61, 92, 73, 80–1, 84, 92, 101,
    110–14, 125–6, 132, 137–41, 157–8, 161
University of Leicester 84
urban change 31–2
urban communities 19–22, 32
urban form, discussion of 121–2

value elicitation 86–7, 148–9, 171, 173
value of infrstructure 164
value persistence 67
values of the community 19, 21, 108
voices from the community 14–16
Voluntary Action Camden 112–13
volunteering 149
vulnerability17, 49

Waag Society 171
waiting lists for social housing 75
walking routes 122
washing machines 44
waste 8, 53–4, 87–8, 97, 99
waste collection 41
waste infrastructure 34
wastewater 2
water–energy–food (WEF) nexus 7, 45,
    86–8, 91–107
water management 138–40, 153, 164
water rates 41
water shortages 45, 86
water supply 2–3, 46
water systems 191
water use 44, 86, 95, 102
water wastage 95
Watson, Carl 138
Watt engine 44
websites 61
'wicked' problems 87
wilderness preservation 24
women, role of 48
working-class communities 18
workshop processes 7, 62, 64, 6, 73, 94–107,
    125–6, 130–1, 146–51, 155–6, 175,
    186–7, 190
worldviews 25
writing down thoughts 173

young processes 100
Yunkaporta, Tyson 25

Milton Keynes UK
Ingram Content Group UK Ltd.
UKHW051942220424
441562UK00014B/387